Gratefully
S M Walton
Sept 1936

Limited Edition
of which this is **Nº 281**

THOSE PARIS YEARS

With the World at the Cross-Roads

THOSE PARIS YEARS

With the World at the Cross-Roads

BY

SAMUEL N. WATSON, D.D.

Officer of the Legion of Honor, France, Chevalier of the Order of Leopold, Belgium, Commander of the Order of Saint Sava, Serbia.

WITH INTRODUCTION BY

WILL IRWIN

NEW YORK

Fleming H. Revell Company

LONDON AND EDINBURGH

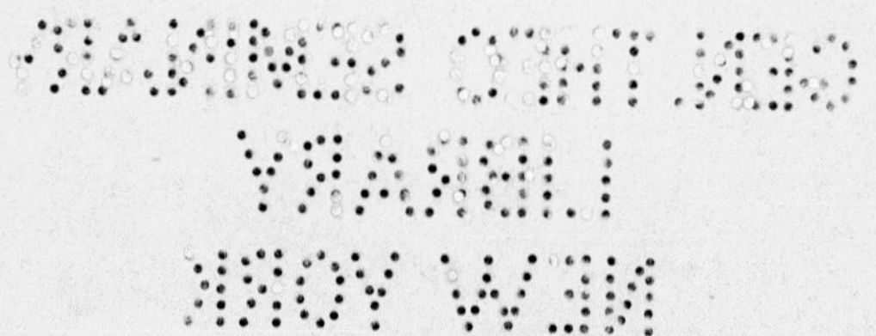

New York: 158 Fifth Avenue
London: 21 Paternoster Square

TO

JAMES HANSON ANDREWS
LAURA LYMAN DAY ANDREWS

and their children

MARION : HELEN : EDWARD.

Those dear comrades of so many days of carefree companioning, when we were young together.

This Record of
the serious and the gay in my life

Is Gratefully Dedicated

To S. N. W.

"The story of your Book sounds so good to me that I can hardly wait to see it in print. I cannot express to you how glad I am that you are writing it. Your matchless tales both of your work at home and of your life in France should not be lost. There are few who can look at life with a serious eye, see its pathos and its need, and still be conscious of its whimsicality and its humour; and only he who can see both sides can give all-around help; or rightly interpret it."

L. L. D. A.

INTRODUCTION

I FIRST met Dr. Samuel N. Watson in April, 1916, which everyone who lived through the World War remembers as "the spring of Verdun"—that period of unshed tears when the Germans, having failed to take the great fortress by surprise, were maintaining their furious attacks in order to bleed France white. We Americans, not yet in the War, were expressing our sympathy for the Allies by gifts of money and supplies to relieve the civilian population. George Horace Lorimer, back in Philadelphia, had observed, in a consignment of second-hand clothing being shipped to France, several boxes of evening dresses—mere cumberers, naturally, of good cargo-space. This, he remarked to himself, was not common sense. I was serving in France at the time as war correspondent for his *Saturday Evening Post*. Forthwith, Lorimer snapped through to me an order for an article telling the American people what France really needed, and what she could worry along without. I scurried from place to place in Paris, and got little substantial information. All our forces of relief had amusing stories about the stuff they found when they opened the cases from America. One enormous box, for example, contained a hundred second-class top hats. They could tell Americans what not to send; as for what to send, and in what proportion, they had only the most hazy ideas. Then, at the end of a discouraging afternoon, I invaded the Avenue de l'Alma and interviewed Dr. Watson.

He was God's gift to the reporter. He knew what he knew and what he did not know. He hadn't done his relief work in Paris alone. He had been scouting through the country, including the war zone, finding out exactly what I wanted to know. "Shoes first!" I remember he said, "The French peasant women, who do the work on the farms nowadays, are going barefooted. Style doesn't matter, but sturdiness does. There must be stocks of old-fashioned shoes selling cheap in America. The French need them. But only the large sizes!" He didn't believe in second-hand clothing at all. It cost too much to transport in proportion to its value. Here again, there must be in the United States much new clothing unsaleable because it had gone out of style, but useful for carrying French families through the winter. I mentioned that instance of the hundred top hats, and he chuckled. "Do you know what became of them?" he asked. "Well, in the old men's homes of France, the inmates are always attending funerals of their fellows. Formerly, only two or three of them had top hats for the occasion. That caused jealousy and dissension. Now, in two homes at least, they'll all attend the funerals properly dressed!"

At this interview, I think, he told me the story, retold in his book, about getting an American harvester for a puzzled department in Northern France. He has forgotten, however, one detail which I have kept in memory ever since. When he had his harvester set up and running, his comrade in this adventure, the French village curé, grew so enthusiastic that he tucked up his soutane and began stacking sheaves behind the machine. Whereupon, Dr. Watson took off his rabat and joined the sport.

He has told how he took me to Millerand, the Minister of War destined to become President of France. He has not told of other eminent Frenchmen whose doors swung for me at his touch. For with both the French and the American Colony, the name of the efficient, agreeable and sterling Dr. Watson was an open sesame during the whole period of the war.

This is the kind of book which fills a professional writer with despair. As he reads it, he finds many things which he would have expressed differently and many others which he would have omitted or expanded. But there is over it all the bloom of the amateur's fine, unfagged enthusiasm—a quality which the professional finds in his own early work, for all its faults, and which he can never recapture. It is more than that; it is a soul-portrait of the old-time American gentleman. Be we better or be we worse, we are not rearing any more Dr. Watsons. Universal charity, faith in the general goodness of mankind, belief that nations will in the end light their way with the lamps of truth and justice —that school of thought seems blasted by the disillusions of the war and of the bad peace. I disagree with many of his opinions on men and measures. For example I still believe that the League of Nations, hampered though it was by its welding with the Treaty of Versailles, might have averted the coming calamity had the United States followed Wilson to the end. As for his League of Peace, attainable when men have new hearts, I submit only that we have been trying that for nineteen hundred years—and look at us! But I would not have him believe any differently. We lost our Dr. Watsons when, somehow, we lost our way. When we find it again we shall, for our good, begin breeding his like again.

WILL IRWIN.

New York City.

FOREWORD

THIS record of my life must be prefaced by a chapter on Ancestors; for the simple reason that no human life is complete in and of itself; the unseen of every life is more than what is seen of it.

Wordsworth writes:

> *"Our birth is but a sleep and a forgetting;*
> *The Soul that rises with us, our life's Star,*
> *Hath had elsewhere its setting,*
> *And cometh from afar!"*

We know very little of that life which we were before we became a baby by the name of Watson—or any other name; but that life, half-glimpsed in moments of revery, is more, much more than half of what we are to-day; that which we bring with us that "cometh from afar" has within its misty self possibilities of an interpretation of this life's mysterious movements which, if we could but read it right, would make clear to us much of which now we say, "I simply cannot understand it."

It is so with my life, I do not understand it: in one sense it is a continuous story, but it is a story which finds its motive more than often in something which I brought with me when I woke here from that "sleep and a forgetting," and that "something" has expressed itself all along the way in an impulsive, unreasoning outreach for BEAUTY, and that word Beauty is but a common term for the whole gamut of sensation, colour, form, perfume, taste, touch—that whole chromatic scale of vibration which makes up the rainbow of Joy.

We say "My life"; but I know that it has not been "my" life; I have lived in it, that is true, but it is far more true that it has been lived for me. It is far more true for all of us that *we are lived,* than that We Live.

Hence Life cannot intelligently harbour regrets. For of all that we call "our life," what was it which made it what it was; what inspired, motivated its thoughts and doings? Who among us can account intelligently for the motives which were the impulses of a long and varied life? I know that I cannot, except in one way only, which is this—Life is a planned Experience, and as such it is a series of *sequences.* There have been turning points in my life, and from the decisions there made have flowed consequences which have made me what I am, but the choice of the ways where the paths turned was not wholly mine, else should I be to-day a bitter rebel; should be, but that I know that I have been a part of a Greater One than I, a greater self Whom I call THE LIFE. My faith for living on consists in this—I firmly believe that I have been better than I knew; and seeing and knowing that, in irrefutable clearness, will be the all-recompensing Vision of That Great Day to which I fearlessly look forward.

S. N. W.

Santa Barbara, Calif.

CONTENTS

Book I

Book II

BOOK I

I

ANCESTRY
912-1854

ANCESTORS are links which tie our individual earth lives to that ingathering of all those life tides from out the unknown past, which have so largely made us what we are.

THE MONTGOMERY LINE

Roger de Montgomerie, so runs the record, was "Count of of Montgomerie before the coming of Rollo," which means the year 912.

The fifth in his line was Hugh de Montgomerie, who married Josseline, daughter of Tourode, Sire de Pont Audemer, whose wife Weva Duceline de Crepon was sister of La Duchesse Gonnor, who was wife of Richard sans Peur, and so great-grandmother of the great Duc William.

The sixth of the line, Roger de Montgomerie was hence a cousin of William the Conqueror, and was one of his right hand men when the time came to invade England; in fact he gave sixty ships for that expedition: for these and other services he was made Earl of Chichester and Arundel, and later Earl of Shrewsbury: the son who succeeded him, Robert of Bellesme, Earl of Shrewsbury, was so bad as to have been the original Robert le Diable.

The fifteenth of the line, Sir John de Montgomerie of Eaglesham and Eastwood, and afterwards of Eglinton and Ardrossan, married in 1361, Elizabeth, daughter and heiress of Sir Hugh Eglinton of Eglinton; and this Eglinton marriage furnished another title to a branch of the Montgomerie descendants; and through this marriage "the estates of Eglinton and Ardrossan passed to the Montgomeries of Eaglesham, who made Eglinton their chief residence afterwards." Sir John de Montgomerie distinguished himself at the Battle of Otterbourne, where James, Earl Douglas, his uncle, was slain. In this battle was slain also Hugh, eldest son of Sir John, the Hugh spoken of in the lines from Percy's Reliques:

Sir Hugh Montgomery was he called,
Who with a spere most bright,
Well mounted on a gallant steed,
Ran fiercely through the fight.

The seventeenth of the line was Alexander de Montgomerie, the first Lord Montgomerie, and it was his son Alexander de Montgomerie, Master of Montgomerie, to whose name is attached the rise of the blood-feud between the Montgomeries and the Cunninghames, the memory of which was vivid even in my early days. It was through this same Alexander, seventeenth of the line, that the family name came to be written in blood on the pages of the history of France. His son, Robert, went to France about the year 1480, and became Seigneur de Lorges, in the Orleannais; he was the founder of the second French house of the Counts of Montgomerie. Robert's grandson, Gabriel Count de Montgomerie, by an unfortunte mischance, killed King Henry II in a Tournament. Despite the fact that it was known to be an accident, as one may read in Dumas' *Joseph Balsamo: "Mais on n'a pas fait pis a M. de Montgomerie pour avoir tue Henry II, dit Louis XV. Il avait tue le roi par accident, Sire;"* and though Montgomerie had been assured of immunity, the fact that he was an active and influential Huguenot told against him, and through the Royal influence at Court, Montgomerie was brought to the scaffold, and was executed in 1576. The last of his male descendants was Nicholas de Montgomerie, who died in 1725.

The nineteenth of the line was Hugh, Third Lord Montgomerie, who was created First Earl of Eglinton by James IV in 1508.

The twenty-eighth of the line was Hugh Montgomerie of Bridgend, who married Katharine, second daughter of Sir William Scott of Clerkington in 1653. A spoon bearing their initials, "H.M."—"K.S." is in the possession of the writer.

The twenty-ninth of the line was William Montgomerie of Bridgend, Hugh's eldest son, who married Isabel Burnett, daughter of Robert Burnett of Lethintie in Aberdeenshire on January 8, 1684. This Robert Burnett was extensively interested in the Quaker Settlements in New Jersey, and became one of the Lords Proprietor of the Province of East New Jersey: his body lies in the Friends Burying Ground at Crosswicks, New Jersey. In 1661 Robert became the owner by purchase of 1/16 of the Province. Isabel Burnett's acquaintance with the new land across the Sea, together with her father's large landed interests there, eventually led William Montgomery, the twenty-ninth of the line, to move his family from Ayrshire to America. In 1701 he settled on Doctor's Creek, in Monmouth County, New Jersey, and gave the name of Eglinton, which it still bears, to his estate; the house is situated about two miles from Allentown, Monmouth County.

The thirtieth of the line, Robert Montgomery of Eglinton, born in Bridgend in 1687, came to America as a boy with his father. He held a magistrate's commission from the King. He married Sarah Stacy of Burlington, New Jersey in 1709. He was a Friend, and his body lies in the Crosswicks Burying Ground.

In the line of William of Bridgend and Isabel Burnett comes John Berrien Montgomery, Commodore in the U. S. Navy, who, in 1846, took possession of the town and harbor of San Francisco, in the name of the United States.

In the line of James Montgomery, spoken of as "Robert's eldest son and heir," comes Harvey Montgomery of Rochester, New York, who married Mary Rochester, daughter of the founder of the City; Brig. Gen. Montgomery C. Meigs, who was Quarter Master General of the United States, and who married Louisa, daughter of Commodore John Rodgers, U. S. Navy; James Montgomery, who was under General Richard Montgomery in his Expedition against Quebec in 1775; and Brig. Gen. William Reading Montgomery, who was noted for his services in the Mexican War, and in the War of the Rebellion.

The thirty-first of the line was Robert Montgomery of

Eglinton, who was born at Eglinton in 1748, where he resided during his long life of nearly 80 years. His first marriage was to Margaret, daughter of John Leonard, in 1771; she died in 1780. Robert then married Elizabeth, daughter of Dr. James Newell of Allentown, New Jersey, in 1788, and whose wife was Elizabeth Lawrence. By his second marriage Robert had two daughters, my greataunt Lucy, and my grandmother Esther; my greataunt Lucy Montgomery I remember well; my grandmother Esther Montgomery, who died in 1856, I never saw. Esther Montgomery married her cousin Samuel Cooke Newell in 1817. Their children were: Elizabeth, who married William Passmore; Sarah, who married Bennington Gill; Robert, who died at the age of eleven; Mary Cooke, who never married; Lucy, who married Theodore Stagg; Hetty, my Mother, who married George W. Watson.

Esther Montgomery who married Samuel Cooke Newell, was thirty-second in descent; Hetty Newell Watson was thirty-third in descent; and I am thirty-fourth in descent from the first of the Montgomery line of whom we have any record—Roger de Montgomerie, Count of Montgomerie, in Normandy in 912.

THE KEARNY LINE

The next line in length which I can trace is through my ancestor Michael Kearny, which runs this way. Edmund Kearny married Elizabeth Fox of Bulligaderie, in the County of Limerick, in Ireland, in the reign of Henry VII, which was from 1485-1509. From him comes a long line: James Kearny married Eleanor O'Brien, daughter of Marrough O'Brien, fourth son of Thurlough, Earl of Thomond, and left issue, etc., and so on down to the fifth in descent from Edmund, who was Michael Kearny, who married as his third wife, Sarah Morris, by whom he had five children, Isabella, Michael, Mary, Euphemia, and Graham. This Michael Kearny settled in New Jersey in about 1712. He was Treasurer of the Province of East New Jersey, 1723 to 1725; held a commission in His Majesty's Navy; and was Clerk of the General Assembly of the Province of New Jersey. His daughter Graham Kearny married my great-great-grandfather the Rev. Dr. Samuel Cooke; so that I am tenth in line of descent from the first of the Kearny line of whom we have record.

A noted son of the Kearny line was General Stephen Watts Kearny, born in 1794, died in 1848; he was put in command of the Army of the West at the outbreak of the Mexican War; was Military and Civil Governor of California in 1847, of Vera Cruz in 1848, and of the City of Mexico in 1848; he is considered by many historians to be the true conqueror of California: he was my grandfather's second cousin.

THE MORRIS LINE

The next oldest line to which I trace lineage is the Morris line. Captain Richard Morris of the Cromwellian Cavalry married Sarah Pole in 1669. They had a son Lewis Morris, known afterward as Lewis Morris the First, who was born in 1671 and died in 1746. In 1691 he married Isabella Graham, daughter of James Graham. This James Graham was born in Scotland, became a citizen of New York, and died in Morrisania, N. Y., in 1701; tradition connects him with the family of James Graham, Marquis of Montrose—he was first Recorder of the City of New York; Attorney General for the Province; member of the Governor's Council; Receiver General of the Province; Attorney General of New England, and member and Speaker of the Provincial Assembly.

Lewis Morris the First was Judge of the Superior Court of New Jersey; member of the Governor's Council of New Jersey, and also of the Governor's Council of New York; member of the New York Assembly; Chief Justice from 1715 to 1733; Boundary Commissioner; acting Governor of New Jersey in 1731; first Governor of New Jersey as a separate Province from 1738 to the time of his death in 1746.

I am sixth in line of direct descent from Lewis Morris the First; and seventh in line of descent from James Graham.

THE COOKE LINE

The Morris Line brings me to my descent from the Rev. Dr. Samuel Cooke, who was my great-great-grandfather. Samuel Cooke was born in London in 1723. He was a graduate of Gonville and Caius College, Cambridge, and was ordained by the Bishop of Ely, in 1748. His bookplate bears his Coat of Arms, as follows:

> "Ermine, on a band cottised gules; three lions pass. guard. or. Christopher Cooke of Thorne, County of Devon, Gent., married Margaret daughter of Richard Curland of Whytfield: had issue Christopher. He was son of William; son of Tobin; son of John; son of Christopher; son of Henry Cooke, all of Thorne aforesaid,—Gentlemen."

The bookplate bears the name:

S. COOKE,
Gon. & Cai. Coll. Cant.

In 1751 he came from England, having been licensed by the Bishop of London to perform the ministerial office in Monmouth County, New Jersey; he settled in Shrewsbury where Christ Church is one of the earliest of the colonial churches, having been built in 1703-1705. The present building was built in 1769, and on the cornerstone are the initials of my great-great-grandfather "S.C.," with the date 1769. In 1775, his life having been threatened on account of his loyalty to the Crown, he left America, on a British man-of-war, accompanied by Captain Philip Kearny, son of Michael, who held a commission in the British Navy, and who accompanied Dr. Cooke to England. On his arrival in England Dr. Cooke was appointed a chaplain in the British Army. Then in 1785 he was appointed missionary to New Brunswick, where he held the first services of the Church in many towns, and where he was instrumental in the building of Old Trinity, in St. John, in 1791.

It interests me to note that in this Morris-Cooke connection there are bishops and deans of the Church of England; some generals and admirals of the American Army and Navy; and some bishops of the Protestant Episcopal Church in America; among these latter are Bishop Bowman, Bishop Clarkson, and Bishop Millspaugh.

On the night of May 3, 1795, Dr. Cooke was returning to his home across the Naswaak River in a bark canoe after having made some parochial visits in Fredericton, his son Michael accompanying him, when the canoe was upset by a sudden squall, and both father and son were drowned. There is a tablet to his memory in St. Anne's Church, Fredericton, in which he is described as, "The First Rector of this Church, and First Ecclesiastical Commissary of the Province."

Among the Cooke memorabilia which have been preserved are sermons written in his own clear hand, and also some letters.

My Cooke line (Samuel), runs as follows:

Samuel Cooke married Graham Kearny, daughter of Michael Kearny and Sarah Morris, his wife. Sarah Cooke, their second daughter, married Elisha Newell, M.D., of Allentown, New Jersey. Samuel Cooke Newell married Esther Montgomery, daughter of Robert Montgomery, 31st of Eglinton. Hetty Newell, their daughter married my father, the Rev. George W. Watson.

THE NEWELL LINE

Tradition has it that Robert Newell, son of James Newell, came to America from Ireland; this is substantiated by the inscription on the tombstone of his son Hugh. The family name was originally de Neuville; this is rendered probable by the fact that a Crest showing a Cup and Dagger has been handed down in the family with the record that this was the Newell Crest, and that it goes back to a Count de Neuville, who was Cupbearer to Duke William.

Hugh Newell married Elizabeth Truax, descendant of the Huguenot refugee, Philippe de Trieux.

My own line is: James Newell (origin Irish). Robert Newell, his son who married Ellen (surname unknown). James Newell, who married Elizabeth Lawrence, daughter of Elisha Lawrence. Elisha Newell, his son, who married Sarah Cooke. Samuel Cooke Newell, his son, who married

Esther Montgomery. Hetty Newell, his daughter, who married George W. Watson, who was my father.

James Newell, who married Elizabeth, daughter of Elisha Lawrence who was member of the General Assembly of the Province of New Jersey in 1721, became one of the Proprietors of the Province of West Jersey.* He was born in Upper Freehold; received his medical education in Edinburgh; but owing to the fact that his graduation coincided with the Great Rebellion, he was obliged to go to London to get his diploma. He settled in Allentown, N. J., for the practice of his profession. He was commissioned surgeon of the Second Regiment of Foot Militia of the County of Monmouth; his commission from the Provincial Congress bears date of May 7, 1776, and is signed by Sam'l Tucker as President of the Congress, and is attested by John Hart

* There is still land registered under the name of James Newell, in New Jersey. At the time of the final distribution of the original Grants amongst the Proprietors, who, by that time by sales and purchases had increased to nineteen in number, there was much land which was considered valueless remaining undistributed; all such land was surveyed and divided into nineteen sections, and these sections were drawn for by lot. The southernmost section of what was then known as Long Island (Beach Haven is now situated on what was Long Island) was Lot No. 19, which was drawn by James Newell: it lies just beyond Beach Haven. I have had the land surveyed, and have verified the Registry of Title. Of the original Lot No. 19. but a few acres remain, large portions of it having been washed out to sea by the tides: but there is a large accretion to the property, which, by the Law of Riparian Rights, belongs to the owners of Lot No. 19.

The Record reads, as a description of Lot No. 19: "BEGINNING at a point in the high water line of the Atlantic Ocean and in the southerly line of the land now of late Baeder Estate, and extending thence (1) along said line, North 39° 52′ west, 1145 feet to a post, thence continuing the same course a further distance of 805 feet to a point in the high water line of the Bay and corner to said Baeder property; thence along the high water line of the Bay the next five courses as follows; (2) south 22° 43′ east 444 feet; (3) south 33° 00′ east 520 feet; (4) south 46° 23′ east 322 feet; (5) south 0° 20′ west 405 feet; (6) south 42° 02′ west 180 feet; thence (7) south 85° east, crossing the Beach, 565 feet to the high water line of the Atlantic Ocean; thence (8) north 37° 35′ east, along said high water line, 200 feet to the place of beginning.

Containing within said bounds, 9.63 acres of land:—as of May 22. 1909.

as Secretary, which latter was one of the Signers of the Declaration of Independence.

Elisha Newell, M.D., son of James, was born in 1755; he married Sarah Cooke, daughter of the Rev. Dr. Samuel Cooke. He was commissioned surgeon of the Fourth Regiment of Militia of Monmouth County at the time of the Whisky Rebellion of 1793; his commission is dated the fifth day of August, 1793, and is signed by R'd Howell as Governor, and Bowes Reed as Secretary.

Samuel Cooke Newell son of Elisha, was born in Allentown, N. J.; he married his cousin Esther Montgomery; they were my grandfather and my grandmother. Thus runs the story of my ancestors on my mother's side.

THE WATSON LINE

My paternal grandfather, the Rev. George Watson, D.D., was born in St. Bees, Cumberland, in England; he was the son of a surgeon in the British Navy. He was pre-eminently a teacher by taste, and began that work as classical master at St. Bees College. From there he went to York where he was head of St. Peter's School, St. William's College, the Minster Foundation. On July 26, 1826, he married Mary Anne Cooke in St. Olave's Church, Marygate, York.

As a matter of record it is well that I note here the members of my grandfather's family: William Watson, lost at sea. Thomas Watson, who died at 80; he had ten children. Mary Watson, died at 70. Susan Watson, died in 1869. Richard Watson, died at 39, leaving two children. John Watson, died at 11. Margaret Watson, died before 1870. Timothy Watson, died at 29, leaving one son. Noble Watson, died aged 52.

THE COOKE LINE (maternal side)

My line of descent runs as follows: Sir Bryan Cooke, of Wheatley Hall, Yorkshire. A younger son who was a barrister. His son, who was a Doctor Cooke. His son, Doctor William Cooke, who married Mary Anne Crowe, daughter of Jno. Crowe, curate of Burwell, Cambridgeshire. Their daughter, Mary Anne Cooke, who married George Watson, who was my grandfather.

Doctor William Cooke died in 1820; his wife Mary Anne Crowe died in 1854; their bodies lie in the same grave in the Churchyard at Great Baddow, Essex.

The Arms of the family of the Cookes of Wheatley Hall are described as:

> Shield, Or; Chevron, Red:
> Two lions, passant gardant, Black.

Here also I should record the family of William Cooke, M.D., and of Mary Anne Crowe, his wife: Mary Anne Cooke, my grandmother, Mrs. George Watson; William Cooke; Louisa Cooke; Emma Cooke; John Cooke; Alice Cooke—Mrs. Peter Jones; Edward Cooke, died as a baby; Eliza Cooke—Mrs. Bloomfield; Caroline Cooke, died as a baby; Edward Charles Cooke.

IT WAS A NOBLE SAYING OF THE LATE LORD CLARENDON THAT "BIRTH CONVEYS NO MERIT BUT MUCH DUTY TO ITS INHERITOR."

II

EARLIEST RECOLLECTIONS
1861-1866

IN TELLING my own personal story in so far as it pertains to a past long gone, I want to qualify my frequent use of the pronoun "I" by this consideration. How much of what we remember is what we really personally recall, or what we really personally had a part in? how much of it is our recollection of what others have told us of what we did, or said, or saw? how much of any story of a distant past, a story written many years afterward is what might be called exact history, and how much of it is a mental picture of what occurred woven in with the occurrences themselves, and interpreted in the light of the writer's later thinking and of his philosophizing about the events as they transpired? Is it possible to tell a story, and re-tell it, and tell it again for years, and not illustrate it by happenings which come in time to be part of the warp and woof of the story itself, and which we repeat again as part of what we knew or saw?

To my way of thinking all of what we call History bears this interpretation, and most of all ancient history: it is a record of happenings coloured and unified by tradition, and impressed with the viewpoint and the reasoning and the explanations of the narrator as the story passed through his mind, taking the impress of his personality on the way; and this comment applies equally to what men call sacred history as well as to what is known as current events. It must be so. An artist paints a picture: he makes it a thing of living interest; and he does this by adding to mathematical fact the colouring of tradition. A picture of bare details would have neither ethical nor aesthetic worth; it would be wholly lacking in appeal; nor would it show us the thing as it really is. For what is what we call tradition? It is really the embroidery to the fabric to give it human worth: it is the fringe which frames the picture in the tissues; but all the while it evidences the existence of the factual something of which it forms a part.

So, for the purpose of making my story more intelligent and more readable I will tell a lot of things in the first person. I will paint the picture as I see it now, without regard to whether I saw the things related, or whether I was told of them so often that they are part of my consciousness of them; without regard to whether I made the bright remarks, or whether I was told the story so often that I now think I did say them; at least I know well that I might have said or done them; they are artistically true, and that is more important to a story-teller than having his details historically exact.

With this disclaimer in advance, I may say that the "house where I was born" was cold, very cold on that windy twenty-seventh of an Iowa February in 1861: all the water for the baby's ritual bath had to be heated on an air-tight wood-stove in Mother's room; in fact until I was quite a boy and had graduated to bathing on Saturday nights in a washtub in the kitchen, as the grown folk did, the Saturday bath performance for me was always "up in Mother's room," and as one was not allowed to go out in the cold until after dinner and after the effects of the opened pores had worn off, one good half of Saturday, which was playday, was wasted on that bath performance; and from that experience I deduce my dislike for baths for a long time afterward.

Lyons, Iowa, where I was born, has as its earliest recollection for me the sight of soldiers lined up in the street in front of the house, "Mr. Lincoln's Men," recruits coming in to the River from the country round about after one of his Drafts; arms were stacked, and the people in the houses along the street were making great pots of coffee and taking it out to them. In this same connection, according to hearsay, a yellow haired boy went out of the gate into the street, and addressing the soldiers, told them that it was wicked to swear.

For years I had two material reminders of Lyons. One

was a set of carved boxwood chessmen in a wooden box, and on the under side of the lid of the box was written in an exquisite hand, "For little Sam; from Uncle Robert." Uncle Robert was Robert Traill Spence; I would like to know more of his story; and I wonder who stole my chessmen; for they are gone. Another reminder of Lyons was a book, bound in red, *The Fairy Tales of Hans Christian Andersen,* and on its fly-leaf was written "For little Sam, from Grandma and Auntie Hickox; the latter's family were friends of my mother, probably kinfolk, and lived in Milwaukee; I can remember some one reading out loud from that book, (Father probably, with many sly chuckles) "What the Old Man does is Always Right." I was christened in Lyons; Bishop Lee was to have done it, but a driving blizzard kept him from coming, so Father took his place. I do not know exactly why it had to be done on that very day; probably it was because "the old Adam in this child" was giving undue evidence of his presence. For I have seen a letter written by Mother to Uncle Bennington Gill, saying, "when you come out to Iowa, please bring several bottles of Darby's Carminative, as little Sam has bad attacks of colic." Darby's Carminative was a celebrated pain-killer for colicky infants in those days, its chief components being paregoric and syrup of senna.

Bishop Lee would have gotten by with my christening in more orthodox fashion than he did on another occasion, when a young mother who lisped badly brought a little girl up to the Font to be baptised by the Bishop. "Name this child," said the great man, and the little mother, completely upset by the dignified presence of this Bishop in his robes with the puffy sleeves, stuttered more than ever, and replied, "Lu-thy, Sir." "Tut, Tut," said the Bishop, "Nothing of the kind; Lucifer is a heathen name; John, I baptise thee"; and so little Lucy had to be John. I have never heard whether the Canons of 1854 had any provision for remedying such an emergency, or whether little Lucy was always John.

My brother George was born in Lyons in 1862. He died at Eglinton, New Jersey, in 1868; and his body was laid in the burying ground of the Presbyterian Church on the Hill in Allentown, where many of his kinfolk's burying-places were. My sister Esther was born in Lyons in 1864; she lived little more than a year; her body was placed in the cemetery in Lyons.

This is the place to recount some events which preceded this Lyons record, and to show how Lyons came to be the place where I was born.

My father was an Englishman, born in the city of York, where the family of my grandfather, George Watson, lived on Marygate, a street near the ruins of St. Mary's Abbey; all the children but my father, were christened in St. Olave's Church, Marygate; tradition has it that my father, who was the oldest child, was christened in the minister, in the font which stands just beneath "The Five Sisters Window." I have been told that my father's great-grandfather, who was an officer in the British Navy, was drowned when the *Royal George* turned turtle on the south coast; and it interested me much, when I was once at Llangollen in Wales to see a table which was made of oak from the *Royal George*. The Watsons must have been strong Liberals who cared little for hereditary glories. There is a tradition amongst us that one of the family after a visit to England being asked about the Watson family, said, "I could find out little about them; there was a bishop among them, and that is good; and as for the rest of them, this may be said, none of them was ever hung for sheep-stealing, none of them was ever sent to Botany Bay, and, Thank God, none of them was ever a Dissenter."

The bishop mentioned must have been an interesting old chap, Richard Watson, Bishop of Llandaff, Wales,—(probably it was from him that my father's brother Richard got his name). Bishop Watson had large estates at Windermere in Westmoreland, (these lands were still in the possession of a member of the family when I was there in 1909). He loved his Westmoreland place, and did not like Wales, so he would "bishop" for a while in Llandaff, and would then betake him to his comfort and his home at Windermere. He won the satiric dislike of his clergy by issuing a denunciatory letter on the subject of Absentee Rectorships. The Bishop bought other properties in the neighbourhood of Windermere in order to increase his holdings. In this manner there came into his possession an Inn at Ambleside known as "The Cock," which was glorified by a swinging sign on which was painted a rooster with wings wide spread. After his Lordship of Llandaff had become the owner, the inn-keeper, thinking to do honour to the new proprietor, took down the Sign of the Cock, committed it ignominiously to the village dust-heap, hung up a new sign-board, whereon one might see swinging to the breeze a brilliant portrait of the Bishop in his robes, and re-named his Inn "The Bishop." There was a small doggery further up the road, whose proprietor seeing the sign-board of "The Cock" in the discard, rescued it, had it varnished anew, and hung it up in front of his place to the dismay of the former owner of the sign; for the sign was so well known and the beer behind it so famous, and the carters coming over the Pass were so used to saying to each other as they met, "Get your beer at The Cock, when you get down," that "The Cock" began to draw much of the patronage. The landlord of "The Bishop" began to feel the loss; whereupon he devised a remedy; he had a hanger painted and swung it underneath his new sign, whereon was painted the Bishop in his Robes, and the sign announced,—"This is the Old Cock."

It was in 1838 that my grandparents, then living in York, bought from an agent what was said to be "a gentleman's estate" in Pennsylvania, thinking that the change to America would benefit the health and fortune of the family. One can well imagine what must have been their visions of "a gentleman's estate" with their quiet scholarly English outlook, when they set sail from the port of Bristol in a sailing vessel to come to America; and equally well what must have been their disappointment when they reached Pennsylvania, for "the gentleman's estate" turned out to be an abandoned farm which went by the name of "Wysox," and was located on the site of a former Indian village by that name. Often have I heard my father tell of the hard life his mother led on that farm. She was gently born and reared;

came from an English city where household help was inexpensive and easily had; her husband's position as an English schoolmaster in a Cathedral School was one of dignity; and in America she found herself of necessity obliged to do everything for the family, cooking, laundering, and all the other household tasks, and even at times she had to prepare the meals for the farmhands who came to help get in the crops.

It was on that farm that my father's later boyhood was spent; and the first money which he ever earned was two York shillings which he got for picking stones from a neighbour's field and piling them up for fencing; with the money he bought a little copy of *Pilgrim's Progress;* my cousin George Watson now has this book bearing my father's signature on the fly-leaf. It was there that Father began his preparation for college; and I have heard Father tell of my grandmother's having an ironing-board set up under a near-by apple tree, and in the intervals as he would run back and forth to the kitchen for the hot irons Grandmother would hear him recite his lessons.

She must have been a wonderfully fine and brave woman, that Grandmother Watson of mine. I can remember her well as I used to see her in Norwalk, Ohio, where she lived the later years of her life. She was a dignified and sober lady; I think of her as I used to see her in the afternoons coming out of her room after her nap and seating herself in an armchair covered with black horsehair; she was dressed in black silk; she had on an apron with violet ribbons let in the edge of it; she wore a lace cap with violet ribbons; she wore silk mitts which half covered her hands; there was always a fragrance of lavender about her; and when she seated herself in that chair and crossed her hands on her lap she possessed a reverential dignity not lightly to be disturbed but rather to be worshipped from afar.

My grandmother Watson's grandfather, the Rev. John Crowe, was a witty man; I wish I might have known him. We have a rhymed invitation to dinner which he once wrote, which is worth preserving in print:

"But, what is here? why, one presents
His most respectful compliments
To Mr. Philip Isaacson,
And if his heart is set upon
Giving his hunger some relief
By bolting down a pound of beef,
Would gladly see him, if he's able
To walk as far as my poor table.
All things shall be in order done
And cleanly cooked exact at one.
I did intend to get a salad
But oil, I know, don't suit your palate,
And the whole town cannot produce
A red or white beet fit for use.
I did purpose to ask another
To make a third; 'twas Bob, your brother;
But he, poor man, on market day
Performs the part of old Dame Gray.
I think, upon a parson's word,
'T is always right to have a third;
And 't is a maxim all through Wales,—
(Don't think I tell old women's tales)
That two can't make a conversation;
But the contrary must be said
Of man and woman when in bed.
For now, supposing two dispute
About the King, or else Lord Bute,
About the House of Commons power
Confining Crosby in The Tower,
And so, like fools, we strip to fight,
Wanting a third to set us right.
Now he, like you, a man of knowledge
Equal to any from a college,
I'll offer my appeal to you
Whether this maxim is not true:
—But here, methinks, I hear you say,
"The parson's surely mad today!
What stuff is here? Do stop, good John!"
No; Faith and Troth, I will go on.
Let prating folk say what they will,
For John will have his humour still.
The Meeting may my ways condemn;
The Meeters, what care I for them?
For tho' they call me wicked sinner,

I'll try if I can't after dinner
A cup of wine and ale afford,
A pack of cards and cribbage board.
Here's to you, Phil, here's fifteen-four!—
'T is time, I think, to say no more.
So I am, with devotion fervent,
Your most obedient, humble servant,

JNO. CROWE
Curate of Burwell,
(Cambridgeshire)

Grandfather's farm of "Wysox" was near the village of Towanda, and in time the village grew up to the farm and the farm land became valuable, so that finally when the family came to Norwalk, Ohio, it was as prosperous citizens that they arrived there; it was there that they had their own home, the last one for them on their earthly pilgrimage. Grandfather early began holding church services in his own house for his family; to these some neighbours came; and when Christ Church, Towanda was organised, Grandfather was ordained to the ministry and became Rector of the Church, still continuing to live at Wysox.

From Towanda Grandfather moved to Owego, New York, where he had accepted the rectorship of St. Paul's Church. I like to think of what that change must have meant to them, to Grandmother, and also to Grandfather, for he was a classical scholar and an educated English gentleman; and Owego was an aristocratic old town with traditions of fine breeding, and families like the Leonard's, and the Pumpelly's and the Bacon's set the pace. It was from Owego that Father left home to go to Hobart College where he graduated in 1851. In 1854 he graduated from the General Theological Seminary in New York; and became assistant minister of St. Luke's Church, Rochester, New York, of which Dr. Henry Washington Lee was then Rector. Dr. Lee was elected first Bishop of Iowa, and he asked Father, who had volunteered to go with him to this new missionary field, to precede him and to organise the work, so far as possible, before the coming of the Bishop.

It was just at this time that Grandfather had accepted

the charge of the Church in Norwalk, and finding it impossible to leave Owego immediately, he asked Father to stop in Norwalk on his way to Iowa and to take charge of the Church there temporarily until he could make his arrangements to come; so that my father was my grandfather's predecessor in that Church, just as I was later my father's predecessor in the Church in Iowa City; and it was in Norwalk that Grandfather finished his earthly ministry. I can remember Main Street in Norwalk, and I can remember Grandfather's house; I can remember Uncle Richard's store and the barrel of New Orleans brown sugar from which I used to get lumps of sticky brown goodness; and I can remember Uncle Richard saying, "Come on, Sam, it's time to go home to dinner," and that meant stopping on the way at the Stoutenburgh house where was found at the gate a radiant vision of beauty, who was one day to be my Aunt Charlotte. I can remember my greatuncle Edward Cooke, who was Grandmother's brother, and his two daughters, my father's cousins who were so good to me. Those nieces were rather old-fashioned and always said Uncle Watson, and Aunt Watson; and Grandmother on all occasions which demanded it, called Grandfather "Mr. Watson."

We Watson menfolk have all of us been rather lacking in parsonical dignity, except in church, where our solemnity of demeanor was, so I think, partly aesthetic good taste, and partly reverence for the fitness of things. And we all of us, neither Grandfather, Father, nor I, could ever let the cut of our garb repress our sense of humour and our love of a joke. (How Father loved to hear and to tell a good story!) One of the Cooke family relates that on a Sunday afternoon when Grandfather had indulged in some precious bit of fun, Grandmother said soberly, "Mr. Watson, I think that you forget what day this is." A little "uncoguid" this may seem to some of her descendants, yet, after all, I think that even an exaggerated regard for the niceties was a finer spirit than the utter lack of reverence for anything which is to-day called "being modern." In his later years Grandfather became blind, but for all that, he still continued to minister in the Church; he knew the services perfectly by heart, and on the Sunday mornings he would have some one of the family read over for him the Psalms for the Day, and the Lessons, and the Collect, Epistle, and Gospel (for the Ante-Communion was an invariable part of the morning worship), and then tapping his way down the street with his cane he would go to the Church, put on his gown or his surplice, and say the morning Offices. In the last days of their lives both Grandfather and Grandmother were confined to their beds which were in opposite corners of their big room, and every morning they said together the Prayer Book Morning Prayer, Versicle and Response being made from bed to bed. To have known my father and to have had such memories of my grandfather and my grandmother was to have an inspiring vision of what heredity and environment might mean. Grandfather died on November 15, 1870; and Grandmother on the 20th of October of the same year; their bodies were laid in a fenced-in plot just back of the Church in Norwalk.

Father was one of four children; beside him there was his brother Richard, and his two sisters, Mary Anne and Eliza. My father's two sisters never married. My Aunt Mary Anne died in Bellevue, Ohio, and I laid her body to rest in the cemetery there. My Aunt Eliza led a busy and deeply interested life as a teacher, beginning her work at a school at Poughkeepsie on the Hudson, which was under the direction of the Rev. Mr. Rider. Later she became associated with Mrs. Sylvanus Reed in the Reed School on East 53rd Street, New York; and when that school passed out of Mrs. Reed's hands, my aunt with one of her friends opened a school of their own in the City. She passed away at Asbury Park, New Jersey on May 11, 1911; her body was laid beside her sister's in the Bellevue Cemetery, and I said the last words beside the grave. My Uncle was for some years a merchant in Norwalk, and there he married Charlotte Stoutenburgh; later he moved to Salina, Kansas, where he went into business; and the first services of the Episcopal Church in Salina were said in his house. He had three children, Charlotte, Eliza, and George (George III), who were all born in Salina. Charlotte and Eliza

(Lida to you) have never married, and have lived in recent years in Norwalk. George married Edith Whittier, and has two children, Jeannette, and Flora; George lives in Cleveland, Ohio. My Uncle Richard was a round and jolly man; and we all loved him dearly; and my Aunt Eliza was the fairy godmother to us all.

After supplying the Church in Norwalk for a time, Father went to Iowa, where with Davenport as a starting point he began work at various river points on the Mississippi, Bellevue and Savannah being among them. Soon after that the new Bishop came, and the active organisation of the Diocese began. He is very clear in my memory, Henry Washington Lee, the first Bishop of Iowa; he used to put me on his shoulder and tell me that he was just the height of Goliath. He loved my father, and out of that association grew one of the happiest relationships of my father's life, his acquaintance with the French family who were Bishop Lee's kinfolk; and from that came my own close friendship with my almost-kinfolk, the George Watson Frenchs of Davenport. George and Anna French have been very close to me in the years that I have known them well, which means since I came to California to live; and to have learned to know and to love George and Anna French is one of the good things which California has brought to my life. Alice French, George's sister, is known to the literary world as Octave Thanet; and his brother Nathanael was both honoured and admired as a jurist in Iowa Courts and elsewhere.

The French family welcomed my father to their home, and Father's engagement to the daughter of the family was brought to a sad close by her death; and when the son of the French family welcomed his little newborn son he was called George Watson French after my father. I have heard George say that when he was a little boy his father took him by the hand and led him over to my father and said, "Son, this is the kind of man I want you to grow up like."

At Bishop Lee's request Father left the eastern part of Iowa to go to the extreme western part, where he settled in Council Bluffs and established the church there, and from there began work in Sioux City, and in Omaha in Nebraska. He made the journey in winter going from Davenport to Iowa City by the railroad, Iowa City being then the Western terminus of the Railroad, and from Iowa City he went to Council Bluffs, by way of Des Moines, in the Government Mail which was an open sled drawn by four horses. I have heard Mrs. Weare who was Father's hostess at Sioux City tell of the time when he first arrived there and came to their house where he was to stay on the occasion of his first church service in Sioux City: she was kneading bread, and she was obliged to ask Father to sit down on the doorstep until she could get her hands out of the dough.

I was at that time in Sioux City in camp with two Regiments of National Guard troops, the Third Iowa of which I was chaplain, and the First Dakota. It was very cold at night, so cold that the water barrels from which we got our water to wash with were frozen over in the morning, and we were obliged to break the ice with a hairbrush. Our Colonel, being the ranking officer, was in command of the Brigade: for his headquarters he had a tent with a large fly to it for his office, and back of that another tent for his sleeping quarters; and in front of headquarters he had a large "V-shaped" barricade built of old railroad ties, in the open side of which toward headquarters was built a large fire and some of the heat was reflected into the big tent. On account of the cold, the Colonel said to me, "Chaplain, you and the Adjutant have your cots brought up here and put them in the big tent in front of mine, and you will be much warmer at night"; which was done. That night after I had gone to bed, "boots and breeches on," I was half asleep with my blankets pulled up over my ears, when some one shook me and said, "Wake up, old man; here's something to keep the cold out!" The "something" was a brown bottle; need it be said that "Barkis was willin'"? As I handed back the little brown jug to the thoughtful friend who brought it, who was the adjutant of the First Dakota, he nearly dropped it. "Good Lord," he said; "It's the Chaplain!" He had thought that he was comforting his colleague the adjutant of the Third Iowa. (Comment: All the officers were present at Church Parade next morning.)

Father made his home in Council Bluffs at the house of Judge Douglass; on Sundays his morning service was in Council Bluffs, and in the afternoon he crossed the Missouri River to hold service at night on the Omaha side; the service was in Papillon, then the county seat and the real town adjoining Fort Omaha. The crossing was on the ferry when the boat could run, and when the river was blocked with ice the crossing was made by the Government Mail which was a sledge when that was usable, and otherwise, when the ice was running, they used a boat on runners which they pushed over the cakes of ice until they came to open water when the sledge became a boat. In Omaha Father stayed with his friend Judge Woolworth. The Judge had a cabin of two rooms, one of which was office and the other was bedroom; there was one bed, and Father and the Judge used to draw lots as to which one of them should have the bedsprings and the blankets and which one should have the mattress on the floor in front of the fireplace; and Father said that he often slept on the floor with his carpet-sack for a pillow and his buffalo-skin coat for a cover. And that carpet-sack! it was a real carpet-bag—I can see it now. It fell to me in after years, and I used to carry it when as a small boy I went to the country when we lived in Burlington to make a visit with the Danner family who were close friends of ours.

The Danners lived on a farm which was traversed by the railroad, and once I thought that I had made my fortune there; I had gathered up abandoned spikes which the section gangs had thrown away along the right-of-way—all I could carry of the rusty old things—and I lugged them home when I went back, carrying them in that carpet-sack mixed promiscuously with my clothes and my "nighty." The rusty spots on my clothes betrayed me; and when I explained that I had found the spikes and that I was going to sell them for "old-iron," I was informed by my dignified family that I was going to do nothing of the sort; that the spikes belonged to the Railroad, and that selling them was stealing. There and then I put a poser to them—"What was I going to do with them?" The solution of that problem in ethics I do not remember. But I wish now that I had taken it myself for solution to the genial President of the "Burlington," and had said: "Mr. Perkins, here are some of your old spikes; my family says that I can't sell them for 'old-iron,' because they are yours, and selling them would be stealing; I didn't know it wasn't all right to take them when they had been thrown away. Please, Sir, what shall I do with them?" And I know right well what the answer would have been: Mr. Perkins would have said, "Sam, that's fine of you to come to me about it"; and I think that I would have had more nickels to buy some of those fat sticks of molasses candy at Runge's for a nickel apiece; and I don't think that the question of ethics would have been raised by the "old-clo' " man who would have had the final disposition of the matter.

That carpet-bag brings me to another story. I was out on the Danner's farm near Burlington, and I was sleeping in a third floor room on a mattress near a window, and in the middle of one night I woke hearing the most awful shrieks which seemed to come from just outside my window. I crept close under the blankets shivering with fear; the moonlight was pouring in the window, but it was a long time before I got courage enough to look out. When I did so what I saw was not calculated to quiet my dread, for I saw a circle of banshees with their heads cast up toward the moon and uttering most fearful cries; and I shut my eyes again and shivered until daylight when the banshees crept away and the shrieking stopped. Morning brought its answer to my troubles of the night. The banshees were prairie-wolves gathered in a circle in the moonlight and howling at the moon about a spot where the body of a dead cow had been buried on the prairie a few days before. I have heard wolves howl in the Morvan in France one night, when my car was fast in the snow after skidding into a drift and I had to sit there five hours till help came, but I have never heard any howling like that of those prairie wolves—the Morvan wolves were timber wolves: And I've known fear too; but submarines in the Estuary of the Gironde, or bombs on the City at night, or even "Big-Bertha," none of these had an "edge" on those prairie wolves for pure unmitigated frightening of the human body. Those war time affairs did not really frighten the real You; they simply gave you a feeling somewhat akin to what the old lady had in mind when she said, "I wish that John would get well—or something." Have it over with, and get done with it, that's the way you felt then.

There were amusing things which happened to relieve the hardness of those journeys, which my father made in and about that Council Bluffs and Omaha country. Claim-jumping was the one unpardonable sin in that day and country, and the Vigilantes executed summary vengeance on a caught offender. At one time Father was preaching in the Court House at Papillon—the court room was on the second floor of a log building and above the county offices. While he was talking a man came forward and handed him a piece of folded brown paper; and Father thinking that it was some kind of a notice to give out put the paper under the edge of the Bible and went on with his discourse. After a time, noticing the man fidgeting around in the back of the room Father was not surprised to see the man come forward with another piece of paper in his hand, and this time, in handing it to Father, he said "Read it!" Father read it; and this is what was written in it; "Hurry up! Preacher, we want to try a man." Father cut the sermon short (probably, as he said, to its advantage) and let the people go with a benediction; and, as the congregation made its way down the stairs they met the Vigilantes coming up bringing with them the claim-jumper, his hands tied behind his back. Before they were out of sight of the Court House, the case was tried and settled and the criminal strung up. It goes without saying that claim-jumping soon ceased to be a popular sport.

During the time that Father was in charge of the church in Council Bluffs, he went East on a vacation and made a visit to his close friend in the Seminary, the Rev. Dr. Edward Foggo, afterward Rector of Christ Church, Philadelphia, who was, at the time when Father visited him, the Rector of Christ Church, Allentown, New Jersey. That was the little white old-fashioned church on Church Street, which I so well remember; and of that church Hetty Newell was the organist. Eglinton was as widely known for its hospitality as were the Newell girls for their charm, and the sequel to this visit to the East was Father's marriage to my mother on September 21, 1859. My mother was very pretty; slender, petite, brunette in type; she had wonderful eyes, and a charm of manner and a gaiety of spirit which were most winning. Beverly Jones, one of our Canadian cousins, wrote me this about Mother:

> "I have often noted a family trait which seems to have descended to your mother, as it did to my mother, from some remote ancestor. My mother had the most penetrating eye, which used to look through me when I did anything which she did not like. Your mother had the same kind of eyes; and if I was 'cheeky' to her as a boy she would look through me in the same way and never say anything, but that eye would 'flatten me out' more than if either of them had shown their displeasure by speaking. I often wondered if that *eye* went through you in the same way as my mother's eye went through me . . . I am sending you some views of Rockford where your mother used to slide down hill in the winter time."

Mother was very fond of her Canadian cousins and spent much time at Brockville, Ontario, where was Rockford (the family place) of which Cousin Beverly wrote; and the Canadian cousins were frequent visitors at Eglinton.

Mother graduated at St. Mary's Hall, Burlington, N. J.; she was distinguished at the school for her musical ability, and her music master there dedicated one of his compositions to her. One of Mother's schoolmates at St. Mary's was Caroline Scheetz, whose son Frederick Scheetz Jones became Dean of Yale; he was my schoolmate at Shattuck.

In 1859 Father and Mother started from New Jersey together to make their home in the West, leaving a place which was more "home" to my mother than any one place can possibly be to most of my readers. Seven generations of her ancestors were born under the same rooftree which sheltered her infancy; every stick and stone of the place was replete with associations and memories; every name of every family for miles around was familiar; and cousins from the first to the Nth degree of kinship were more or less constantly coming and going; for Eglinton was the replica of an old English Manor Hall with its doors wide open with hospitable welcome to all our kinfolk. More than once do I remember our sitting down at dinner in the dining-room at Eglinton with twenty at the table, and all of the twenty relatives in some degree of kinship. It was with leaving all this behind that Mother came to that border-town on the Missouri where her life was to begin anew; and what the resultant homesickness must have been after the first novelty wore off no one of us of her kinfolk can realise. I have been homesick; it is an ache which finds no relief; no wonder that no one of us ever fully knew till long afterward what Mother gave of life to life, when she made a home for a family in that wild new world of the Western plains.

Their first stop was in Chicago where Mother bought supplies for her housekeeping; some of the china which came from "Burley's" I have with me still. From Chicago they went to St. Louis by train; from there to St. Joseph by boat on the Missouri; and from St. Joseph they went to Council Bluffs by stage coach. The only tradition which I have of the life in Council Bluffs is the story of a fright which Mother had when she looked up from her sewing (probably sewing for me, for I was then "on the way"), and she saw an Indian in paint and feathers looking in at her through the window. From Council Bluffs the family moved to Lyons, Iowa, and it was there that I arrived vocally upon the scene; from Lyons we moved in 1866 to Burlington, another town on the great Mississippi; and it is in Burlington that my own story really begins in conscious memory.

III

BURLINGTON DAYS

1866-1874

BURLINGTON was really my only home, until I came to California; although I always felt myself at home at Eglinton. I loved the place like a home, which means that I was always glad to go back to it, both in bodily presence and in memory. That is my definition of "home" —a place to which you always love to go back; and Burlington had always that attraction for me.

Father was Rector of Christ Church on the corner of Fifth and High; and we lived first on Fourth Street, in what we always called the "Clark House"; later on we moved to what we called the "Hedge house," just next to the big house on the corner of Fifth (and I think it was Columbia) where Mr. Thomas Hedge, Sr. lived, and between that and the house which Thomas Hedge, Jr. built for himself after we moved there, and after he married the lovely Mollie Cook. The Clark house was a good sized red brick house set up high from the street with terraces and a stone wall; on the south side was an alley; the street was a dirt road, and a sea of mud when it rained, and the alley was the same. There were alleys all over the town cutting the blocks in four; and those alleys!—they were the happy hunting ground of pigs, and sometimes cows; there was no city ordinance controlling the free roaming of such domestic pets; there was no sewer system and no garbage collecting service; the garbage was deposited in the alleys by every one and the pigs and the cows did garbage service free of charge. Wooden sidewalks were everywhere; and one would often have to wait a moment when about to cross an alleyway until Mrs. Pig and a tribe of little piglets availed themselves of what one willing accorded them, the "right of way."

But Burlington was a fair place, for all that these were primitive times and there were some funny things about it. It had VIEWS. Never except in my Oriole House in Montecito have I lived with such a wealth of view as we had from the windows of "Mother's room," the upstairs southeast corner room, of the "Clark house" in Burlington. The long stretch of the Mississippi from the "Cut-off" to Vinegar Hill, miles wide when the river was in flood, and with sandbars showing at times of low water. And what I saw from those windows in Mother's room!—boats, and boats, and more boats; the two ferries that ran across the River to East Burlington, the *Flint Hills* and the *Shokoquon*. The Railroad did not cross the river when we first went there to live; one had to take the ferry across to East Burlington, and then wade through sand and pine log bark up to the East Burlington Station of the C. B. & Q. when we went on one of our pilgrimages to the homeland in Jersey. And then the big boats! and they were really *big* boats. I could tell every one of them by the shape and colour of its pilot-house, and by the sound of its whistle—the *Phil Sheridan,* and the *Tom Jasper,* and the *Hawkeye State,* and all the rest, which were big side-wheelers. Then there were some fine big stern-wheelers like the *Diamond Joe;* and there was the whole fleet of towboats and raftboats, log-rafts and lumber-rafts. Oh, a river town was a place for a boy to grow up in. They say, "Pity a boy who has never known life on a farm," and I say so too; but I say also, "Pity a boy who has never grown up on the banks of a real river like the Mississippi"; and I knew both, for we went back to the home farm at Eglinton nearly every summer. It was one of those log-rafts which taught me to swim. Just above the town there was an inland passage, a sort of bayou, or as we called it a slough *(sloo),* and the stern-wheelers with their tows of logs, which they did not tow but pushed, used often at high water to take that cut-off in order to save time. Just after emerging from the cut-off and being close to the right bank, the head of the raft would be well inshore, and then the raftboat would have to push the rear end hard and sharp in order to swing the raft out into the channel again.

There was a sand beach on the main shore just where the cut-off ended, and this was a favourite place for boys to swim; but, for me, it was against parental orders to go into the river. There was a bathhouse on floats in the river just in front of the town, and once a week I was given ten cents to pay my way at the bathhouse. It seemed to me an awful waste of good molasses candy in the potential to spend that money just to go in the river, when most of the boys went in the river for nothing. (And if I mention that molasses candy at Runge's, big fat sticks for a nickel, every old Burlington boy will know what I mean; if I mention them more often than seems necessary, the modern reader is asked to remember that even now-a-days doctors say that children need sweets). Well, the sequel needs no telling; I took to going in the river with the other boys; and one day when a stern-pusher came along with a big string of logs and swung it in close to the shore and all the other boys hopped on, I went with the rest; I was thrilled and fascinated. Then the head of the raft swung out from the shore, the boys jumped off and made for land, and what I heard was, "Jump, Sam! Jump, you little fool!" For a whole minute which seemed an age, the problem flashed through my mind, what to do, for I knew I really could not swim. Should I jump and risk drowning, or should I stick by the raft and go on with it down river in sight of all Burlington, and me with nothing on but "my birthday suit"; the scene sometimes repeats itself even now in my dreams. But in the end modesty prevailed; I jumped, made half a dozen paddles dog-fashion toward the shore, went down, came up, went down again, paddled some more, and then was dragged out thoroughly water-logged by two of the bigger boys, was rolled on the sand, hung up by the heels, slapped on the back, and finally when I got my breath back was encouraged to go into the water again. And, then, wonder of wonders, the thrilling truth came home to me—I COULD SWIM. From that moment the fascination of the river was on me in real earnest; Old Man River called whenever I could run away from the good little boys of the neighbourhood with whom I was supposed to be playing. But the summer Iowa sun was hot on youthful backs, and one day Aunt Mary said to Mother, "Hetty, just look at this poor boy's back and shoulders; he's all sunburned; you must get him some thicker waists to wear." But the rest of the family were not so easy as Aunt Mary, and after a due application of the "third degree," the truth came out—I had been in the river. "Have you not been told that you must not go in the river until you can swim?" I was asked. My dearly beloved family did not realise what they had done by that question; but I did, and I took advantage of it; their question "gave me the edge," and my reply was, "But I *can* swim; just come down to the bathhouse with me, and I'll show you." They were good sports, my family; they accepted my challenge; and "I show'd 'em," and won my freedom, as many another had before me, at the risk of my life, little realising what a small boy drowned could mean to his family, nor what it had cost to "born and raise" him. Not that I would have cared much in those days, for as I think of it now, I must have been a selfish little beast; and my chief concern was that there would have been no more swimming in the river and no more molasses candy at Runge's.

Father was an epicure; he knew all about good things to eat, and he knew how to pick them out. There was a market down near Valley Street to which the country people brought their produce, and in the cool of the morning about six o'clock Father would take a big market-basket and go to the market and come home again with a basket brimming full. I had often begged to go with him, and as often had been told "No." One morning when Father was on his way to the market, whom did he see but Sam, in his nighties, sitting on the low stone wall at Fourth and Columbia Streets, at the end of the Robertson place. If the fascinated reader would ask me to tell what followed, rather than repeat the sad tale, I would prefer to reply in Latin. Father used to tell the story of an Eton boy who had been flogged, and who was standing in one of the hallways, arm against the wall, head on his arm, and crying. Queen Victoria was visiting the school that day, and when she saw the boy, she stopped and said, "Why, my lad, what is the matter?", and the boy replied *"Infandum regina, jubes renovare dolorem"* (O Queen, you order me to renew my awful hurt). Father loved Latin, and Latin jokes, and he told this tale of a boy who used to come to him and to some others of his schoolmates and beg them to translate his Latin poetry for him just before class. Thinking to get rid of him in future, one day when this line occurred in the lesson, *"Romanos rerum dominos, gentemque togatam,"* they translated it for him, and he went into class with this translation of it; *Romanos rerum*—a Roman nose is a rare thing; *dominos*—damn the nose; *gentemque togatam*—and the gentleman that's got him.

Another sight which I had from the windows of Mother's room which thrilled me was the building of the bridge. The C. B. & Q. Road ran from Chicago to the Mississippi; then from the Mississippi to the Missouri was the old B. & M.; but in time there came an empire-builder, C. E. Perkins, and in August, 1868 the Mississippi was bridged, and the two roads became "The Burlington"; and the trains came across right in sight of our windows. It was a wonderful sight to see the first little dinky engines crawling out over that spider work of a bridge; and then work trains, and then passenger and freight trains. The building of that bridge was a great piece of engineering in those days; it was first of all the vision of a constructive mind, and then the accomplishing of an engineering feat of giant proportions. There were mud-banks for approaches, and a shifting current always at work eroding both banks and channels; there were piers to sink in deflecting swirls of water, and accumulations of mud and débris to reckon with whenever high water changed conditions; and how to place the piers with reference to the "draw" so as to make navigation safe in those whirling waters, so that big boats like the *Phil Sheridan,* could pass through the "draw" at all waters. I was thrilled when I saw it being done, and I am more appreciative of its meaning as I look back at it after all these years. And to make that bridge safe for boats to pass was a first essential, for there was no north and south transportation from Burlington in those days except that which the river afforded. Those were the days of which Mark Twain wrote such vivid pictures in his river stories; and passengers and freight, north-bound or south-bound, had to wait on the levee or on the wharf-boat until the steamers came. Piers and docks were impossible on account of the current and the varying levels of the water; and so all loadings and landings had to be made by a landing-stage let down from the boat. You could never tell exactly when a boat would be in. One of my most vivid memories of river days is of a trip northward by boat on the river. The agent on the levee said, "She'll be in about 8:00 o'clock this evening"; so by 6:30 we were all packed up and had had our supper; at 7:00 the trunks started for the levee on a "dray," and we followed them in the omnibus which had been notified to come for us and in more than ample time we reached the landing. Eight o'clock came and no boat; there was no telephone, nor wireless, and except from the largest towns there was no possibility of getting word as to the boat's whereabouts by telegram; and there would have been no way of getting the word to our house if word had been received; so to go to the levee and wait was all that there was to be done. We could not go home again for there was no way of getting there and back, and no knowing either when the boat would come, and that the last boat for a week. The boat was the *Hawkeye State,* and she was a beauty. Oh, the splendour of her "saloon"—the long salon between the staterooms with the tables set the length of the boat in between the staterooms, all of it splendid in white and gold and scarlet and mirrors, and overhead the quivering and the jingling of the lustres about the oil-lamps which lit it all as the engines throbbed and set the great palace adriving up the stream. We were impatient to go. Would she ever come? Night grew darker and colder. "Come here children and put your wraps on"; and finally heavy-lidded eyes gave way to slumber long delayed past the usual "eight o'clock bedtime"; and then, "Wake up children; the boat's coming!" First the whistle before we could see anything; then a scarlet glow in the sky; then coming around the bend by Vinegar Hill a blaze of lights; and we knew that Providence had been kind, and that we were going after all. I have crossed the Ocean many times, sometimes on giant liners like the *Lusitania,* but I never had again such a thrill as that which that first river trip on the *Hawkeye State* gave me.

My schooldays began in Burlington. Father taught me Latin while we lived in "the Clark house," but I remember but little of that first educative experience except that the Latin Books were bound in sheepskin—Anthon's Cæsar, and Anthon's Latin Dictionary; and what little I remember of them is that I liked the smell of the leather. Thus early I seem to have begun to feel the pull of sense-perception.

Public Schools in Iowa in those days had small attraction for one like my father who had been brought up with English ideas of thoroughness in education; they were fairly inefficient types of mass education which gave no chance at all for individual instruction but obliged all the children to go from grade to grade at a pace which was fixed by the dullest of the lot. As a consequence I was sent to Mr. Graff's school, a private school, in a wooden schoolhouse on the south end of the Robertson property, on Columbia Street just off Fourth. In this story I am putting in the names of streets just as I remember them after more than sixty years of absence, and I may locate some of them inexactly, but that is the way in which all history is written, as I have before remarked; the main fact is that there was a street there, and that it had a name, and that I went to a school in the neighbourhood; and that is exactitude enough for any reader or writer of history. Mr. Graff was a precisian; there were no debatable things with him; you could not be half-right and half-wrong with Mr. Graff, and the present day sloppy moral code would have had short shrift if enunciated by any of his scholars in his presence. There were no excuses for non-performance; you knew your lesson or you didn't; you were eating that apple on the sly behind your desk, or you were not; and the one crime, worse than the crime itself, in his eyes, was lying about it. For girls, punishments were perforce limited in possibility of variety and performance (for Mr. Graff was a chivalrous man, with a delicate courtesy toward woman-kind) and consisted of standing in a corner, back to the school and face to the wall. For boys it was different; their punishment was a beating, on the hands with a ruler, or with a stick on that part of the anatomy most prominent, with the result that sitting down was uncomfortable for some time afterward; and the instrument of punishment was selected with due regard to its intended use. The instruction given the unlucky culprit would be; "Take this knife, and go out and cut me a stick; not an old dried one, but a tough limber one!" I well remember a certain boy whose name I could give, and I hesitate to do it for fear that he might challenge the record on grounds of historical accuracy, who having been warned of a beating to come on the morrow, took the precaution of putting on an extra pair of trousers. The punishment was administered with no faltering arm, but the little rascal was so foolish as to grin in the face of the labouring teacher as the strokes came down. A superficial exploration sufficed to reveal the fraud on the public, and (Mr. Graff had no sense of humour in such a case). S—— (I almost gave his name) was instructed to retire and remove the impediments, and come back for more.

Yet Mr. Graff's school was the best school in Burlington. Judge James D. Smyth speaks of him as "our rugged instructor Graff," of whom it may be said, as of Goldsmith's village schoolmaster that, "If severe in aught, the love he bore to learning was in fault." It was the sort of a school which a river town of that day needed; it taught boys and girls, especially boys, lessons with a thoroughness which could be found nowhere else; parents were grateful for it, and as for me, I am grateful for it too. For Mr. Graff taught me arithmetic, and that was a triumph; I do not know any one else who could have done it; it was the only mathematics which I ever learned; for the rest of my scholastic days I consistently and shamelessly flunked "Math." And more than a merely scholastic training was had in that school; Mr. Graff was a character builder; boys and girls who could not stand real training went back to the public schools. So called modern methods are apparently more merciful, more understanding, more sympathetic; but they partake of the lacks in modern home life and home training; they are soft; the reaction to them on the part of youth is a tendency to exaggerate self and its cries for consideration. My diagnosis of the causes for the wobbliness of this American generation is that precedent and environing life has failed in cradling it in the idealism of a lovable and livable family background; and has also failed in inspiring it with that loyalty to something beyond itself and its cries of self in which strength of character finds chiefest support.

I remember well some of my schoolmates at Mr. Graff's, Frank and Arthur Adams, and the Robertson girls with their appleblossom fairness, and the Brooks girls from South Hill.

I did fairly well in the school, largely because I did not like what went with not doing fairly well. I was always a sensitive individual, too much so often for my own good; and my worst offence was neglecting to learn "a piece" to speak, and for the third and last time to perpetrate that sad apology in rhyme:

"You'd scarce expect one of my age
To speak in public on the stage."

And again I quote with full assent Judge Smyth's words; "I consider Mr. Graff's instruction as of the very best that I ever received anywhere."

We had neighbours when we lived in the "Clark house" on Fourth Street, whom I bear in grateful memory. Just next to us on the south lived the Mathes family, German people of the good old sort; there were many like them all down the Mississippi Valley, and Burlington had many of them; the kind of Germans who, even in that day, rebelled against autocracy and imperialism; Germans of the Carl Schurz type; never were better friends and neighbours than they. The Mathes family made me welcome to their table, and they did have such good things to eat; and from them I learned my beginnings of the sonorous tongue of the Fatherland. And on the north of us lived Fred Becker, a bachelor, and his two maiden sisters; they taught me to love the traditions of old Germany; I thought of them often when I visited Germany years later, the kindly, jolly, comfortable Germany that I first knew; and one of the bitter things of the War to me was to realize how the heart of the German people was being wounded by the results of the blinded ambitions of their leaders. The Beckers were gentle folk; Fred Becker was the principal liquor dealer in Burlington; and the Becker house and garden at Christmas and at Easter with *Lebkuchen,* and the Easter rabbits leaving eggs for children under every bush were full of joys for us small folk.

Near Fred Becker's store was the wholesale grocery of John H. Gear, who had beautiful daughters. Senator Gear he was afterward. I used to go down to that good smelling emporium of his and make my way back to the office which was partitioned off in glass from the mainstore, and I would find the big man himself, and hold out to him what was wealth to me and tell him that I came to get a nickel's worth of Brazil nuts—"nigger-toes" we called them in those days. And I would come away with a great cornucopia, symbol of plenty, filled to running over with a quarter's worth of spoil for a nickel, just because John H. Gear's heart had a place in it for small boys. I wonder if grown folk were to realize how sympathy and understanding makes the world a more joyful place for little folk, and whether that impulse would not perpetuate itself throughout the world of adults of which children are the making in years to follow.

While we were still in the "Clark house" there came to Burlington a young Englishman by the name of Berkeley. His father was the vicar of Southminster, and he was a younger son, so he came out to Canada to find his fortune; but Canada offered him nothing; and in some way he drifted to Burlington. Father was always an Englishman at heart and feeling. I have often thought that he would have found life infinitely congenial if the way had opened for him so that he could have gone back to England to live and work there: he was naturalized here and became a citizen late in life not for any other reason but that he might render a service to a dear friend; but birth and inborn traditions of life kept him English still. I question seriously whether there is not such an inherent difference between natural relations and assumed relations as to make the naturalization of the foreign-born an attempt to accomplish the impossible; it is impossible to change racial traits, to graft a new present on an old past, simply by signing a document or by giving verbal assent to declaration of new loyalties. I speak to the point; I lived the life of the French people for years. The Chief Justice of France once said to me: "Better than any foreigner who has ever to come to live among us, you have come to feel and realize the meaning of France"; but he knew, and I knew that I could never become a real Frenchman; and, knowing France as intimately as I do, I know perfectly well that it is impossible to make a Frenchman into an American. Those who decry nationality must face stubborn facts. Each nation is an entity, a personality; each nation has its own gift to give to one corporate humanity; each nation enshrines in its heart a gift for all life, just as a reliquary is both a symbol and a creator of devotion; all human life would have been infinitely poorer without the treasures which national and racial character have engendered and brought to birth; and those contributions to life's larger meaning are not cosmopolitan in origin or spirit. Shakespeare was an Englishman as definitely as Homer was a Greek, and not only an Englishman but an Englishman of a given time in England's story; Wagner was a German, no spirit but the Teutonic inbreathing of life could have entoned his vibrating melodies. Nationality is back of them, found utterance in them both; no other background but their own national life could have inspired them to bring their immortal contributions to the enrichment of all that human life has of vision and joy today.

And now for the young Englishman whose coming to Burlington started me on this train of thought. It was because Father was an Englishman at heart that he took such a liking to this young Berkeley compatriot, and got him a job under Bob Burdette as a reporter on *The Burlington Hawkeye*. And to those who do not know the *Burlington Hawkeye* let me say that it was the biggest small town newspaper, and the liveliest and the wittiest periodical in all the West. And for the same reason, in course of time, Maurice Berkeley "came to our house to stay." He studied with me, for Father found that Maurice seriously longed to become a minister, so Father prepared him in his Latin and Greek, and in due time Maurice went to Nashotah, graduated, was ordained, and his first work was in Keokuk, Iowa, as assistant to Father's good and cherished friend, Dr. McIlwain, the Rector of St. John's.

Father's birthday present to me on my twelfth birthday was a Greek Grammar, "Professor Hadley's almost perfect grammar," as it has been called.

My sister Mary was born in the "Clark house"; a frail and a delicate child; that fact as well as her naturally appealing nature made her very dear to the family; she was known as "Pussie" Watson. I remember a portrait of her done on porcelain by Monfort & Hill, of Burlington, which is a thing of exquisite beauty.

As I think of those Burlington days, over for me, more than sixty years gone, I marvel at what a strange thing memory is, and what details it clings to! There was a public park one block in extent near where we lived; and I can remember the names of most of the people who lived in the houses which faced the Park; there were the Denises, and the Touzalins, and the Hedges, and the Robertsons, and the Smyths, and the Armstrongs, and the Lanes, and the Greens; and then near us in the other direction were the Rhodes, and the Nelsons, and the Garretts, and the Schramms, and the Tracys, and the Adams, and the Pollocks, and Miss Lorraine, and the Harbachs, and the Cooks. And here I must pay a sincere though passing compliment to the first girl who ever made a deep impression on my youthful heart, Lulie (Louise) Cook; she was my young ideal of loveliness, and my heart was at her feet, but I don't think that she ever felt urgently inclined to pick it up. When years afterward, as Louise Carson, she asked me to dinner at her house I found her as attractive as ever, and I complimented myself on my youthful good taste.

We had a baseball team there on North Hill, composed

of the boys and girls of the neighbourhood. One day when I was taking lunch in Santa Barbara at the house of Mrs. E. S. Otis, General Harbach asked me where my home town was, and I told him that Burlington was the only place which I ever had thought of as home; and the General said that his family were Burlington people. "Was Betty Harbach one of your family?" I asked. And the General said, "She was my little sister; did you know her?" "Yes," I replied, "Betty Harbach was the pitcher on our baseball nine." My great chums in the neighbourhood were Frank Adams, and Charlie and Walter Schramm. How well I remember them all after all these years—the Schramms, Henry, Lucia, Charlie, Walter, and Ralph; and the Adams, Fanny, Ed, Arthur, Frank, Maud, Daisy (Genevieve), and Gail! Again I think, what a thing is memory! to keep all their names in mind along with my grateful memories of them. There is there something of the meaning of a home place.

IV

EGLINTON, NEW JERSEY
1859-1874

SUMMERS took us most often to that other home place, Mother's old home in New Jersey, "Eglinton." Robert Burnett's original house must have been built on what is now the Eglinton farm shortly after his removal to America; for among the references to the place in old records there are these:

"Frame work of wood addition hewn from forest in 1690 by order of the proprietor Robert Burnett of Lethintie, Aberdeenshire, Scotland.

"New Brick addition built by Robert Montgomery in 1773.

"Mark of cannon ball shot four days prior to the Battle of Monmouth, by the British, June 24, 1778, then under command of Sir Henry Clinton, who was retreating toward Sandy Hook, General Washington and the Patriots in hot pursuit."

It is evident then that the first house there was built prior to 1690; it was of frame, and was situated on rising ground at the head of a lovely valley of more than seven miles in length; tradition has it that this house was situated in the lower part of the grounds (as we of today remember them) where the red lilies were; and that it was burned. In 1701 William Montgomery and his wife, Isabel Burnett Montgomery, crossed the ocean with their young family and settled on lands deeded to William by his father-in-law; the instrument reading that:

"Robert Burnett of Freehold, in ye County of Monmouth within the Eastern division of Nova Caesarea . . . and William Montgomery, his son-in-law, . . . one hundred pounds current silver money, . . . part and parcel of a certain tract of land belonging to ye said Robert Burnett, lying on a creek commonly known and called by the name of Doctor's Creek, and is also that plantation and tract of land whereon the said William Montgomery now dwelleth."

I have had in my possession three deeds on parchment, which were transfers of some of the original lands of the old estate: one from Robert Gordon, of Cluny, conveying ½ of 1/24th part of the Division of New Jersey, dated 1705; another from Clement Plumstead of London, in the thirty-fourth year of Charles II., conveying to Robert Gordon undivided 1/12th part of New Cæsarea; and a third whereby John Heywood of London conveyed to Robert Burnett of Lethintie, in the thirty-fifth year of Charles II., an undivided 1/24th part of East New Jersey. It was in 1706 that William Montgomery built his house of Eglinton; and it was in 1773 that Robert Montgomery, great-grandson of William built the Eglinton which I remember, the house in which Mother was born. The note which is quoted above, "New brick addition built by Robert Montgomery in 1773," implies that the part of the old house built of local brick and covered with frame is part of the house of 1706; and the tradition of a fire would account for the new addition, which is of old Flemish bond, and one of the finest pieces of brickwork in this country. An old record says that the red bricks (of the original house) were made on the farm; the bricks with the black ends were imported from Scotland. There was a pentroof running around the house just below the second story windows; and it was by one of those windows that my great-grandmother Montgomery was sitting when a cannon ball came through the window, passed over her head, and lodged in the woodwork on the opposite side of the room. Another cannon ball struck the house just to the left of the front door and knocked out the ends of four bricks; that ball, which is now in the Historical Museum at Freehold, used to hang by a chain just above the hole in the brickwall when I was a boy at Eglinton. General Clinton's forces must have been marching in an easterly direction following the old Shrewsbury Road; and the guns must have been fired from the hillside above the meadow. There are two traditions which give colour to the story; one of them is that a boy sitting on the gatepost at the end of the Lane jeered at the British Battery which was in retreat, and that the officer in charge ordered a gun to be wheeled about and fired at the mansion; another is that one of the coloured boys about the place refused to tell whereabouts in the orchard the family silver was buried, and that the British put a rope about his neck and strung him up to a limb of the big walnut tree in front of the house to frighten him, but finally let him down when they found that he would not tell. That walnut tree on which the big bell hung is impressed on my memory by the fact that I was once knocked over by the effects of a bolt of lightning, which struck the tree and felled a limb from it.

In going from Burlington to New Jersey we crossed the river on the ferry, and then took a train, all daycoaches, for Chicago; there were no Pullmans and no diners; so we carried provender for the way in lunch baskets, such as hard boiled eggs, cold fried chicken, and rolls, as I now remember the menu. But what I do remember most clearly is the oil lamp arrangement with a boiler fitted into the top of it which we carried to heat the baby's milk on the train; it was my job to carry the thing, banging my little legs at every step; and I despised it, even the smell of it, when it was back home again in the closet under the stairs. Once when we stopped at a station where there was a lunch-counter, Aunt Mary got off the train to get a cup of tea for herself and to bring one to Mother. The train started to shunt some cars to another track, and I thought that Aunt Mary was left behind; in a moment I ran to the end of the car, jumped off, rolled down the cinder-clad right of way, picked myself up, and ran down the track to the platform, crying, "Aunt Mary! Aunt Mary!" at the top of my voice. Aunt Mary always took the most loving care of me, and was very gentle to an often wayward boy; and I think that if any other member of the family had been left behind, that I would have borne it with becoming equanimity; but when it was Aunt Mary it was a different thing. In Chicago we changed to an eastbound train which took thirty-six hours to make the journey either to New York or to Philadelphia. In Philadelphia we stayed over night at a hotel, and my first recollections of Philadelphia are the ferries crossing the Delaware to Camden, which I saw from the windows of the old Ridgeway House. From Philadelphia we crossed to Camden and took the old Pemberton & Hightstown Railroad to Imlaystown, or to Cat-Tail (which I believe is Sharon now) where the horses from Eglinton met us. I liked it best when we went by way of New York where there was an over night stay, then the next day a trip down the Bay by boat to South Amboy, on which boat was a big fat coloured woman who sold candy and other delectable dainties; then from South Amboy we took the Camden & Amboy Railroad to Newtown and drove four miles to Eglinton. I can see now the "carry-all" with a team of shiny horses all brushed and groomed waiting for us. It was on one of these trips by way of New York that we stayed with Mrs. Stillman, the mother of James Stillman, Senior, the great banker (Mrs. Stillman had been a schoolmate of Mother's), and it was in that house that I saw a real bathtub for the first time. I told Mr. Stillman about it once when he visited me in Paris; and he told me of his memories of Eglinton when he had visited there.

I could write a book on Eglinton alone; but this is to be only a boy's memories of his mother's old home. One of my memories of the house is of a Sunday afternoon; it was hot outside but a breeze was coming through the big hall with its doors both front and back open; there was a green slat door at the south entrance, and Uncle Ben was asleep on the big mahogany sofa with the haircloth upholstery and a newspaper over his face to keep off the flies; I was flat on my "tummy" on the floor in front of the big door, reading the *Country Gentleman*—I read it yet and I like it better than any other periodical which comes my way.

The Eglinton folk of those days were first Aunt Lucy, Miss Lucy Montgomery; she was Robert Montgomery's daughter and the sister of my grandmother, Esther Montgomery Newell, and it was she who inherited Eglinton. Then there was Cousin Eliza Lawrence; Elisha Lawrence was member of the General Assembly of New Jersey in 1721, his daughter Elizabeth Lawrence married my great-great-grandfather, Dr. James Newell, and Cousin Eliza Lawrence was the daughter of Elizabeth Lawrence's brother.

This Lawrence-Newell connection brings to me a bit of unrecorded history of great interest. In the year 1778 Major André came to Allentown bringing with him letters of introduction to Dr. James Newell from Mrs. John Lawrence of Burlington, and asked Dr. Newell to give medical service to André's brother who was ill. The brothers were hospitably received and cared for at Dr. Newell's house in Allentown, where they stayed for a day and a night; then getting word that the American troops were advancing rapidly in that direction they left very early in the morning in a carriage belonging to an invalid lady, a Mrs. Wykoff of Philadelphia, which Major André borrowed on account of the extreme illness of his brother (whom Mrs. Newell thought too ill to be moved); this carriage Major André caused to be returned to its owner after he had reached South Amboy in safety. In the hurried departure at an hour before daylight, one of the spoons from Major André's campkit, which had been used as a medicine spoon for the invalid, was left on the mantel-shelf of the room which they occupied in my great-great-grandfather's house; this spoon bearing the Crest of the André family is in my possession.

Another of the Eglinton folk who was very dear to me was my great Aunt Susan Newell, my grandfather's sister, and I cannot write of her even after all these years without a feeling of deep emotion; I was her brother's namesake, and I was always her "little Sam"; and she had always a special measure of affection for me. She was Susan Faesch Newell; and the name of Faesch brings in some interesting history. Among Aunt Sue's papers there was one which reads:

"Michael Kearny was married three times; his first wife was Joanna Lenox; his second wife was Elizabeth Britton, by whom he had a son Philip, born at sea just before the arrival of the parents at Philadelphia; his third wife was Sarah Morris, who was the mother of Isabella, Michael, Euphemia, and Graham Kearny. Isabella and Michael both died single at an advanced age, and are interred in a burial place at their farm which was called 'Irish Lot Farm,' and is a few miles from Morristown, New Jersey. Euphemia married a Mr. Leonard, and left one daughter Susan, who married a German gentleman, Mr. Faesch."

So that is where Aunt Sue got her name Susan Faesch. Another paper reads:

"Extracts from a note-book kept by Susan Faesch, who was born Susan Leonard; then follows a long list of dates of birth of the various members of the Kearny family; then,—Married to Mr. Faesch April 23, 1790. Departed this life on the 23rd of May, 1799, my affectionate and dearly beloved husband John Jacob Faesch."

The following is from a newspaper clipping:

"Died at Boonton on Friday evening last, John J. Faesch, Esq., one of the judges of the Inferior Court of Common Pleas of the County of Morris, aged 70 years. His remains were brought to this town on Sunday, and attended to the grave from the house of David Ford by a numerous procession."

Another "Extract" from a book kept by Susan Faesch:

"Mr. Trigant: 1808, March 19., To service of my black woman Peg from 19th Sept. last to this date—

6 months at $5 per month	30.00
By cash paid her	6.25
Balance	23.75

March 30, Received from Mr. Trigant
$23., six shillings
Received from my black woman Peg since her
freedom, One hundred and four dollars."

Aunt Susan Newell always kept up a close connection with our Canadian cousins, of whom was the family of David Ford, just mentioned. Anastasia Cooke married David Ford, and from them comes our connection with the Fords, the Jones', and the Bogerts. Isabella Cooke married Col. Harris W. Hailes, of whose line was Mrs. Stairs; Elizabeth Newell, Aunt Sue's sister, married Hon. Wm. F. Odell, and from them is our connection with the Odells and the Bowmans.

Finding myself in St. John, New Brunswick on a summer vacation in 1906, I made the acquaintance of the then Rector of Trinity Church, St. John, the Rev. Dr. Richardson, now Bishop Richardson, and by his courtesy I was asked to preach at the Annual Church Parade of the Regiment of Royal Fusiliers which was at that time in garrison at the place. At a later date, in 1907, I returned to St. John to speak at the Annual Meeting of the United Empire Loyalists, the descendants of those earliest English settlers, who first established themselves in the Maritime Provinces; and at that time I was the guest of the Rev. Dr. Raymond, who made me a gift of the valuable record of early New Brunswick history called *The Winslow Papers*. Later when Dr. Richardson had been made Bishop of Fredericton he asked me to officiate for a time in Old Trinity, the church which was established in St. John by the Rev. Samuel Cooke, my great-great-grandfather. I was occupied then with the building of St. Paul's Church, in Akron, Ohio, and I felt that I could not leave that work even for a time; but the invitation appealed to me very strongly, for the atmosphere of that part of Canada, with its old world flavour, was most congenial to my tastes. If I could have accepted it, it would probably have resulted in my making a home for myself ultimately in that part of the world; and then, I would not have gone to France, but that is another story. It is well written:

"laisser errer son imagination est inutile: les hommes sont aveugles d'avance en ce qui concerne l'avenir et sur le bien et sur le mal: les philosophes parlent du libre-arbitre, mais en effet il n'y en a pas: on croit faire ses choix, mais la vérité est que l'on suit aveuglement le chemin de son destin."

It was on that first visit to New Brunswick, and then to Nova Scotia, that I made the personal acquaintance of our Canadian cousins in Lower Canada, Mrs. Stairs, the Odells in Halifax, and the Bowmans in Windsor. Our visit to Fort Massie, as the house of the Odell cousins is called, is a bright spot in memory, and I cherish the recollection of the charming hospitality offered us there by cousins on whom we descended as "a bolt out of the blue." And our visit to the Bowmans at Windsor is another happy memory; cousin Annie Bowman, another second cousin, made us most welcome to their home, Littlecourt. We came to Windsor by train and took an open carriage for the drive to Littlecourt;

on the way I asked the driver to stop at a bank as I wished to replenish my petty cash by drawing on my Letter of Credit. While I was in the bank, the old Irishman, who owned the carriage and who was a well known character of the place and acquainted with all the leading families, turned round on the box and said to Jeannette: "Excuse me M'um, but are the gentleman who just went in there any kin to Mr. Charlie Odell?" (Mr. Charlie Odell being a cousin of my mother's) "he certainly looks most like him."

I later made the acquaintance of another Canadian cousin, Beverly Jones of Toronto, when I went there to officiate at a Church Semi-Centenary, at which time I was his guest; and from that time on he remembered me regularly with most interesting letters. He was born in 1839 at Brockville, Ontario, and he was in his 95th year when he passed away. He visited his office almost every day up to four months before his death. He was known in the family as "the grand old Man," so cousin Sidney Jones writes me. Beverly Jones' outstanding achievement was the establishment of the Provincial Industrial Schools for boys and girls; and he gave a part of every week to visits for counsel and encouragement to these young protégés.

This is the place to mention briefly in passing some of the other interesting relations which have come to me through the Morris-Cooke connection. Bishop Clarkson I remember personally; it is a memory which dates back to 1871. We were on our way back to Iowa from our summer visit to Eglinton, and on reaching Chicago we found ourselves in a scene of utter desolation. It was the time of the Great Fire which ravaged Chicago. Dr. Clarkson, afterward Bishop of Nebraska, was then rector of St. James' Church at Cass and Huron Streets, where he had won the devotion of the people of the entire city by his helpfulness to every human need. Not knowing what to do or where to lodge or where to eat, we drove out to see this cousin of Mother's; and we found him. I can well remember the picture; it is so vivid from the appeal it made to my small boy's eyes; Dr. Clarkson was in the street where his church people had set tables, and he and they were serving breakfasts of bread and coffee to all who came; and they came by the hundreds. Our connection with the Clarksons comes in this way: the Rev. Joseph Clarkson married Grace, daughter of the Rev. Samuel Cooke; their daughter Harriet married the Rev. Samuel Bowman, whose daughter married Bishop Vail, Bishop of Kansas. Samuel Bowman was made assistant Bishop of Pennsylvania in 1858. The Rev. Joseph Clarkson's son, Michael Cooke Clarkson married Louisa Harper, and it was their son, Robert Harper Clarkson, who became Bishop of Nebraska, and had for his See City Omaha, where Father had held the first church services when Omaha was but a trading post, and Papillon was the county seat. The Battle of Gettysburg was fought upon the farm where Bishop Clarkson grew up as a boy. Bishop Bowman was Bishop Clarkson's uncle, and he married my grandfather's own cousin; so Bishop Clarkson and my mother were second cousins.

It is in this connection also that I can claim kinship to the family of Mrs. Elwell S. Otis. She was Louise Bowman, a resident of Santa Barbara, when I first went there to live; it was my privilege to say the Church's word of committal when she had passed to rest; and to her and her family, to Mary Isham, Laura Elston, and Louise Wagner I feel a nearness of kinship and a warmth of gratitude which this printed page cannot express. It is interesting also to note that General F. W. Sladen, who was at one time on the Staff of General Otis, married Elizabeth Lefferts, the daughter of Elizabeth Morris Lefferts who did such a superb piece of work in the compiling of the genealogy of Lewis Morris the first, from which many of the data in this book are taken. Mrs. Sladen is seventh in descent, as I am seventh in descent from Governor Lewis Morris. The first funeral service at which I officiated after I took charge of the Church in Paris, France, was that of Anna, Comtesse de Montsaulnin, also a descendant of Lewis Morris; and her children the Comtesse du Luart, and the Comtesse de Gourcuff were among the charming acquaintances of my Paris days.

I cannot put into words my feeling for Eglinton, and my lasting gratitude for the welcome which always awaited me there by all my kinfolk. Once I thought that I would try and buy the old place back and go there to live, so that some one of the family might own it, but that filial hope is now gratified in that two cousins, Robert L. Montgomery and his brother, now own the old homestead. Eglinton means to me Uncle Ben, and Aunt Sarah, and Lucy, and Albert, and Clarence, and Hetty, and Joe. Uncle Ben always kind to me; Aunt Sarah so good, so gay, with her pretty dancing curls; Lucy and Hetty and Albert like big brothers and sisters; and "young Joseph," my chum and playmate. When I think of those days long past, and of the meanings for good which these others put into my life then, I feel sure that they know now how deeply I cherish their memory, and how keen is my sense of gratitude now, which in those days of my immaturity I neither knew how nor thought to express.

We boys slept on the third floor in a big room which was called "the sky parlour"; two big beds were there, four-posters, with sacking-bottoms to hold the mattresses,—(sacking-bottoms, Reader, are sheets of sailcloth with eyelets in the edges, and held in place by ropes laced around wooden pegs in the bed frames). The sky parlour was more than half of the third floor of the great house; the rest of the third floor being what was called "the garret"—and what a garret! It contained the accumulations of a century or more, books old and new, clothes old and new, trunks full of everything and anything; and what a resource was there for a rainy day. I say that we boys slept in the sky parlour; but I remember that once when there was an overflow, Joe and I slept in a trundle bed under Uncle Ben's and Aunt Sarah's bed. The fruit at Eglinton was wonderful; I have never seen its like anywhere—apples, bough-sweetings, molasses apples, sheep-noses; and then pears, harvest pears, lying so thick on the ground under the tree just back of the ice house, and the wasps and the bees sucking the honey from them; and seckel pears, big trees full; and peaches with a mealy cream coloured flesh and a deep brown pit; and cherries, blackhearts best of all, cherry trees as tall as the house and full of black cherries; and then in the lane coming up to the house there were big trees of wild cherries, and these were Aunt Sue's especial predilection. She would bribe Joe and me to pick baskets full of them, and then she would put the cherries in demijohns with some sugar and fill the waste spaces with applejack: and, Oh, the cherry bounce which resulted therefrom! And our reward would be gingerbread, big thick chunks of sticky, luscious stuff which Aunt Sue made herself and which she kept in a cupboard in her own room; I've never seen the like again.

It may interest the reader to know the *traditional* derivation of the word demijohn, which was originally Dame-Jeanne. The story goes that there was a Normandy hostess whose inn was famed for its good cheer, and her name was Jeanne: she had wicker coats made for her big glass wine bottles in order to protect them from careless handling; and from Normandy Dame Jeanne has come the name of demijohn for wicker-coated bottles. He who may be inclined to cavil at the space allotted in this tale to good things to eat and drink should be reminded that this is a small boy's story of the "good old days," and of the things which appealed to him.

Eglinton was two miles from the posttown which was Allentown, and it was to Allentown that we went to do the errands, Joe and I. It was a quaint old town; it is so still; a backwater off the path of progress because the railroad did not come there. There was one Main Street on which were all the stores; Hankins' where we took butter and eggs to trade; and Neely Vanderbeck's, and Dan Savidge the harness-maker. I owe Dan Savidge a debt of gratitude. I was not allowed a horse to ride; it was too hard on the horse; that old maxim "Up hill, Spare me: Down hill, Spare thee" meant nothing in my young life; so my steed was a little red mule; she could run, that little mule. Down at the end of Main Street in Allentown was a gristmill run by water power; there was a millpond and a race; and just beyond the mill was a hill. One day I was coming down that hill toward the town riding as fast as my little mule would go, when, crack! went the stirrup strap on the left side. I slid off on the back of my neck lighting almost between that little mule's front feet. She stopped in her tracks, and looked down at me as if to say, "It's lucky for you, Boy, that I have more sense than you have." Two of the men from the mill came out and picked me up and dusted me off, and with painful steps and slow I made my way to Dan Savidge's shop. Dan knew me well; he knew what would be coming to me if the folks at home learned what had happened to me and how it happened; so he mended my stirrup strap and rubbed dirt in the stitches so they would not show; then he helped me into the saddle, and by the time those two miles from Allentown to Eglinton had been traversed I was over the shock and feeling better, though I was lame for days; but the family never knew till long afterward how their wisdom in not letting me have a horse to ride had been justified.

Years afterward I had a chance to remember Dan Savidge's friendship and to return it pleasantly. There came to my house in Akron, Ohio, one evening, a boy and a girl—they were scarcely more than that—and asked me to bless their marriage; they were strangers there, they said, and they had no witnesses with them; they had just come from the East; and the boy said that his name was Savidge. An echo of the long ago seemed to sound for me. "Where in the East did you come from," I said. "From Allentown, New Jersey," was his reply. "And who were your relatives there?" I asked. And when he mentioned Dan Savidge's name, it was like a breath from the faraway homeland to me. I made it a general rule not to officiate at the marriage of people whom I did not know unless they brought witnesses whom I knew; but here was once when I cast principles to the winds; and I was glad to be witness and all else necessary, and to ask God's blessing on Dan Savidge's kinsman and the girl who was willing to join her young life to his.

Another figure which stands out most clearly in those memories of other days is Asa Wills, the "village blacksmith"; it was not "under a spreading chestnut tree he stood," I think it was an elm which shadowed his shop; he was large and portly, ruddy and good natured, looking in every line the typical English village squire. A visit to Asa Wills' meant a chance to go to town; true, it involved swishing a brush made of a horse's tail about the legs of the animals being shod, to keep the flies from tormenting and to keep the horse from stamping during the shoeing process; none the less, the work was light, and a visit to town meant a nickel for the candy shop.

Allentown had three houses which are clear in my memory. The Imlay-Fisk house was the grandest; it stood flush with the street; it had fan lights over its hall doors; there was a garden with box hedges at the back; the parlour walls were covered with wallpaper made in France and put on in little squares, and I remember the original bill for the paper, framed and hanging on the wall. There were two pretty nieces, Emma and Julia Gordon, who added to the attraction of the house for me.

Then there was the house where Cousin Susan Debow, and Cousin Margaret Buckley, and Cousin Mary Leavenworth lived; they were sisters; their grandmother was Margaret Leonard and their grandfather was Robert Montgomery of Eglinton, who was my mother's grandfather. Their house was filled with beautiful things inside; it was a house where boys had to "mind their 'P's and Q's' "; but there were always good things to eat coming, so we got by with it; and that house, too, had garden hedges of box; and how fragrant those box hedges were on a warm day!

I think that there is no sense perception which leaves more lasting records than does the sense of smell; it has a power of calling up a consciousness of the past which is wonderful. There are odours which come to me now, that give me a vivid mental picture of places and of happenings which are long years away in time. There is the perfume of a box-hedge, for instance, and I am a small boy back in Allentown; there is the perfume which means Ivory Soap, and I am back at Eglinton on the back porch, where there was a copper wash basin and a roller towel and a cake of soap and a big oak pitcher of cold water (it was a copper bound pitcher in this case) "fresh from the well," and I am cleaning up before going in to dinner; then there is the smell of Arbor Vitæ trees in the warm sun, and I am at Eglinton going down an evergreen bordered walk which led to a little white house well known but not mentioned in polite society in those days; though in these our less fastidious but more clean minded times, Chick Sale has had no qualms in writing a book about it.

During the Great War when Mary Gladwin, of Akron, was in Belgrade as a nurse, we sent her out some cases of supplies, and in one case we put a dozen big bottles of Lavender water; and she told us that sometimes when a badly wounded soldier boy, or one who was terribly ill with fever, was wavering betwen the Here and the There, a piece of gauze wet with this fragrant Lavender and put to his face would waken old echoes and win him back to life again.

There is another house in Allentown of which I carry a clear picture in my mind. It is the house where Mr. Carroll lived, the parsonage of the Presbyterian Church up on the Hill; it faced the church whose rolling meadows of green lawns stretched down to the millpond; and those lawns were the blessed resting place of the bodies of so many of my forebears. My little brother George's body was laid there too; and the church was the sanctuary of my kinfolk's lives long before there was an Episcopal Church on Church Street. Mr. Carroll was a valued friend of the Eglinton family, and he and his were always welcome guests at the old place; I remember him well. But my liveliest memories of that House on the Hill are attached to Mr. Carroll's nephew, Ed Newton, who was a boyhood companion often in those joy filled summer days when life knew no "depressions," at least none that affected boys; we played together; we did all that boys can do on a farm, Ed, and my cousin Joe, and I. Ed is now a celebrity—A. Edward Newton as he is known to literary circles; his must be "the pen of a ready writer," for there is fascinating spontaneity in all that he writes. It was a great pleasure to me to welcome Ed and Babette to my Oriole House in 1931; nothing in years has given me more of an uplift than their visit; it was not only their personal charm which they both have in large degree, but it was the spiritual impulse which I got from their visit. Ed and I met and talked as if the days between then and boy time meant nothing; we took up living just where we left off so many decades ago. Now I know that space and time have no actuality, no power to divide, and that personality is imperishable in its essence.

V

MINNESOTA AND SCHOOL DAYS
1874–1879

IT WAS in 1874 that summers at Eglinton were no more for me, for in that year I left Burlington, Iowa, with deep regret and went with my family to Red Wing, Minnesota, where Father had accepted a call to be Rector of Christ Church, as successor to his oldtime collegemate, Edward Randolph Welles who had been made Bishop of Wisconsin. It was a new kind of work which Father took up there; the population of that part of the West had a large Scandinavian group. Swedes and Norwegians who had their own Lutheran Churches with services in Swedish and Norwegian, and also their devoted pastors conducted schools for the children in which all the instruction was in the languages of the Old World. But in time the children drifted into the public schools and soon forgot their Swedish and Norwegian; so that so far as their homelands and their home tongues were concerned, a generation grew up which "knew not Joseph." The Scandinavian people were all used to a liturgical form of worship in their churches; Confirmation was a dignity added to child life which appealed to them. The Episcopal Church seemed to them much the same as the Church in which they had been brought up; and as a consequence Christ Church, Red Wing, came in time to have the largest Scandinavian congregation in America.

There were also quite a number of Indians in the congregation, Chippewas who lived in tepees in the river bottoms; they made a scant living by fishing and hunting; they used to come into church on a Sunday in single file following their Chief, and on Easter Day the collection plate would be piled with bead-work which was all that they had for offering. One source of gain for these Indians was the abundance of wild pigeons, carrier pigeons, now almost extinct, although flocks of them have been seen here in California in recent years. These pigeons nested in the cottonwoods along the bayous, and when the squabs were developed but not yet ready to fly, the Indians would tip over the nests with long poles and bring the young birds into town to trade. More than once I have seen an Indian kneeling in the stern of a "dugout" (a canoe made of a log hollowed out by chipping and burning) and the whole of the dugout, from bow to stern, would be piled full of wild pigeon squabs. These Indians would come to the rectory, enter without knocking as they would into a tepee, go into Father's study, bow, say, "How! How!" squat on the floor, and take off their wet moccasins, and hang them on the fender in front of the open fireplace to dry; in due course of time they would reverse the process, and go out saying "How! How!" again; and usually taking with them some gifts which the kindly pastor sent to the women and children.

My own stay in Red Wing was brief. We went there in 1874, and in 1875 I was sent to Shattuck School at Faribault, Minnesota, and from that time my wanderings began. I have said that "home" is a place to which you want to go back when you are away from it; and I had left home, for me, when we left Burlington. I wonder if adults ever realise what such changes mean to children. And so going away to school was not a grievance to me, rather it was a relief, for homesickness for the place I loved was still upsetting my equilibrium; to such an extent, in fact, that I think the family welcomed the chance to shift the responsibility of a boy who evidently did not fit where he was, to another authority and training. It was to Shattuck School and to my teachers there that I owe most of what was constructive in my young life. My scholastic education, apart from the Latin and Greek which Father had taught me and the arithmetic which I learned from Mr. Graff, was not only begun but largely finished before I left Shattuck, and all that I have learned since was based on that foundation. I am not really proud of any accomplishment in my whole career; but I had a deep thrill of satisfaction, on going back to Shattuck to make an address at one of the commencements after the War, to see white tablets on either side of a doorway bearing the names of Shattuck boys who had rendered service in the Great War, in the order of their graduation. And while it may not be said that "Abou-Ben-Watson's name led all the rest," yet my name was very near the top; I think that I was second in years of the men who rendered service "over seas."

I have known few teachers anywhere of finer calibre than those at Shattuck. First there was Professor Champlin, dear "Old Champ," a man who could teach mathematics to anyone who was half way intelligent; he did not succeed in teaching me algebra to any great extent, but he did not mind that, for I don't think that he really loved algebra himself; geometry was his pet prize, and how he could teach it! He made even me enthuse over geometry, though I don't consider geometry mathematics at all, it is a branch of logic. He had us learn by heart all the theorems in Davies' Legendre, learn them by Book and Number, so that he could say, "Watson, Book III: Theorem 6." And Watson would have to stand and recite it word for word; then "Go to the board and draw the figure and write out the formula"; and if you did not remember the formula just as it was written but could make up a formula which would carry the demonstration, he was all the more pleased.

Then there was Harry Whitney, dear old "Whit"; I think that he did more to make Shattuck great than any other one man in its long story: he was a Shattuck boy himself, and he loved the old School; it was his very life; and what a blessing it was that he could stay by it to his last days! He taught me German and made me love it; I can repeat from memory to-day Goethe and Schiller and Heine and Fichte, that I learned from him. Is there anything in all literature with a more majestic roll than *Das Lied von der Glocke?*

"Fest gemauert in der Erden
Steht die Form aus Lehm gebrannt";

I have not looked at it for years, and I know it all still. And "Whit" was my Latin professor; note the distinction, please; I said that he *taught* me German, but it was Father who taught me Latin. When I went to Shattuck at fifteen I had already read Cæsar, and Virgil, and Ovid's Metamorphoses. Think of it! They are now banned by the censor in this our hypocritical and supersensitive America; but in my clean day they were select diet for small boys; and I had also read Cicero's Orations, and Sallust, and probably something more; but at any rate "Whit" had an easy time of it with me so far as Latin was concerned.

And then came a new breed of teachers at Shattuck. "Champ" and "Whit" were of the Old Guard; but some of the new ones were fine, especially Camp in Greek, and Pyle (John Gilpin) in English. Greek was an easy proposition for I had had a good start at that; and English was easy too, for Pyle knew how to teach it as well as write it; he quickened my love for etymology which had already had good beginnings in my Latin, *"Unde Derivatur?"*; and his training in English was so good that when I entered college and would have made a complete flunk in algebra, they let me through on condition that I pass special examinations in English and in German. That college was an educationally living thing and not a mechanized grist mill.

Shattuck is a military school, and we were under West Point men, regular Army Officers, Lancaster and Danes, of the Third Artillery. I have come to have a great regard for the Third Artillery, the Fifth Cavalry, and the Seventh Cavalry, which has come from my association with some of their officers.

There is an active propaganda going on at present against military training for boys. In speaking on this subject, I speak *en connaissance de cause,* for I know war. I saw four years of it in France at close range and at its worst; I had four years of training in a military school, and for a time I was chaplain of a regiment of the National Guard. The contention that military schools, military training in schools, the R.O.T.C., and student training camps, tend to create war loving instincts in boys and encourage brutality in conduct is in my sober judgment, an opinion which is the product of an exaggerated, unreal, and fictitious pacifism; by that I mean that it calls itself pacifism, and is nothing of the kind. True pacifism—and I claim to be a pacifist in this sense—is a deep and reasoned faith in peace as the very foundation of those values which are the meaning of the life of man or nation. And I know neither man nor nation so earnestly peace loving as those who know war, and know what it is, and know its ways and methods. It was an American General who said that "War is Hell"; and those of us who lived through the four years of the Great War and saw it firsthand know well that he spoke the brutal truth. Such men do not love war; their military experience and their military training have not made them brutal; and the tactical lessons given to boys and young men in military schools and training camps have precisely the opposite effect from what is claimed by their opponents.

Military training inculcates a sense of order, of right, of duty above all else; under its influence a boy comes face to face with a known duty, and that duty is for him, for the moment, the supreme imperative; instantly, without question,

"Their's not to make reply,
Their's not to reason why."

And just as he is trained to protect the weak, to defend the right, by his life if need be, so is he led to realise that that peace by which his country can alone live its fullest life must be his own life's meaning and motive. War is the very destruction of all that a soldier holds dear; of all that he is taught by his training to consider of first importance in life. I look on my own military training as that in my life which gave me self-command, and which prepared me best for facing uncompromisingly every difficult situation in which the exigencies of living ever placed me. And I can say unhesitatingly that whatever I have been able to accomplish in the way of constructive or directing work in my life had its possibility of accomplishment in that habit of instantaneous, unquestioning obedience to the duty which faced me, that Shattuck School was founded to teach.

Do I then maintain that every boy should have military school training? I do not. It all depends on the individual boy; for some boys it is the finest possible kind of education; other boys would profit more by a wholly different type of character building. For a school is primarily a character education rather than a brain education; it is an individual education rather than a mass education. Every school worthy of the name has a character of its own; it is an entity, a personality in the upbuilding life of the nation. For the boy whose need is the acquirement of self-control, whose need is to learn to value duty above impulse, I rank military training very high in its possibility of developing and bringing out the most of a man that is in him. Military training cultivates a spirit of self-reliance in a boy rather than a spirit of subservience and of dependence on others. Sooner or later any boy in the batallion may become an officer if he serves sufficiently long and sufficiently well; and as such he is put in a position where he must exercise responsibility, and make instantaneous decisions affecting others as well as himself; and I consider that sort of training as of inestimable value to our American youth.

It may be that just because this was the sort of training which I most needed myself I contrast college with school in favour of the latter. I got infinitely more out of my school days than I did out of my college days; in fact I am of the opinion that college training, as it exists at present in our American life, is a very questionable experiment for the American boy. This statement is both experience and observation, and it is confirmed by the testimony of many college heads. Life is too strenuous a game to-day to justify putting in four years of it in a boy-training, much of which is non-essential and non-productive. I have talked with numbers of college students in recent years, with the distinct purpose of learning from them just how large a percentage of their college years was given to real scholastic work and what percentage was given to "college activities" and various other kindred side issues. The result is that my conviction has been made all the more sure that if a boy could have two more years than the usual course at a first rank boy's school, graduating in course and remaining for two extra years of an extended course, purposely designed to fit him for his after work, whatever that might be planned to be, and then could go directly to the professional school of his choice to prepare there for his life-work, or else to a *real* university for postgraduate work, or directly into business, we would have helped our young manhood in an immeasurable degree towards efficient living, as compared with our present methods. This proposed plan would put the boy into business or into a professional school in time to save for him the two years which I think are often wasted.

As it is to-day, the boy graduates from a "prep-school" after four years there; he puts in four more years in college; an additional four years in a professional school, making twelve years in all of scholastic work, and if he enters school at fourteen or fifteen he is twenty-six or twenty-seven years old, still being supported by his parents, before he can get to work at all. And often he must wait another two or three years before his profession will yield him a living for himself, to say nothing of a living for another, so that he will in all likelihood be twenty-nine or thirty years of age before he can marry and take his place in upbuilding that human society which is his vital reason for existence. I hold this method to be a dangerous procedure for the average young human animal, and furthermore it is a waste of what ought to be some of the finest and most joyous moments out of life at a time when that life is capable of its finest idealism, and is most fitted to develop a kindred idealism in human society.

VI

COLLEGE AND POSTGRADUATE WORK
1879–1884

MY CLASS at Shattuck was 1879; and from there I went to Trinity College, Hartford, Connecticut, where I entered sophomore. Father picked Trinity as a college for me because he was an Alpha Delt, and there was a good Chapter of Alpha Delta Phi at Trinity, and at that time the Alpha Delta Chapter at Hobart which was Father's college had given up its Charter. I say that Father picked the college for me; but I am certain that the choice was guided by that same overruling influence which has ever chosen for me hitherto, and always will; for Trinity gave me a kind of training which I might not have had anywhere else that I would have been likely to go.

I have commented on the fact that I got more out of school than I did out of college, and one reason for that was that I went to college too well prepared in every thing except mathematics, and it was a foregone conclusion that that science would ever be "a lost art" for me. In school I had to work; in college it was all too easy: I had read all the Latin and Greek which any average college course prescribed; I knew German so well that I was excused from attending the German classes; I had had fine grounding in English rhetoric and in philology; the result of all this was that I liked what I liked and what I was capable of understanding; and as for the rest of it I gave it up in dumb despair.

My roommate, Clarence Kurtz, to whom my easy things were hard, would win mathematical prizes with solutions of problems which he would write backwards and forwards and sideways; I did not envy him his power and skill for I knew that such things were not for me; and I went to some of my classes with the type of preparation, or lack of it, which

I once used to try with Father when he was teaching me Latin or Greek; but with Father my bluff never worked, and he would look at me half sorrowfully and half regretfully and would say, "Well, Son, trusting to your former ignorance again, I see." And that is just the kind of "trusting" that I made use of all too often during those days of half joyous, half dubious progress toward attaining a college education. Those were days when a college course was an affair as invariable as the course of the planets; such things as "optionals" were never heard of. Who would "opt"? not boys certainly, they were not considered capable of it; we were like the historic character of the dim and misty past of whom it is written,—

"Methuselah ate what he found on his plate,
He ate it because it was chow"

We took education as it was provided; and what was not learning could at least be considered discipline. And it is true that Trinity gave me a training which I very much needed, which was in fact essential to my after-work—, and that was training in social *savoir-faire;* and I got that training chiefly from the "brothers of A.D.Phi." The students at Trinity in my day were an exceptional lot of fellows; they had manners and they had breeding above the average; and one of the things which was early learned on going to Trinity was that there are certain things which "simply are not done." I had never found that attitude among boys before; and because boys are humans they are herd animals and run with the herd. And I learned a lot at Trinity scholastically; all apart from the initiation which I got into social *savoir-faire;* for there were good men on the faculty then; and some of them I remember most gratefully. My own favourite was "old Brock," Doctor John Brocklesby, who was our Professor of Physics. That was a subject which appealed to me immensely; and Dr. Brocklesby was a past master at teaching physics. The class sat on long benches in his lecture room, half surrounding the tables which bore the instruments for the experiments which were performed in our presence; these benches were stayed by long slats about eighteen inches below the seats and running parallel to them; and by putting one's heels on one of these slats and exerting the lifting force of the leg muscles one could rise in the air a foot or more above the bench. It was on a day when some interesting experiments with Leyden jars had been made, in the course of which an overcharge and consequent discharge of electricity had shattered the jar that some mischievous genius among us gave the familiar signal for a concerted bench raising, and all on the bench rose in the air like a line of automatons, and the ancient bench collapsed. Dr. John looked around, and said, "What was the matter with that bench?" and some wit said, "It must have been overcharged, Professor"; with his quizzical grin Dr. John came back with this, "It'll be charged in the bills." The best of all for me was when Dr. John would ask me to stay after class and help him arrange the instruments for the next day's lecture; that was real college instruction. As one once said of a Williams College President who would take a boy for a walk with him in the woods: "Mark Hopkins on one end of a log and the student on the other end—that's education."

There was much of that personal contact between faculty and student at Trinity. It is a possibility in a small college which cannot be too highly valued, the coming in contact personally with the big man, with the professor himself. The greatest of such contacts that we made was the coming to know on human terms a man whose loving friends called him "John of Connecticut," Bishop John Williams, a prince among men, a really human man; a scholar, a philosopher, and yet a boy at heart; he would come to our rooms and talk and tell stories by the hour. He was our lecturer on the Philosophy of History, and years later when I came to read Allen's *Continuity of Christian Thought,* I found myself on familiar ground. Bishop Williams was a real Connecticut churchman. He once said when asked if he were going with other bishops to London for a certain Conference: "I am too old, and I have read history too well to begin pilgrimages to Lambeth at my time of life."

My college fraternity meant more to me than all my other

college experiences, and its influence on my development was marked. The Alpha Delta Phi tradition has always been maintained on a high level, and the leaders of our Phi Kappa Chapter were exceptionally fine. The seniors of the group used wisely their position and their influence by counselling the younger men with a view to keeping the credit of the Chapter high in matters of scholarship and morale; furthermore they were wise mentors in all that concerned that most attractive and welcoming social life which Hartford offered to the college student. Coming as I did to the college, a western plainsman, I learned a lot from my Alpha Delt contacts which I could have learned in no other way; and that is college fraternity life at its best. In 1881 in my junior year I made Phi Beta Kappa; and in 1882 I received a parchment wherein the world was advised in most elegant Latin that I was possessed of the degree of Bachelor of Arts and was entitled to all the rights and privileges thereto pertaining.

On graduating from college the teaching profession opened its doors to me. I was offered work at Holderness School at Holderness, New Hampshire; at Harcourt Place Academy at Gambier, Ohio: and also the position of the instructorship in Greek at Seabury Divinity School. As it was by that time determined that I was destined for the ministry of the Episcopal Church, I took the position at Seabury, where in addition to a small stipend I had my living and my theological education.

It was my father and my mother who gave me the only "call" which I had at that time to enter the work of the ministry; and the strongest influence in the "call" was my mother's earnest wish. I believe that she thought her Samuel was destined from his earliest beginnings to follow the prophetic footsteps of his father and his grandfather; and I bless her for her faith in me.

There are two kinds of "calls" to a lifework. Some have had an imperative inner urge to follow a destined course; and others for whom the only "call" has been that the way opened in that direction and there was no other way which opened, so they followed the path of least resistance. The latter was my case. I have grown, hopingly grown to value and to seek for those mystic impulses which are so precious to those who gain sufficient spiritual stature to contact them; but this has been only in the later years of my life; in my earlier years I was both by heredity and by training an intellectual pragmatist.

At Seabury I enjoyed teaching Greek. I was by inheritance a teacher, and I knew Greek so well that I found keen satisfaction in teaching it to others and in making possible for them their further advancement. And at Seabury I had another joy, the thrill which comes from widened horizons, from seeing new meanings. This came to me from the instruction given by Professor James McBride Sterrett; he was an independent, fearless, unshackled thinker, and he helped me greatly toward spiritual freedom.

In my second year at Seabury I found that the severity of the winter weather was telling on my health; so I entered the University of the South at Sewanee, Tennessee, with the beginning of their 1884 term, and remained there until June of that year. At Sewanee the Professor of Ecclesiastical History was Dr. Gailor, now Bishop of Tennessee, and later to become my Diocesan when he was made Presiding Bishop. My association with him at Sewanee began a friendship which was the prelude to a closer intimacy in the Paris of the first days of the War, in 1914. Dr. Gailor was a wonderful interpreter of ecclesiastical history; I count it as the chief blessing of my student days to have been taught to read the story of the past from men like Bishop Williams and Bishop Gailor, both of them scholars who interpreted history in the light of facts, and never considered that ecclesiastical heredity called on them to make facts fit themselves into preconceived theories. Dr. Wilmer and Dr. Du Bose were also among my instructors at Sewanee; both of them men who were essentially lovable personally, and whose guidance was most helpful to a mind just growing its thinking wings. The whole atmosphere of Sewanee was delightful; and I look back upon my stay there with deep appreciation.

VII

IN MISSOURI AND IOWA
1884–1897

MEXICO, MISSOURI

WHEN I went to Seabury to study, Bishop Whipple was the head of all the work at Faribault; he confirmed me as a boy at Shattuck; and it was only natural that I should have become one of his candidates for Orders. But when I found that Minnesota winters would preclude my working there Bishop Whipple transferred me, at my request, to Bishop Robertson of the Diocese of Missouri. It was in Missouri I received deacon's orders in 1884, and there that I began work as a missionary on a stage route covering two counties, Audrain and Ralls. After my canonical examination in June 1884, at which ceremony the officiants were Dr. Runcie of St. Joseph, Dr. Cameron Mann, afterward Bishop of South Florida, and Dr. Ethelbert Talbot, who became Bishop of Bethlehem, and who also became my Diocesan when he was made Presiding Bishop. My deacon's orders were conferred in Grace Church, Kansas City, on Trinity Sunday, 1884, and the next day I betook myself to my new duties as "Vicar in ordinary" of Mexico, Missouri, and parts adjacent. I was ordained priest in the little Church in Mexico, and I remained there until 1886.

While I was on duty in Mexico another part of my life's story began. I was married on January 7, 1885, to Jeannette Grace, daughter of James Nevil Watkins and Ellen Grant Watkins. Mr. Watkins was an Englishman by birth, born at Banwell near Bristol; and Mrs. Watkins was a Canadian from Montreal of Scotch ancestry (Grant-MacLean). Father and Mother came to Kansas City at this time, and Father and Dr. Cameron Mann officiated at the marriage; and the day of the marriage Jeannette and I went to Mexico to begin work and life together.

A missionary post in an interior Missouri county was a good experience for a beginner, and Audrain County was at that time a sort of border region, half Old South and half New West; it was just north of "the Kingdom of Callaway" as Callaway County was called, where precedent took precedence over principle, so far as matters of neighbourhood dealings were concerned, and no better law could be invoked than "We've always done it that way." The church building in Mexico was a new structure of brick, and I was the first to minister in it. It lacked much in the way of adornment, and that fact brought me my first lesson in diplomacy. A devoted lady in the congregation offered to give a brass altar cross; in my innocent ignorance of the fact that an "ornament" of that type might evoke questions of dogmatic theology, and not deeming for a moment that there could possibly be any objections to it being used, I accepted it and gave it a place in the little chancel where it lit up the surroundings with a golden gleam of colour. The Sunday morning which followed brought an issue: the Senior Warden offered emphatic objection as he had full right to do. The two wardens of the church were splendid men, both of them; the Senior Warden was Fred Llewellyn, a Kentuckian with a Southern Episcopalian's feelings on the matter of the appurtenances of ritualism, and with a Welshman's tenacity; and the Junior Warden was Judge Lackland, also a Southerner but of the suave and easy-going type. I was in a dilemma. I did not want to hurt the sensitive nature of the giver of the gift, and I did not want to give in to what seemed to me only personal prejudice; so after the morning's interview with the Senior Warden, whose Protestant and protesting opposition held firm, I went, in the afternoon to have a conference with the Junior Warden. I sputtered and talked about rights, but Judge Lackland set me straight by saying: "Now what we want to do is to get this little church going; we want people; we want Fred; and as Fred is the main issue in this question because he means the best interests of our little church, don't you think you'd better let Fred have his way? You can catch a darn sight more flies with molasses than you can with vinegar." The Judge won, and I tried the "molasses" way; and Fred Llewellyn was my devoted supporter from that time on.

The Campbellites, as they were called in the Southwest, were the strongest congregation in Mexico. On one occasion they arranged to have a special preacher come for a series of meetings; he was a man of a most combative turn of mind, and he used his most forceful arguments to demonstrate the validity of the claims of his Church; he knew his Bible with his finger tips, and he could flip over the leaves and in an instant light on any text he wanted to find. In the back of the church at one of the evening meetings, there was a Methodist evangelist of the type which was called in those parts a "locust-preacher," meaning thereby a circuit rider. He took notice that all the Campbellite brother's arguments were reinforced by New Testament texts; whereupon, taking advantage of a pause in the flow of pulpit eloquence, he rose in his place and called out: "Brother, if you'll let me up in that pulpit, I'll muss up the front part of that book for you."

In 1885 I was nominated by Bishop Robertson to The Washburn Memorial Fund Trustees to receive a gift of books. The Rev. Dr. Washburn had created an endowment to be known by his name, the income from which was to encourage some of the younger clergy of the Church to read and think; the choice of the men who were to receive the benefit of this gift was left in the hands of some of the bishops. A list was sent me of a large number of titles from which I was free to make my choice of twenty-five volumes; one only restriction being made which was that Robertson's Sermons and Allen's *Continuity of Christian Thought* must be among the books selected. To this gift from the Washburn Fund, and to the two books here named I owe very much; the reading of these books was for me like the clipping of a bird's wings and leaving him free to fly by himself in a limitless sky. I had grown up in my religious thinking under the tutelage of the vicarious system of theology; no sermon was justified which did not present "the whole plan of salvation"; there were *ne plus ultras* in doctrine, the questioning or even the reinterpreting of which was banned;

thinking was allowable only within set pales; and I felt secretly guilty when my mind ventured beyond the "thus it is written"; and Allen and Robertson set me free. Never since have I known a joy of the spirit greater than that of the spiritual liberty which those two men gave me. To feel guiltless in giving my own interpretations of life free range; to stand on my own intellectual feet and speak the truth as I saw the truth must be for me—that was the opening of a door into new possibilities of power. For years Allen's methods of interpretation guided my thinking, and Robertson's visions moulded my preaching in substance and in method. I wonder of how many thousands the same thing might be said. And this is a tribute chiefly to the man who had the vision to see what a small sum of money wisely guided in its expenditure in stimuli to thinking could do to make it possible for numbers of religious teachers to learn to "speak with authority, and not as the Scribes," men who must win vision for themselves if others are to gain it from them.

My stipend in Mexico was raised to $90 a month at that time; and my last year in Mexico was one of the very few years in my ministry when my stipend paid my living expenses and still left me a little surplus to put by as savings. For when I left Mexico I had a few shares of Stock in a Building & Loan Association which I had bought out of surplus earnings.

IOWA CITY, IOWA

In 1886 I was made Rector of Trinity Church, Iowa City, Iowa; and in the summer of that year we began an interesting life there. At first we lived in lodgings; then for a year we lived in a rented house; and the year following we moved into the rectory which was next the church: this rectory had a bathroom upstairs—my first bathroom—and it had a hot air furnace in the cellar. Iowa City was a town of great interest. First of all, it was the seat of the State University, and that meant that it was the home of a group of men of unusual talent and ability; furthermore, my living there gave me the opportunity to keep up scholastic work. Iowa City was distinctly a university town, which means that it was small enough so that the University dominated the town; this was a great advantage both for the town and for the University. The greatest event in University life during my Iowa City days, as also for my life in relation to the University was the coming of Charles A. Schaeffer as President. Dr. Schaeffer had been Professor of Chemistry and Dean of the Collegiate Faculty at Cornell; he was a broad-minded man of wide scholastic vision; he had had an experience which qualified him to cope ably with the difficult problems of administration which a semi-political institution of learning presented; and he had a quality of seeming to bend, yet without yielding, which brought about the results he sought with no sacrifice of fundamentals on his part. The President's house was a centre of social and intellectual life hitherto unknown in Iowa City; and this was made possible by the gifts which the President's wife brought to a task which was as difficult for her as was the President's for him. Mrs. Schaeffer was Evelyn Schuyler, a woman of unusual grace and charm, qualities which were the setting for a brilliant and versatile intellectuality. Official receptions at the President's house were what the term indicates; but the dinners which preceded them were never dull, for Mrs. Schaeffer had the gift of "assorting" her people, as the French put it. I never was a guest at a party of the kind which was *mal assorti;* I always found myself next to some one who either had something to say, or who, better still perhaps was a good listener. And it should be noted that many a politico-educational impasse was solved at those dinners which had failed utterly of solution by endless argumentations in committee.

There was a family in Iowa City who welcomed me as an old friend, although I had never known them before going there to live. Years and years before, in Owego, N. Y., my grandfather had officiated at a marriage ceremony which united the families of two of the older residents there; and in course of time the young couple, Mr. and Mrs. Charles Ransom, came to Iowa City to make their home. Years later my father christened the daughter of this couple; and when I came to Iowa City to take charge of the church there, the first marriage at which I officiated was the marriage of this daughter, and in time I christened her children. This is an unusual record for America, that three generations of one family should minister to three generations of another family.

Years more passed and one day in Paris, Lovering Hill, one of Charles Ransom's grandsons whom I had christened in Iowa City, came to Paris and was at our house as a guest; he had been serving on the Serbian Front, and Jeannette and I were the first persons whom he had come to know, who could tell him of his old home where he was born and of his people; for he had left there in boyhood and had been educated in Europe as a boy. Charles Ransom was the autocrat of the neighbourhood; he had education, wealth, and character. There was an Englishman who did odd jobs of gardening about the town, and one day a fellow townsman of Mr. Ransom's saw this man occupied in (what was called) skinning the turf from a stretch of green pasture land across the street; it was a beautiful piece of rolling woodland which belonged to Mrs. Ella Lyon. This gentleman, Mr. Rigg, called to the gardener man, and said, "Bob, I don't want that done; it makes the place look ugly." In those days making a lawn was done by laying square blocks of turf on prepared and levelled ground instead of the slower process of seeding; and blue-grass sod was plentiful and easy to be had. "Do you hear me, Bob?" said the gentleman, as there was no interruption in the process of devastation. "Yes, Sir," said Bob, and drove off with his cart. In an hour or so, however, he was back and at the same performance. "Bob, didn't I tell you that I didn't want that done?" "Yes, Sir," said Bob, "but Mr. Ransom told me to come and get this sod for his lawn." "Well," said Mr. Rigg, "who is Mr. Ransom anyhow? he's made of dirt like the rest of us, isn't he?" "Yes, Sir," said Bob, "Yes, Sir, Mr. Rigg, but you know there's odds in dirt, Sir." This same Bob was one of my parochial responsibilities, so on one occasion I ventured to suggest the desirability of Bob's being confirmed. "What's that, Sir," said Bob. I duly explained. "Oh, that's all right, Sir," said Bob, "I don't need it." "Why not," said I. "Why, Sir," said Bob, "it's this way; I was christened when I was a baaby in the Old Country; and I had the other thing done to me afore you come, when Paason Judd was the minister."

The Lyon family meant a great deal to us in our Iowa City life. Mrs. Lyon, Sr., was a woman of strong character, and she was the centre of an interesting family of which she was the matriarch. Her son Lois was the Junior Warden of the church; he was a man deeply imbued with a sense of beauty, and he loved to work out his beauty instinct in craftsmanship; he did beautiful things in wood and metal and some of them I have with me to-day. His wife was a little lady of delicate beauty and gentle charm, and her children grew up to call her blessed. One of her sons has inherited his father's strong and sensitive fingers; he is a craftsman of a scientific profession, a dental surgeon who has made a name for himself in Santa Barbara.

It is a great pleasure to me to meet or to know of boys whom I knew years ago and who now as men have arrived at positions of responsibility. Richard Lyon is one of those boys; and there is another of them here in Santa Barbara, Edward Clinton; I knew him well as a young fellow in Iowa City, son of a widowed mother, and a clerk in a clothing store where I used to make my purchases: his unfailing courtesy won him friends there; and to-day he is one of the leaders in the mercantile life of Santa Barbara.

There is another man of note in our national life whom I knew in Iowa City, and thinking of him leads me to speak of the choir in the church in Iowa City. Dr. James Grant Gilchrist was the trainer of the choir and the organist of the church; and one of the boys in the choir was William D. Connor, now Major General Connor of the United States Army, and superintendent of the U. S. Military Academy at West Point. Dr. Gilchrist was one of the most versatile geniuses whom I have ever known. He was a brilliant and cultivated musician, a surgeon of unusual skill; he was a writer on scientific subjects; he was colonel of the Third Regiment Iowa National Guard. I studied surgery with him; I was Chaplain of the regiment of which he was the Colonel; and he was the organist at my church. He was a purist in music; he had absolutely no patience with anything which was commonplace in the rendering of the services; his choir would have done credit to any city. For him the church and the services were simply a background for the musical setting, and the sermon was at all times an interruption, and sometimes an impertinence; and I am not wholly certain but that often he was in the right in that opinion.

The Dey family were very good to us: they took us to their home and hearts when first we went to Iowa City. Peter A. Dey was from the same college as my father; and that was a tie at once. He was the Union Pacific's first chief engineer in the early days, and I have heard him spoken of as "the man who wouldn't steal a railroad"; his unswerving integrity blocked at one time a move for certain unfair proceedings in the development of a Western road; in Iowa he became one of the Railroad Commissioners of the State, a position in which his opinions carried influence and authority.

The Senior Warden of the church was Solomon Coldren, a man of wonderful balance and judgment; he was my next door neighbour, and he and his family were our constant friends. A nephew of his, Clifford Coldren, has now become one of the important men in the management of the Quaker Oats Company in Chicago.

During my Missouri days I gained the friendship of Ethelbert Talbot, Rector of the church at Macon, and the head of a boys school there; he was one of my examining chaplains, and he presented me for priest's orders. It was a treat for me to go over to Macon from Mexico for a Sunday and to officiate there when the rector was away on a missionary errand. He had a coloured factotum, commonly known as Uncle Billy. Uncle Billy would come into your room in the morning before you were up, to light the fire and to get the shoes to clean; if you did not wake up and turn over and speak to him he would rattle the fireirons until you did. He had known a boy who came from an interior Missouri town and who had grown up under Talbot's influence, and who had been ordained; and it was announced that he would officiate in Macon on a given Sunday. On the Sunday previous the occupant of the prophet's chamber said to the dark ministrant at the fireplace, "Uncle Billy, I hear that Mr.———— is to preach in the church here on Sunday next: I suppose you are going to hear him." "No, Suh, I ain't," said Uncle Billy. "But, why not," said the occupant of the bed. "You've known him so long. I'd think that you'd like to hear him." "Well, Suh, it's dis way, Suh," said Uncle Billy; "If I goes to de chu'ch and sees dat gemman a standin' up dere in dat pulpit and a expoundin' ob de Scriptures, I couldn't never help fum thinkin' 'bout dat tex' which says, 'Dey ain't no good kin come out o' Lazarene.' "

From that old association of Missouri days with Talbot, it came about that when he was made Bishop of Wyoming he wrote me a letter full of enthusiasm for his "People of the Plains" and telling me of the thrill of life in the Great Out of Doors, and offering me the position of Dean of his Cathedral at Laramie. I had always been keen on out of door living, so I accepted his offer and went out with high visions of new work to do.

It was on Commencement Day of this year at the University of Iowa that I received a signal honour, and my information of it came to me in this way. For some reason I had been prevented that year from following my usual custom of attending the commencement. As I was returning home from the errand which had called me away, I met a friend who greeted me as "Doctor"; and on seeing my astonished look he said, "Why, didn't you know that they gave you a 'D.D.' this morning at commencement?" I am right in calling it a signal honour, for it was one of the very few degrees of "D.D." which had ever been given by the University up to that time, and it was announced at the commencement that the degree had been awarded "on the nomination of the Scientific Faculty." My association with the Scientific Faculty was one of great importance for me; in fact I may well say that that association was a very real part of my education. There were men on that faculty who were scholars, students, original thinkers; men like Andrews, and Calvin, and McBride, and Nutting; and from the medical group men like Boehring, and Gilchrist, and Woods Hutchinson; their study group was called "The Baconian Club"; they made me a member of it, and one of the conditions for membership was that the proponent should be actively engaged in scientific study of some sort.

So at the mature age of twenty-eight I became Doctor of Divinity; and then a cathedral dean and set out for Wyoming.

That was an expedition which ended like many another crusade. A few months of life in Laramie made us realise that we could not stand the altitude, so I resigned to become Rector of St. Paul's, Des Moines, Iowa. Here in Des Moines I found old friends, and made new ones. George F. Henry had been a colleague in many an Iowa Convention; and he made much possible for me in the Des Moines Church. Simon Casady and his wife who was Rose Conarroe (she was one of the loveliest of women) made their home ours. And here must be placed the record of another boy who has made a name and place in the wider world—Tom Casady, now Bishop of Oklahoma, was one of my Des Moines choir boys. Another Des Moines friend who has become a man of note is Marcus Kavanagh, now Judge of the Superior Court of Cook County, Illinois; he was Lieutenant Colonel of the Third Iowa when I was the chaplain. Des Moines brings back other happy memories, our friendship with the Hubbell's, and the Hippee's, and with Oliver Perkins. I officiated at the marriage of Mary Windsor and Fred Hubbell; and the Countess Wachtmeister, who was Beulah Hubbell, was one of my parishioners in the Paris Church when I went to France. The people in Des Moines were more than good to us, and I might have stayed there many years longer; but I had not regained my health fully after the Wyoming experience, and I found it necessary to take a complete rest for some months. So feeling that I could not do justice to the growing work in Des Moines I resigned, and spent a whole summer idling in the Wisconsin pine woods; after which I took up work at Iowa City again, and remained there until 1897. Thus it was in 1890 that I took up again my associations with Iowa University life.

It was during this second stay in Iowa City that a suggestion came to me, which had a strong appeal for me at the time. Years before, as a boy, I had gained the friendship of Charles King, Captain King, and later General King; he was a near relative of Madame Waddington and of Miss Henrietta King, who were afterward valued friends of my Paris days. I had a letter from Captain King in which he strongly urged me to make application for an appointment as chaplain in the United States Army. The spirit of adventure came on me again, and I took up the matter seriously. Captain King said that he would see to the necessary endorsements from the Army side; leaving it to me to secure such endorsements as might be needed from bishops, and from men of influence in Washington. The result was that papers were filed on my behalf by General Schofield, Commanding General of the Army; by General Flagler, Chief of Ordnance; by many of the bishops; among politicians by our Iowa senators, Senator Allison and Senator Gear; and by J. J. Richardson, Secretary of the National Democratic Committee; and others. In the summer following the filing of these papers I went East to visit Father and Mother at Swedesboro, and at Mr. Richardson's suggestion I stopped in Washington to see the War Office and to find out by personal interview what the situation was. Every one whom I saw was most cordial. I was asked to luncheon at General Schofield's; and at the War Office I saw General Flagler and the Adjutant General; the latter told me that there ought to be no question at all as to the chaplaincy; that my recommendations outvalued any that had come to the office in years; and he asked me to go with him to see the Secretary of War. The Secretary of War was Mr. Lamont; and his comment was, "If the appointment rested with me I would sign the commission to-day; but the matter is wholly in the hands of the President; so far he has refused you; but I'll see him again to-day and tell him of my personal interview with you, and I'll ask him personally to appoint you. If you will come back and see me again to-morrow I may have favourable news for you." The President was Mr. Cleveland. On the following day I saw the Secretary of War again. He said, "The President refuses the appointment; he says that the Episcopal Church has already more than its share of chaplaincies; that there are good men on the list from among the Presbyterians; and that he proposes to fill all vacancies existing during his remaining short term of office from among them." It was characteristic of Mr. Cleveland; I had always admired him personally; and his consistent refusal diminished in no degree my high regard for the President. The Secretary of War said to me further, "There is a vacancy in the Navy, and if you will take that, I will see that your commission is issued to-day." That would have meant years of absence at Sea; and I did not feel justified in making that decision; so I declined the offer, with deep appreciation of the Secretary's friendship.

On my way from Washington to Philadelphia and Swedesboro, the car in which I had found a seat was invaded by a host of young people, and a young lady stopped by my seat—the only vacant place left—and said, "May I sit here?" She told me *en route* that she was a member of an Opera Company which had been playing in Washington, and that they were on their way to Atlantic City for a week of opera on the Pier. During that week Father and I went down to Atlantic City for a week of salt air and sea bathing. One night we went to the Pier to see the opera, and saw there the young lady of the train who was a *première danseuse;* the day following we saw her again trying to induce a diminutive pug dog to take a liking to the surf. A month or so after my return to Iowa City I had a call from a young man who asked me to officiate at his marriage; he said that he was Musical Director of a Company which was playing a week of Light Opera at the Iowa City Opera House; and he asked that the marriage might take place at the rectory. At the appointed hour the young couple arrived, and as soon as the girl came in she said, "Why, I've seen you before"; it was the young lady of the Pier and the surf. Jeannette had the house full of flowers and asked them to stay to luncheon with us. When she took the girl to her room before luncheon was served and to do some pretty things for her, the girl broke down and cried, and said, "Please don't think that I am foolish, but this is the first time that I have ever been a guest in a private house; I was literally born on the stage; my mother was an actress; and stage life and hotel life is all that I have ever known." We heard from her from time to time afterward; and then later had word that she was seriously burned in a fire in a theatre.

PRACTICING MEDICINE

The next event of moment in my life was the result of reading a book by Dr. Jacob Gould Schurman called *The Ethical Import of Darwinism.* This subject had been troubling me for some time, and I was not satisfied with any solution of the question, which had come to my knowledge. As a consequence I decided to do some investigating at first hand and took up the study of biology at the University; and from that went on to histology, pathology, and anatomy; and as these are the foundations of a medical course I found that a hereditary hangover in the way of an inclination to the study of medicine was strong in me. My ancestors, Samuel Cooke, James Newell, and Elisha Newell on my mother's side were all medical men, as were also my great-grandfather and my great-great-grandfather on my father's side. So I followed up my microscopic laboratory work by taking lectures and clinics in the medical departments of the University, and in 1893 I received the degree of Doctor of Medicine from the University; and in due course I went before the State Board of Medical Examiners, passed their examinations, and received a license to practice medicine.

One of my treasured possessions, a book which I often use, is a souvenir of my graduation in medicine—William Cullen Bryant's *Library of Poetry and Song;* and on the flyleaf there is this inscription:

Dr. Watson, with love and congratulation
from
Ethelind and Margaret Swire.
March 14th, 1893.

Ethelind and Margaret Swire were two of the dearest little playmates one could ever have; their father and mother, Roger and Edith Swire, were our close friends, and we loved the children dearly.

My questions as to the ethical import of Darwinism were a serious issue in my mind. I was in that stage of life when ethical imports were grave concerns on which decisions must be rendered by myself to myself, then and there: I had studied Darwin, and Huxley, Spencer, Tyndall and Wallace, and I felt an inner urge to make up my mind for myself whether a type of materialistic determinism was to sweep away all possibility of confidence in the decisions of an intuitive conscience; what, in the final issue, was to be the basis of morals. The results of my studies I embodied in some papers which I read before the Baconian Club of the University. Years afterward on a day when we were guests at *déjeuner* at the Château de Pontault-Combault, I was talking to Monsieur Emil Boutroux, the eminent French philosopher, and he asked me what my title of "Doctor" signified. I told him of my studies in biology and morals, and of my conclusions; and Monsieur Boutroux told me that in the same year he was pursuing a similar course of study, to arrive at the same results.

The Château de Pontault-Combault is of especial interest because it once belonged to Madame Sans-Gène, who was in real life Madame la Maréchale Lefebvre. She was at one time a *blanchisseuse* of Paris. To be near Lefebvre, whose military rank was then Maréchal de Logis, she became a Vivandière in his Regiment. Lefebvre who was a brave man was promoted from one rank to another; distinguished himself at the capture of Dantzig in 1807; was made Maréchal of France and Duc de Dantzig. The former vivandière, now Madame la Maréchale, offended the *grandes dames* of Napoleon's Court by her franchise and her utter independence of dress and manners and they combined to bring influence on the Emperor to relieve the Court of her presence: so Napoleon gave her the Château de Pontault-Combault which she much wanted. The play by her name gives an interesting picture of Madame Sans-Gène. There is a fascinating story called *Le Fils de Madame Sans-Gène*; and in the Château one may still see the closet where the mother kept the uniform of her boy. The Château is now the property of Monsieur Xavier Leon, the Directeur of the Review of Metaphysics and of Morals.

In 1896 I found that doubling in work, and the consequent strain of microscopic study had seriously affected my eyes, and examination showed that in my left eye there was a threatened detachment of the retina; with the result that I was advised by oculists to change my work for a time. To the question what I should do, the advice was to get more out of door life; open an office and practice medicine. This advice came at a time when it seemed almost providential; for Father had resigned his work in New Jersey, and was undetermined as to where he would settle. When he left Red Wing he took the rectorship of Christ Church, Swedesboro, New Jersey, an old Colonial Church in what had been one of the Swedish settlements on the Delaware. The Swedes who were early settlers on both sides of the Delaware River brought with them their ministers and their Church; but as this was British Colonial territory these ministers of the Swedish Lutheran State Church received their stipends from the Church of England Society for the Propagation of the Gospel in Foreign Parts. In time as the Swedish language came to be less and less spoken by the people the ministers of the Swedish churches, under the leadership of Nicolas Collin, advised the Swedish authorities that it would be advisable that these churches be turned over to the Church of England, inasmuch as they had long received their support from that Church; all of which was done, and these Swedish Churches became parts of the Church of England in the Colonies. This old Colonial Church in Swedesboro with its dignified architecture and its conservative customs pleased Father much; it was also a relief to get away from the strain of Minnesota winters into a mild climate; and, for Mother, it was a joy to be in Jersey again, even if it was South Jersey. One deprivation which this move entailed on Father was the necessary separation from old friends in Minnesota, chief of whom in his affection and regard was the Rev. Elisha S. Thomas, Rector of St. Paul's Church, St. Paul, and afterward Bishop of Kansas. Dr. Thomas and my father were close akin intellectually, and spent many of their Mondays together, which was a great pleasure to Father, for this was one of the few great intimacies of his later life. Out of this association of Father's came my own friendship as a boy with Nathaniel S. Thomas, now the retired Bishop of Wyoming, who has his home here in Santa Barbara near me. Nat married Edith Prince, a woman of fine presence, keen mind, and great personal charm; and their being here has added much to my life in these later years.

In Swedesboro one of Father's vestrymen was Dr. L. F. Halsey, the typical "good physician" of the countryside; I always think of him when I see that well known engraving which pictures the doctor leaning over the bedside of a child. Dr. Halsey's son, Joseph G. Halsey, a dental surgeon who lived in the old Halsey home in Swedesboro, married my sister Mary; and so an old friendship became a closer tie. Joe Halsey was a gentleman in all that the word implies; I have never known a man more considerate of his womankind, nor could I imagine one more suited to my sister's character; for them both refinement was of the very essence of living.

It was in 1896 that Father resigned the Church in Swedesboro and accepted my invitation to come out to Iowa, and for some months Father and Mother and Sister Mary and my Aunt Mary made their home with us in the Iowa City rectory. Then when I found that I must give up church work for a time, Father was made Rector of the Iowa City Church in my place; and for the second time in the family history father succeeded son; for Father had charge of the Norwalk Church for a time till Grandfather could arrange to come from the East to take it. I then went to Chicago for some postgraduate work at Cook County Hospital; and on returning to Iowa City I bought a house and opened an office for the practice of medicine. Thus my medical studies had opened the way for me to render Father and Mother a very real service when it would be most worthwhile.

In Iowa City Father passed three years of what were among the happiest of his ministry. After three years of work there Father's health began to fail, and he resigned the church and moved into a house which he rented from our good friend, Mr. Lyon. Before moving time came there was a Confirmation in the church at the Easter time; it was the last class which Father presented, and he said of it that it was the one Confirmation class that he was really ever proud of, for they were all volunteers. At that service Father broke; and in a few months more he was gone; no serious ailment, but he simply felt that he was through. Mother survived him some years. Their bodies were laid to rest in the cemetery in Iowa City; I said the committal for them both, as I did also for my Aunt Mary whose going preceded Mother's. In noting my gratitude that I was able to render Father and Mother some measure of a grateful return for all that they had done for me, it is due that I make record of all that Sister Mary meant to our older folk, Father, Mother and Aunt Mary; her loving care of them, her patience and her devotion to them cannot be expressed in words. They were worth all of it, and more, for they were very rare souls. Mary Cooke Newell was an aristocrat in every fibre of her being, brave, fine, and lovely like a bit of old porcelain; and my little mother was a saint. I can see her now with her little black leather book of Devotions (Dr. Hook's) in her lap; and her hour of morning meditation, of real mystic devotion, was the strength of her day. Mother would not have known what the word mystic stood for, but she was one.

What a wonderful blessing is what we call death! What an opener of blind eyes it is! It surely is that for those of us who wait; for as time and distance make materiality to fade, only the spiritual presence remains, and we see them for what they are. Useless for us to say, "If I could have seen! If I could have known!" We simply could not; they had grown to spiritual stature beyond us; and now, by their help, we have grown also. Let us be grateful for the vision and see in it, limited though it be as yet, some pledge and promise of what they shall yet mean to us when a new birth to a new life shall have "knit severed friendships up."

My medical venture was a success, as was also my venture in real estate. My income from my medical practice was more than my income had been from the church; I sold my house for more than I paid for it; and when the oculists told me that the eye danger was averted I accepted the offer of parish work again.

VIII

St. PAUL'S, CHILLICOTHE, AND, ST. PAUL'S, AKRON
1897-1912

CHILLICOTHE, OHIO

THE parish of Chillicothe in the Scioto Valley was a very old one. Old St. Paul's consisted of an old square brick church with a rectory on one side and a parish house on the other side; then there was a chapel for a large settlement in the east end, and a chapel for coloured people in the west end; there was an assistant, and after a time a deaconess who was ordained by Bishop Vincent in St. Paul's. It was in 1897 that we settled in the old rectory; a gloomy old house it was, and yet I have some delightful memories of our life there. More genuine gentlefolk than the people of that old town I have never known.

Chillicothe was originally the capital of the Virginia Military District, and was settled by Virginians. When Virginia ceded the Northwest Territory to the Federal Government, she reserved such a portion of the land lying between the Scioto and the little Miami rivers as would suffice for the location of the bounty warrants of her Revolutionary soldiers. These warrants simply called for so many acres of land. So across the mountains they came, with their carts and wagons and carriages and horses and often with their coloured dependents, and after finding a surveyor they proceeded to locate as many acres of land as their respective warrants called for. This "locating" was done under the old statutes of "Metes and Bounds" so many rods to a watercourse; thence so many poles to a hackmetack tree. The land was selected by each claimant according to his ideas of its fertility, no attention being paid to any possible aftercomers nor to any possible roads to be built in the future; with the result that many of the tracts were long and narrow and winding—what were known as "shoe-string tracts," often following the windings of little streams. When in aftertime conveyances of these lands were made by sale or by mortgage deed, the deciphering of these instruments required more than the skill of the proverbial "Philadelphia Lawyer"; for he would have been lost in such a maze. Only the trained judgment and pathfinding sense of a Scioto Valley lawyer, who was by long experience habituated to such puzzles, was competent to decipher them. The land of the Valley was alluvial soil and river debris and it was of unparalleled fertility; the sight of it from some of the hill tops was of such beauty that lovers of the country were led to say, and in time to believe, that it was here in all truth that God had set the Garden of Eden. For me, I am still of the opinion that the old saying, "God could have made a fruit more delicious, but He did not," should be reserved for the strawberries which were grown in the Scioto Valley.

St. Paul's Church, Chillicothe dates back to 1817, and was the outcome of visits made by Bishop Philander Chase, then Bishop of Ohio. It is told that on the occasion of one of his visits to the Valley he held services in the County Court House, and as there was no vestry room available, a noted jurist observed the proprieties of the occasion by standing in front of the bishop and holding up a large bandanna handkerchief while the dignitary put on his satin and lawn. The fitness of things, the decorum which precedent called for were ruling motives in the old town even when I lived there. If ever there were a community where the maxim, "It simply isn't done," had a sanction which gave it the force of law, Chillicothe was that place. There were "first families" there, and always had been, and what they did set the pace. The ice man came to the house one day in late autumn; it was necessary for him to go through the kitchen to reach the inner sanctuary where stood the icebox. The cook said, "You all ain't gwine to come traipsin' through my nice clean kitchen with yo' ol' muddy boots much longer." "What you mean by dat?" he said. "I means dat we all's gwine to quit takin' ice pretty soon; I heard de Missus say so." "Huh," said the ice man, "you don't know what you talkin' 'bout; all de big bugs, dey takes ice all wintah"; and cook replied, "I'll has you to know, mistah man, dat we all's such big bugs in dis house dat we doesn't has to take ice all wintah fur to prove it." They had great pride of family, of their "fambly," those "cullud help," who once came from Virginia. We came home late one afternoon to find some cards and an envelope on a silver tray in the hall; it was the tray which surprised us, for usually when we would ask Jane why she did not take the tray to the door for cards the reply would be, "Oh, Miss, Ah guess Ah done fo'got it." But this time evidently she had not "done fo'got it," for there were the evidences of virtue on the table on the tray, and behind the portieres between the dining room and the hall was the dusky guardian of proprieties waiting for our comments with a sublime consciousness of acquired merit. And this followed "Jane, did some one leave these here while we were out?" "Yes'm, Yes'm, Ah reckon dem are de tickets foh de M———— weddin': Ah peeked out dis little window beside de doah, and Ah seen dey cullud man a prancin' up de walk wid dem things on a silvah waitah, an' you bet Ah hustled back an' got ou'ah waitah for to put 'em on. Ah wasn't goin' to have dem folks a-puttin' anythin' on ovah us."

My vestry room attendant was not a judge like the Bishop's when he first came to town, but a most dignified coloured man. I am giving his name here in full letters, and I know that he will feel honoured where he is, in the best kind of a heaven, to know that I remember him with affection, and that I am so writing it down in my Book. William Hill was a tall man, very black, very white of hair; he dressed on Sundays in a long-tailed, dark-blue coat with metal buttons; he knew all the nobility and their proper places in the pews; he respected their tastes and prejudices; and they remembered him on Christmas Day when William stood at the church door, face wreathed in smiles, and bowing to each one with the grace of an oldtime courtier —for people went to Church on Christmas Day then. Shortly after we went to Chillicothe I was coming up the brick walk beneath the elm trees which led from the street to the rectory, and William was on his knees, back to the walk, trimming the borders, and talking to himself. And this is what I overheard him saying. "Ah thinks dese heah new ministah people gwine to suit St. Paul's. 'Peahs to me like dey got style, and dey got 'ligion, and dey got sense; most gen'ly when folks got style dey ain't got no 'ligion; and when dey got 'ligion dey gen'ly got no sense." Seeing a handsome carriage and a pair of black horses driving away from the gate one day just before I reached home—for those were the joyous days when a noble pair of horses furnished motive power for gentle folk—I said, "William, who were those people who have just been here? I suppose that they were some of the pillars of the church";—"No Suh," said William, "Ah don't just call dem folks pillahs; Ah calls 'em buttresses; dey suppo'hts de church fum de outside." On the day of the Battle of Santiago in the Spanish American War I heard "Uxtry!" being cried upon the street, and as soon as I heard the news I told William to ring the church bell; he complied too leisurely to suit my enthusiasm, and when he came out after a few moments of solemn ringing I said, "William; that's no way to ring a bell to celebrate a Victory; I want you to go back there and ring that bell long, and fast, and loud." "Yes, Suh," said William, "Ah'll do it ef you says so; but ef dey's goin' to be any moah uv dese heah Vict'ys, I'se gwine to quit de job. Ah mos' broke mah back ringin' dis heah bell when Gin'l Lee surrendered." One morning, sitting at my study window, I heard William outside; he looked up and saw me and remarked, "De Doctah's gwine to have a good dinnah to-day. Ah heah's de cook a-singin' some good ol' Mefodis' hymns." Soon he was running water into a tin pail from the hydrant in the garden; he would lift up the pail look at the contents, then throw them out. "What's the matter, William; do you want a drink?" I said. "Yes, Suh, Ah want's a drink," said William, "but dis heah water 'd be a lot bettah if it had a few hops drawed frew it. Ah nevah could drink just watah, Suh. Ah's got one o' dese heah i'on constitutions, and just watah always rusts mah throat."

There was a gentleness and a peace about life in that old town that I never knew the like of anywhere else. I often used to think that when I should retire I would like to go back there to live out my days. But it is well that I never could do it, for there is no disillusionment like trying to live over a rare experience of the past and to try and repeat one of life's joyous chapters; you simply cannot do it; it is never the same the second time. You have changed, and they have changed, and the place has changed; you are doomed to disappointment if you try it; far better to "kiss it good-bye," and to put it away in the top bureau drawer with some tissue paper and some lavender flowers, and to remember the precious things and to forget the bitter ones, and to say Thank God for them both.

In time I was called to the church in Cumberland, Maryland, where Hewitt Reynolds would have been one of my flock had I gone there. It has been one of the privileges of my life to be associated in Santa Barbara with Hewitt and Annie Reynolds; Hewitt a schoolman of the finest ideals, and Annie Reynolds the type of woman whom it is a privilege for boys to come in contact with; it meant much to the boys of their school to see the infinite attractiveness of refined and gentle womanhood. I did not go to Cumberland because the Chillicothe people offered me another rectory; they bought a house on Fifth Street which was a lovely place to live in. Yet for all that the old rectory next the church had its disadvantages, it has its cherished memories for me.

Father came there to be with us for a time. As he began to fail in health my mother and my sister wrote me that they thought it would do him good to get away from Iowa City for a change; so I went out there and brought him back with me to Chillicothe where he stayed with me for some weeks. One day while he was there he was lying on the lounge in my upstairs study, a room which looked out over the garden, and he had been asleep. As Jeannette came in to see if he needed anything he woke up, looking utterly bewildered, and said, "It must have been a dream; I was a boy, and back in England again; and looking in that window—I thought it was the window of the house in York —I saw a gypsy looking at me, a dark man with gold earrings and a red handkerchief about his head." Here is the sequel to the story. On the floor in front of the couch on which Father was lying there was a rug which Grandmother had brought to America from their house in York when the family moved to America. Father went to sleep looking at that rug which he had known as a boy in England, and the sight of it woke up memories which had been buried decades deep, and which translated themselves in dream life into actualities. Is any deed or vision or thought ever lost? Is it all recorded for ever in the imperishable records of vibrations which neither cease nor die? What is memory? What are dreams? Where is the substance of memory on which records of spirit meanings are written so ineffaceably that decades after all physical substance has changed and changed again, scenes of long past days are clearer to sight than happenings of yesterday?

One Christmas time before we left the "old rectory" Mother and Aunt Mary and Aunt Eliza came to Chillicothe to make us a visit; they were the kind of gentlefolk to appreciate the old town. Once after we had moved into the Fifth Street rectory they came there to visit us, and Mother became very ill at that time; it was the skill and care of my good friend Doctor Hoyt which won her back to life again. Charles Hoyt was another of the "good physicians," whom it has been my privilege to have as counsellor and friend. He had two lovely boys when we lived there, and I once asked him, "Doctor, I notice that neither you nor Mrs. Hoyt ever scold the boys or reprove them, yet they seem to do as you want them to do. How do you manage it?" His reply was, "I have made it a custom to go to the boys' room every evening, and just after they have gone to sleep I sit down by the bedside and talk to them in a low voice; I make suggestions, but I never blame them; I never call a thing bad or let them feel that I think less of them for having done it, but I simply point out a better way. And if I notice that they are restless or showing signs of wakefulness I stop until they are in that borderland of the first light sleep before taking up the lesson again. I have often made tests to see if they had any waking memory of my visit and always with negative results. Often on the day following I have noticed one of the boys make a start to do something which my counselling of the night before had touched on, and I have seen the boy seemingly hesitate, and then follow the line of conduct which I had indicated as better." It should be noted that all this was years before Coué or his work had been heard of in this country.

That Fifth Street rectory had a garden which is green and fragrant in my recollection, even after all these years. There were grape hyacinths of the deepest blue under my study windows. There was an apple tree in the garden the like of which I never saw elsewhere. The vision of Holy John was of a tree which bore twelve kinds of fruit, yielding a fresh crop month by month; and that apple tree of which I write bore four different kinds of apples, beginning in early summer to complete its bounty late in the autumn. It had been grafted to these different sorts so long before that the grafts were like limbs of the great tree; and the latest of its blessings were big water-cores. I wonder if any of my readers are old enough to know what "water-cores" are like; they would drop on the ground and break open and the heart of them was so filled with luscious juice that it was transparent. This tree was taller than the house, and I have looked out into it from the attic windows when it was simply a glorious radiant sea of pink and white, and my heart would melt into that vision of beauty, until I came to realise what one sight of the Kingdom of Heaven is. There was a papaw tree in that garden which bore the largest papaws that I have ever eaten. That Fifth Street house, with the one exception of my Oriole Nest in Montecito, was the most livable house which I ever had, and my study there was just what a study should be. It was to that house that there came once a little girl, a very little girl, a shy little girl; she was our *filleule* and her name was Aurilla Douglas Brigham; she was Jeannette's sister Nellie's child; and from that time on she had a place in every home which we made and was welcome whenever she would come; the charm which she brought with her is a lasting and a fragrant memory.

Our nearest neighbours on Fifth Street were the family of William McClintock; there was "Miss Petrea," as she was always called, a lovely woman, I have seldom seen her like; and her father and mother were people whom it was a privilege to know, gentlefolk of the old School, kindly, generous in thought and in deed. Mr. McClintock was a Methodist; but that term carried with it no limitations to his sympathy and his kindliness. At one time we had word that Percy Haswell (Mrs. George Fawcett) was coming to Chillicothe to play in the local theatre. We had known her well at Siasconset in Nantucket where we often went for a summer holiday; so we wrote asking her to be our guest while she was in Chillicothe. In her letter of acceptance she said, "I have written the manager of the theatre to reserve a box for your use on the night of my play." The manager wrote me: "Miss Haswell has asked me to provide you with a box for Saturday night; I would most gladly comply; but a soapbox is all that the house affords in that line. However I am most happy to send you, with this, tickets for two of the best seats in the theatre." "Percy" played on Saturday night with a grace and a charm which is vivid in my memory after all these years; I have never seen an actress on the stage who charmed me more. She was our guest, and on Saturday night we took her to the theatre and brought her back in a real carriage at a very questionable (for West Fifth Street, Chillicothe) hour on Sunday morning; and the carriage, the horses, and the coachman were Mr. McClintock's. He had said to me, "Doctor, I would rather that you did not take a common hack for your guest on Saturday night, so I am asking you to let me have the pleasure of sending my carriage for you." I learned much of the fineness of Faith from Mr. McClintock. He began to fail in strength and for weeks before the end of earthly days came for him, I used to go over each evening to sit with him and have a prayer with him; he said it comforted him greatly. You see we were neighbours in the best sense of the word.

I had a close friend in the Minister of the Walnut Street Methodist Church in those days. On the occasion of the Wesley Bicentenary he asked me to speak in his church on John Wesley, his mission and his meaning for England, an invitation which I most gladly accepted. I asked Dr. Courtney what sort of dress he would prefer that I should wear at the service in the Methodist Church. His answer was, "I think that it would be a fine courtesy if you would wear in our church what you wear in your own"; so I stood in the sanctuary of the Methodist Church in surplice, hood and stole, and told the people my vision of the story of St. John of England. Shortly after this Dr. Courtney came to St. Paul's and gave a most inspiring picture of John Wesley's training in the Church of England. Before coming he had said to me, "I would like to wear just what Wesley used to wear. Can you fit me out?" I have a beautiful picture of Wesley in cassock, gown, and bands; and I had them all for my good friend Courtney to wear. One of the finest letters which I ever had from Bishop Tuttle (then Presiding Bishop) was a hearty appreciation of that Wesley Commemoration in Chillicothe.

How to write of the friends in Chillicothe who gave us so lovingly of their best! Where to begin; where to stop! The Senior Warden, Thomas Marfield, was very good to me, as were all his family. He had such abounding faith in me that he sanctioned as a matter of course anything which I wished to do churchwise. He had a witty and attractive daughter who came home one Palm Sunday morning and said to her father who had been detained from the service; "Well! and what do you think your Dr. Watson did this morning?" "Well, what was it, Daughter?" "Why he walked up the aisle with a crown on his head and a palm in his hand. What do you think of that?" "I never heard of anything like that in our church before, Dear," said my Senior Warden, in his slow sober way. "But I know that the Doctor must have had some good reason for it." And I said to myself when I heard the story, "A man has a great inspiration for living his best when anyone has a faith in him like that."

Clifford Douglas was the Junior Warden. I hope that I have it right this time; I have already written Douglass with two "s's"; and I know that all these Douglas' are very sensitive about that final letter of their name; but if I've made a mistake this time it's not my fault. I have just looked up Anne Douglas Sedgwick in *Who's Who in America*, she is of this same tribe, and one "s" is all that is allowed her there. Clifford Douglas was a man whom one could respect and admire and love all at the same time; and that is a great deal to say of a man and a contemporary: and as for Lucy, his wife, she was—well, my adjectives, even my American adjectives, are lacking in expressiveness suitable; keen intelligence, fascinating gaiety, charm of manner and personal beauty were in her all combined. I fully appreciate something which was once said when we were at dinner together at a friend's house in Dayton and my neighbour at table said to me, "You are the only man here who has not at some time asked Lucy Douglas to marry him; and the only reason that you did not is that you were not here soon enough."

Albert Douglas was another good friend, the leading lawyer of the community, a man of influence and position; it was through him that the call to Chillicothe came to me. My last official act in Chillicothe was to officiate at the marriage of Grace Douglas, Albert's beautiful daughter. The Senior Mrs. Douglas—Madame Douglas, as she was called—opened her home and her heart to us most graciously; and to go into the entrance hall of her house where on a hat-rack hung Dr. Douglas' hat, just as he had left it there when he passed through the last Great Door, was to have a glimpse of a depth of filial reverence and of family feeling which was very lovely.

Again I am thinking of the Nyes and the Saffords. The Nyes lived in a big house on West Second Street—Mrs. Nye, and Dora, and Virginia; together with Aunt Hattie, the Mrs. Towne who was so like my own Aunt Eliza; it was a house always full of a charming hospitality, and it was a family of fine old traditions. When I remember people who came from Marietta I think that it must have been a choice place, so many worthwhile people came out of it. The Saffords were another family of distinction; they lived in "Tanglewood," a charming place with a hillside garden; and the daughters of the house were as fair to look upon as the house was attractive. Mrs. Safford was an appreciative friend; I have at my hand a little book in which is written "A Happy Xmas for Dr. Watson, with love from his old friend Mrs. Safford. Tanglewood, 1902." One day Mrs. Safford gave me a volume to carry home with me; it was by Principal Caird; and when I reached home (it was a Saturday afternoon) I sat down at my desk in my study and picked up the notes which I had made ready for my Sunday morning sermon in the church and read them through. Then, for the first time, I glanced at the contents of Principal Caird's book; and I said to Jeannette, "Plagiarism does not exist: listen to this and follow it along in my sermon notes," and I read sentence after sentence almost alike, and occasionally one in the identical words. It has long been my belief that we live footfast to the earth but head free to a spiritual and intellectual atmosphere which knows no limitations of space, and I question whether it has time limits either; so that thinkers of everywhere who have attuned themselves alike receive kindred impulses from out its vasty deep.

The Storys too were my most generous friends; the Clark Storys were my comrades when we began golf together on the old Race Track, and I was the first President when we formed a Golf Club. Mary Story did something for me which no one else ever did, she chose me to be her godfather when she was christened. Most generally godfathers are wished on you by your elders for purposes of their own, and you take what is given you and say nothing, except sometimes to cry out in protest; it is a wise child who knows enough to pick her own godfather. The Walter Storys too were devoted friends and made much possible for us in the church.

Speaking of that first of my Golf Clubs, I was initiated

into golf one summer at Wequetonsing by Bishop Tuttle who had a summer cottage there, and I brought back from Michigan my first golf clubs. After we had started the club in Chillicothe I had a visit one day from Willie McGregor, a professional of note, who told me that he was turning out some fine clubs and that he would like to furnish the incoming members of our new club with their kits; and as a sample of what he could do he would like to make me a present of two of his best clubs, made to my measure. "Barkis was willin' "; and the clubs are here in California now, a Brassie and a Driver, the heads of the clubs spliced on to the shafts, and the shafts of a second growth hickory so snappy that if you ever hit the ball fair, without pull or slice, it would go into "the middle of next week"; and equally the slice or the pull would be just as fierce if your stroke was poor. Another peculiarity of these spliced shafts was that when the glue which held the splice dried out, sometimes the head of the club would part company with the shaft and would go sailing down the fairway after the ball, to the great satisfaction of the gallery.

The Bennetts were another old family in Chillicothe whom I hold in grateful memory. Alice Bennett was the choir leader. When I first came to St. Paul's the choir occupied some proscenium seats in a large box stall at the head of a side aisle. When it was decided that the choir should be vested and occupy seats in the chancel it was Alice Bennett who made it all possible; much of my work there was made possible by her devoted allegiance. Another member of this family whom we were proud to claim for old St. Paul's was John Bennett. He came to his own when he published *Master Skylark.* And Harry Bennett, both writer and scholar, gave me constant aid and understanding help; his "Hats Off! The Flag Goes By!" made his name known at home and abroad. When the Field Service of the American Ambulance Hospital acquired a house on the Rue Raynouard and went to the Front as an independent unit, an American Flag was presented to the House by Mr. Clarence Mackay, whose beautiful mother, Mrs. John

Mackay, was one of my devoted friends in France; and at the dedication of House and Flag I was asked to read a poem in French about the Stars and Stripes. I could find none that was suitable, so I translated into French Harry Bennett's "Hats Off!", and used it for the ceremony.* Another member of the Bennett's whose homecoming was always a holiday when she came for a vacation from Wellesley where she was a teacher was Martha Bennett.

And so the list grows as I let memory range over those years from 1897 to 1903. Their names are not forgotten —Ireland, Boggs, Minshall, Bell, Pearson, Hathaway, Sears, Minear, Brimson, Miesse, Howson, Downes, Houk, Mills, Smart, Smith, McDougal. I would like to pay a personal tribute to each one of those who made my life in the Scioto Valley so fair a recollection, and who were so very good to me and mine. I would like to tell of the founding of the Sunset Club, of which I was one of the initiators; of my cordial relations with the masonic fraternity in Scioto Lodge No. 6.; and of my visits to Cincinnati for the dinners of the Society of the Colonial Wars, of which I was chaplain for a time.

It was in 1903 on a summer Sunday morning that I noticed in the church two men whose faces were strange to me. In the afternoon they came to the rectory to see me; and in the coming years they became my close friends; they were Charles B. Raymond and Karl Kendig and they were vestrymen of St. Paul's Church in Akron; and as a result of their visit we went to Akron to live.

Leaving Chillicothe meant leaving Bishop Vincent, and that meant much to me. For a clergyman to be associated in work with a Bishop with whom he is always in complete harmony in every move whether it be diocesan or parochial; to be admitted to his Bishop's counsels; to be made welcome to his house in closest intimacy; to share his plans for diocesan work and legislation—all this is so rare a privilege that words cannot tell what my heart would say; and this was my relation to my Bishop of Southern Ohio. I admired Bishop Vincent as an administrator and as a preacher; I

*See page, 276.

was grateful for his cordial friendship so freely given me. But the deepest chords of my heart were set vibrating when I was with him in his family life and at his table, in his study in the evenings, saw his thoughtful care of his invalid brother, saw his gentle deference to his sister, and above all saw his tenderness to his dear aged mother when she would come into the study to bid him good-night—that is what it meant to a presbyter to be a part of the human life of his Bishop. I am deeply grateful for all that Bishop Vincent means to me, and my life has been the finer for it. Bishop Vincent succeeded by right of seniority to the office of Presiding Bishop but he did not accept the charge. That fact reminds me of the number of Presiding Bishops with whom I have been associated. As a presbyter of the European Jurisdiction I was transferred first to the then Presiding Bishop, Bishop Tuttle; then I passed automatically to the charge of Bishop Garrett, Bishop Talbot, Bishop Murray, Bishop Anderson; and now I am attached to the jurisdiction of Bishop Perry. My good friend, Bishop Leonard, was another who inherited the Presiding Office by right of seniority, and declined to accept the post.

AKRON, OHIO

The change from Chillicothe to Akron was another marked epoch in my life. Chillicothe was a dream away town, Akron was the keenest of industrial communities; in Akron, among other things, I learned to be a business man. Bishop Leonard, at whose suggestion I was called to Akron, gave me the most hearty welcome; it was a welcome with a hereditary feeling in it: he had been a boy in Owego, N. Y. at the time that my grandfather was rector there: and, in time, I became for Bishop Leonard, as I had been for Bishop Vincent, Chairman of the Diocesan Committee on Constitution and Canons, the only diocesan office which ever had the least attraction for me. In Akron my first welcome came from a family all of whose members are very dear to me. When I made a visit to Akron to look the field over and to determine whether I ought to accept the work or not, I was a guest at the house of Mrs. Helen

Raymond, long one of the most devoted friends of the Church; and the gentle courtesy of the members of that household was a strong factor in making me feel that we could wisely make the move.

A short time after we were installed in the rectory, Jeannette showed signs of fatigue, partly consequent on the strain of breaking up one home and settling another one, for she dearly loved Chillicothe. One of the first to notice it was Mrs. George T. Perkins, who said to me one day, "Your dear wife is tired out and needs a rest; I am coming for her with the carriage this afternoon and she is coming down to make a visit until she picks up again; you can keep your office at the rectory and come and make your home with us for a while, and we will make her well." Deep feelings cannot be set down on paper. I can only say, looking back at it from this distance of many years, that no visit which I ever made was a greater blessing; it made life new again. Our welcome came from all the family, from Colonel and Mrs. Perkins; from their daughter Mary and her husband Charles B. Raymond; and from their children, Mary and George. Colonel Perkins was a great man; great in heart, in character, and in constructive ability; his daughter Mary resembles him in all essential traits; and Mary and Charlie Raymond have been to me all that a brother and a sister could have been. Charlie Raymond, while in a measure relieved of his heaviest responsibility in the active management of The B. F. Goodrich Company, of which Colonel Perkins was the creative and long the administrative head, is now giving his time and his executive ability to the direction of the affairs of Cottage Hospital in Santa Barbara, of the Santa Barbara Foundation, and of the First National Trust and Savings Bank of this city. Mary Raymond is a leader in all that pertains to the City's interests in music, in drama, and in art. I have known them both intimately in all the stresses of strong lives; and rarely is one given the privilege to know the inner meaning of lives like these, for whom opportunity means but the other name for sharing with others, and to whom difficulties have been but a school for courage. And Mary

Raymond has an undaunted spirit which has ever won my constant admiration.

The Senior Warden of the Church when I went to Akron first was Judge Marvin; he was a man whom every one respected, and he became a hearty friend. At a dinner which was given for the furtherance of the church's interests, the Judge paid me a compliment which was much to my liking, in eulogizing my friendliness of attitude toward the other churches of the city. He illustrated his point by saying

"I was once required to give a decision in a case in Court which involved some properties situated in a part of the country where most of the people were settlers who had come there from Sweden. After a journey by train I was met by the Sheriff of the County, who drove me to where the property in question was located. On the way we passed by a country cross-roads the corners of which were occupied respectively by a church, a store, another church, and a school house; and I said 'Sheriff, how is it that they have two churches here? it does not seem that there are enough people hereabouts to well support even one of them.' 'I don't know, Judge," said the Sheriff, 'but here is one of the local characters, we will ask him.' Then calling to the man who came up to us, 'Ole, the Judge here wants to know about your churches.' 'Yes, my friend,' I said, 'I want to know how it comes that you have two churches here for this little settlement?' 'Wal, Judge,' said the man, 'Daas account deefferance releegion.' 'Difference of religion?' I said. 'What kind of a church is that one?' and I pointed to the one on the right hand corner. 'Daas Looterann Church, Judge.' 'And that other one,' I said, pointing to the church on the left hand corner, 'What kind of a church is that, Ole?' 'Oh,' he said, 'daas Looterann Church also.' 'But,' I said, 'you just told me that you had two churches here on account of differences of religion, and now you tell me that they are both Lutheran Churches. Where does the difference of religion come in?' 'Waal, Judge,' said Ole, 'it ees thees way: daas church ofer dere, he believe as all trouble come in world from Ev-ah: and dees church, he believe as Adam was damn fool from bayganning.' "And," said the Judge, "I have long been wondering just which one was right; in fact the theological differences between ecclesiastical splitups are much like that, in my opinion, many of them; and to a humble jurist like myself they are too deep to fathom; and I am glad to see that our rector does not take them seriously enough to let them militate against good fellowship and community service."

Another warden was George W. Crouse, a man deeply interested in the Akron Church. When we came to the building of the new St. Paul's, his faith in the move and his faithfulness in furthering the project were essential elements in its success: the Crouse Memorial Organ was a tribute to the family name.

This reference to the building of the new St. Paul's brings in another name of interest, that of Ohio C. Barber, the longtime head of The Diamond Match Company. One evening he was at the rectory at dinner with us, and after dinner he was walking up and down the long living room, hands behind his back, digesting a postprandial cigar, and looking at a lot of sketches of churches which had been sent me by Mr. Coolidge of Shepley, Rutan and Coolidge of Boston (I had known Mr. Coolidge in Maine one summer). Mr. Barber turned to me and said, "Doctor, how much will be the cost of such a church as you propose to build?" I told him that the cost would be about $75,000. "And how much can your people raise?" "They have $60,000 in sight," was my reply. "It is not enough," he said; "Tell them that if they will raise $75,000 an unnamed friend will give $25,000 additional; that will then make $100,000, and with that sum you can build such a church as you should have." Needless to say that the Vestry accepted the offer with enthusiasm and set about at once raising the necessary money. I went East for a vacation; Mr. Barber went to Europe. When I returned I found that the $75,000 had been subscribed; and I took the first opportunity of seeing Mr. Barber and telling him that our part was done. My reception was most cordial; even more than that; Mr. Barber was enthusiastic; he said that he was ready to do something infinitely finer than he had at first proposed. And this was his proposition—"Tell your people that I want to build a church in Akron which will be a historic monument; it will be built after the general design of the Church of the Madeleine in Paris. Mr. Burnham of Chicago will draw the plans; I have made all the arrangements with him, and all that you and your people have to do is to buy the ground and make it ready and I will build the church which will cost at least $400,000." My Vestry were as dubious about this proposal as they had been enthusiastic about the first one. They were business men with a wide outlook, and the first thing that impressed them in the matter was the probable cost of the upkeep of the building proposed; it would be a monument and a wonderfully beautiful thing for the city; but monuments are expensive to maintain. Secondly, it had been hard work to raise that $75,000, and they naturally hesitated about expending it all on a building site and walls and drives; as trustees they felt that their cash expenditure should be balanced by some contractual security guaranteeing that, in the event of the generous donor's meeting with financial misfortune they would not be left with a large piece of ground, a larger pile of stone, and no church. So the matter "went to committee"; our legal advisers and Mr. Barber's legal advisers took the matter in charge. In the meantime Mr. Burnham had drawn the plans, and they were glorious; not a replica of The Madeleine, but a Greek temple of perfect proportions exteriorly, and within adapted to the worship of the Episcopal Church; and it was my privilege to guide this adaptation.

When the plans were completed I went to New York, as Mr. Barber's guest, to consult artists and sculptors, as to the decorations of the building within and without. One element of the plans called forth much discussion and woke some strenuous opposition on the part of some of the old fashioned folk. There was to be a crypt with burial vaults beneath the building: Akron was not used to crypts, and some of the good people could not happily think of themselves as saying their prayers with a crypt beneath their feet, even though the blessed remains therein bestowed were roomed in chambers of solid stone. I think that in time we would have gotten by with the crypt, but a much more serious matter came up; the lawyers failed to find a mutual ground for agreement; a demand for guarantees on the one hand was met by objections on the other side; and in the end the conclusion as expressed by one of the wardens was, "We'll build a church for ourselves"—and we did. I've never really deeply regretted the breaking of that iridescent vase, the plan for a Church of The Madeleine in Akron. With ample—and that means all that the word conveys of meaning—with ample endowment to provide, so far as such provision can be made in advance, for the care in perpetuity and for the upkeep of what in France would be a *monument historique,* the creating of that dream into a reality would have been a wonderful thing to have shared. Furthermore, it would have been in accord with a conviction which came over me, the first time that I saw what Akron was and was destined to be, that the beauty side of life and of living needs emphasis in an industrial community like that; that the worship of God needs to be so exalted by the very material signs and evidences of concrete structure that the passer-by cannot escape the lesson. He would be struck in his imagination by such a building saying to him, this beauty, this solidity, this massive creation means GOD; he would meet that impression as he came from the manufacturing districts, where the immense constructions of industry never ceased telling him of the power and the might of material things; and it would be a lesson so told that it would mean a people's spiritual uplift, just as a lofty spire inevitably lifts a man's thoughts heavenward.

Ohio Barber was very good to his friends, and he counted me one of them. I was in his office one day shortly after I had had a small amount of money unexpectedly paid in, and he and his secretary were counting over some bonds which were stacked on the desk so high that the secretary could hardly see over the top of them; they represented the underlying securities of a Corporation which Mr. Barber and some of his friends had taken over, and he told me what the bonds had cost them, and what return they would make on the investment. My reply was the trite remark that, "It takes money to make money." "That need not be so for you," said Mr. Barber. "There will be an uneven number of these bonds left when we have made our division of them amongst us, and you may have as many of them as you want at the price that we are paying for them." "How safe are they?" I asked. "I have older folk to care for out of my income from what investment funds I have; and I cannot take any risks." "Well," he said, "if at any time you do not want them, just bring them back to me, and I will take them off your hands at the price you paid for them." I readily agreed to that proposition, and I took some of the bonds. All went famously until a couple of years later those bonds defaulted their interest, and the bank where I had placed them as collateral on a loan called my attention to their depreciated value. That very morning I met Mr. Barber on the street, and after the usual cordial greeting, he said, "What's the matter? is anything worrying you?" I evaded the question, probably rather clumsily, and he said, "See here, is it those bonds?" I told him that the bank had most courteously suggested their replacement, at least in part, in my collateral account. "Then, why did you not do as we agreed?" he said. My reply was that I would never hold a friend responsible for the outcome of an act of kindness which he might have done for me. "Well," said Mr. Barber, "if we're to keep on being friends, you will bring those bonds up to my office this morning." So, I went to the bank, and asked the President if I might have the bonds. "Certainly you may have them," he said, "but, will you tell me what you are going to do with them?" I told him that Mr. Barber had said that he would take them off my hands. "And he'll do it, too," said the banker. When I went to Mr. Barber's office a short time later he said, "Have you brought those bonds, Doctor?" I handed them to him. He gave them to his secretary and said to her, "Check up these bonds; reckon 7% interest on their face value and also on the coupons from the date when the interest stopped, and write the Doctor a check for the full amount which he paid for them, plus the unpaid coupons, and the interest on the entire amount."

The bank here mentioned was the National City Bank of Akron, a bank which carried me financially during the War and during the whole of my life abroad. And I must record here my tribute of gratitude to the bank for that service, as also to Nelson Stone and to Harry Williams for their unfailing kindness and courtesy to me during the many years of our association.

My first financial start in life was given me in Akron by Andrew Noah, who was at the time the Treasurer of the Diamond Rubber Company. A few thousand dollars was left me as a legacy, and being in Mr. Noah's office one day, I asked him where I could place it to best advantage. "Why not buy some Diamond Rubber Stock?" he said. "I would like to," was my reply, "but I am told that there is none to be had." "There is none on the market," said Mr. Noah, "but one of our directors has some stock which he will sell; and I can get some of that for you." And that stock was the beginning of what I hoped would be my provision for my years of retirement.

The Golf Club in those days was on property owned by Colonel Perkins, and the fees were very modest; but when it was decided to lay out a new course elsewhere and to create the beautiful property now known as the Portage Country Club, the expenses began to climb. One day as we were playing the old course Andrew Noah said to me, "Have you taken out your membership in the new club," "No," was my reply, "that will be out of my reach financially; I cannot afford to buy the necessary stock for membership." "That's easily arranged," said Mr. Noah, "I've had to subscribe to a number of shares, and I'll transfer one share of the stock to your name, and then all you'll have to provide for will be the dues." So I became a member of the Portage Country Club; and that share of stock I still have. Just before I went to France to live, and while I was arranging business matters for an indeterminate absence, I went to see Andrew and took him the stock certificate, which he had placed in my name and told him that as I was going away from Akron I thought that I should return it to him. "Not at all," was Andrew's reply, "that was a gift; you keep the stock; it is a certificate of partnership in valuable real estate, and some day it may be worth some money." I am hoping that the prophecy comes true.

To the west of the grounds of the club is what is now the home of Harvey Firestone, the creator of the great business which bears his name. When I lived on Forge Street and the Firestones lived on Fir Street, they were my near neighbours, and their little house on Fir Street has many charming memories for me, memories of christenings, and confirmations, and a marriage—and, a birthday party, and the birthday party was a lovely one. It was Harvey Senior's birthday; and the lovely mother of the three boys (which were then the family) had arranged a celebration, and we were asked to share it. "Little Harvey" as we called him—now Harvey Junior—was at the table; the two younger boys were upstairs and in bed; but when the cake with all its trimmings and blazing with candles was brought in the father asked to be excused for a moment. And he went upstairs to come down shortly with two handsome boys, all rosy with their first sleep, one under each arm, and the boys had a part in blowing out the lights and in making the wishes; it is as charming a memory as I have out of a long life.

It is in the sharing of such joys that the charm of a parson's life consists; the being one with a family in their most intimate hours, one with them in both their joys and their sorrows; the seeing men who are leaders of affairs when the burdens of competition are cast aside for a moment and the man in all the simplicity of his real self appears. It was in his little study on Fir Street that I came to know the deep sensitiveness and the strong sense of responsibility, which a man of business can experience, when Harvey Firestone told me of what it cost him, heartwise, to see a factory in which *he* had been the factory, where he knew his men and they knew him, turned into a Corporation, and he himself alienated to an office apart, and other men come between him and his workingmen.

In that little study on Fir Street another thing happened which I remember with amusement for my part in it. I was asking Harvey Firestone about the possible placement of a few thousand dollars which had come from the payment of a loan belonging to Father's estate. He said, "Look out that window, Doctor. Do you see that little car which I just drove up in: it is being put out by a Mr. Ford of Detroit; it has a future before it. Why not buy some of the stock of that Company?" Hold your breath for the sequel! Did I buy any of that stock? I did not, and it was within financial reach. "Is it to laugh?", or Is it to cry? Well, this was another time that financial fortune sat on my doorstep, and I simply said, "How do you do?" and "Good-bye." Have I any real regrets? Not one. My life has been full of friends, and that means a life which has been rich beyond the power of money to buy. "Riches take wings," but friends remain. I have been brought well on into the seventies, always cared for by those who have borne me love; I have had enough with which to do for those whom I loved, when they had need; and I do not know that any other way would have been better.

Harvey Firestone, Junior, was one of my colleagues in the Church in Akron; and the thought of that reminds me of how men whom I knew in their lesser days have grown to great days. One of my former choir boys is a bishop; another of them is a major general in the Army of the United States; my colleague in the Church in Paris all through the War is a canon of St. Paul's Cathedral in London; and Harvey, who was one of my altar boys, is now vice-president of one of America's great industries. Those altar boys in the Akron Church are a most happy memory. The choirmaster had decided that the boys who were available could not do the musical work which, in his opinion, the service called for; so it became a question as to what I could do for a group of boys to which I had become much attached, and who were gathered with the idea of their forming the nucleus of a boy choir. I simply could not let them go, so I called them altar boys, and gave them work to do in connection with the church and the services, and they took their functions most seriously. One of those fuctions was the arranging of the font for baptisms, the carrying of the napkin, and holding the Prayer Book. One day one of the boys who had not as yet officiated at that ceremony was reminded by his mother that he was "on duty" for the day, and that it was time for him to go to the church. "I don't want to go, Mother," he said. "But why do you say that, Son? you always like to go to help Dr. Watson; and Harvey is going." "That's all right for Harvey," said Joe, "he's done it before, and he knows how; but I don't know anything about baptisin' babies; I'll go next time." When I say that those boys were my colleagues, I mean just that; it was wonderful what they did for me. It was a large church; I had no assistant for a time; the boys were eager to help in every way: and more than in their church work they helped me; they made me their friend and their confidant, and I got from them my best lessons in boy-philosophy.

One day when I was at luncheon the little housemaid came into the dining room, and said, "Doctah, I knows dat you cant see nobody when you'se eatin, and I done told de little boy dat; but dis heah's one of you' altah boys, and he said he knew you'd want to see him, so I jes let him in, and he's in de study." She was right; it was one of my altar boys; he was on his way to school from his home on Fir Street, and he had an important question to ask me, "Was it right to play marbles for *keeps?*" Now I render tribute to his home training as well as to any influence which I had had on the boy that that question became for him a moral question; but that he should bring the question to me for counsel and advice seemed to me a wonderful mark of confidence. It seemed to me then that I had before me a problem of life in its entirety, not just a question of marbles; that playing marbles was simply playing the game of life on a smaller stage; and that for me to hold that lad's confidence at a moment when he had entrusted to me a problem involving a question of ethics just as important as any which might come to him in his whole after life was both a duty and a privilege. So, after a moment's thought, I said to him, "All right, boy; play marbles 'for keeps' all you want to, provided that you play a clean game; no bad language, no quarrelling, no cheating, no playing with fellows who are not honest and clean and sporty." And the sight of his honest frank face with the real feeling of partnership looking at me out of his eyes is with me yet; and what he said by looks was something which he probably could not express then in words, and it was this—"It means a lot to a fellow to have a big friend to come to who understands boys."

Most people treat children—many people treat their own children—as if they were either hopeless little idiots, or else were creatures with the same reactions as adults; whereas they are neither the one nor the other. Children, if they are normal children, live in a world which is all their own. It is one of the penalties of growing up for most people that they leave that world of the child life so far behind them that they simply cannot understand why a child cannot see things just as they do, and that they expect that the child will of course understand the grown-up point of view about things; whereas to most children the grown-up point of view is unreal and fictitious and meaningless, and leaves out of consideration much which, for a child, are the matters of prime importance. Children are full often strangers where they should be most at home, that is with their parents and in their families. I have seen the look on a child's face which pictured what Wordsworth meant when he wrote:

"Full soon thy souls shall have her earthly freight,
And custom lie upon thee like a weight,
Heavy as frost, and deep almost as life."

Children simply don't understand grown-up customs, which are really, many of them, nothing but reasonless conventions or artificial habits,—the outcome of "trying to be like the Jones'es." Their joys and sorrows seem trivial to grown-ups, who look upon them as childish whimsies to be smiled down upon from the standpoint of superior wisdom;

whereas the grief of a little girl whose doll is broken is just as *real*—as real in its own way—as is the grief of a mother who has lost her child. There is a perfection in every stage of life; a child, for a child, is as perfect as is a man for a man; its emotions are just as real. And, because child nature is new, fresh, unhurt, injustices, and above all the injustices of misunderstandings, cut deeper than any which come in later life. Many a child goes into manhood or womanhood, bearing the unhealed hurts of the misunderstandings and the helpless fears of their younger days. It is ignorance that did it; that is true, but it is none the less an ignorance which entails consequences which are a handicap to many a child for all its earthly days to come. One must be a child at heart, even in one's maturest years, to make the most of that blessed privilege, the companionship and the confidences of the younger folk. I am well along in my seventies but I do not think that I will ever grow old in spirit; for I still find young folk nearer to me than are most older people.

Akron brought me the friendship of other men who felt that their business was part of a living life. One of these was George R. Hill. I said to him one day, "George, you are carrying too heavy a load: why don't you get clear of this business and let the others take over the heavy work; it will break you physically if you don't let go." He said, "Doctor, I'd do it to-morrow if it were not for our responsibilities to our stockholders; I feel that I must stand by them." George's feelings were not of the surface type; they were deep waters and still; yet sometimes they came to plain sight. I remember well the day that I christened him; it was in the old family home on Arlington Street, his father's and his mother's home, and afterward his home and Alice's. The congregation were two, his mother and his wife: and George's decision to make this outward act of allegiance to the faith of a Christian as to life's meaning seemed to me then to be a tribute to them, in part. I speak of this just as I spoke of my own decision to go into the ministry because of my mother, that I may bring out this fact—I am certain that we often find God and His meaning to us enshrined in our devotion to some other life beside ours, and that in reverencing them we reverence Him; we give our allegiance to the love which is the near-to in outward seeming, yet it is none the less an allegiance to the Infinite Love which is the Heart of All Life. God is very far off to some folk; it is hard to say to God, "'I love You"; but, if we can couple with that the love of some one nearer the Godward meaning remains the same. The Catholic's deep feeling for the Mary Mother has little of theological appreciation mingled with it; it is rather the human heart going out to some divine and understandable nearness. My own ministry found its first and deepest meaning for me in this, that in doing what Mother wished for me I was doing what God wished; and I have seen this written true in many another life.

George Hill's niece, Evalyn Kendig, and all her family were very dear to us. I say *were,* but I really mean are. The fact that I am writing history does not alter the fact that intimate relationships and affections do not change with time and distance. When I write of "children whom I have known," though they be grown up like Karl and Evalyn Kendig's children and may have children of their own, they are still children to me. There is something of eternity in the unchanging character of affectionate memories. And the Zilioxs, Sam and Kathryn—when I think of them, it brings to mind what I once read, that Heaven will be a community where we can have about us all who have been and are dear to us.

I would like to tell of many others who made our life in Akron worth the living, and who were our helpers in building the new St. Paul's—for that is what we went to Akron for. Their names come quick to memory—Goodhue, Brewster, Paige, Bloomfield, Saalfield, Adam, Smith, Mell, Manning, Gladwin, Jones, Latta, Good, Crouse, Stanley, Houser, Lawson, Oenslager. The list would be too long to write in its entirety, but the record of their helpfulness is written on the stones of the church itself. For it was an achievement, the building of that church, and we were grateful for the opportunity. The Crouses—the three Georges—broke the ground; Fred Jones found the architect and watched over the construction; in time the building was completed; then Bishop Leonard consecrated it. And then we went to France.

IX

TRAVELS IN EUROPE
1909-1912

THE beginning of our France-going came about in this way. First, we got used to going to Europe by going on vacations with "the Jimmies," which means the Andrews family,—James H. Andrews and Laura his wife (as they put things in Biblical chronologies); then Marion, Helen, and Edward, children of the aforesaid: and always to be remembered with them are Mr. and Mrs. Edward Day, who are Laura's father and mother. One summer we went to Fisher's Island with them, and sailed in the good Yacht *Amelia;* another summer we went to Hyannisport and sailed in a centreboard shallow-draft sloop and bought lobsters from the lighthouse men. Then in 1909 we went to Europe. Mr. and Mrs. Andrews had decided on a summer in Great Britain; and on a certain Tuesday evening we went out to Westwood to wish them *bon voyage.* Before we started back for the other side of town Mr. Andrews said to me, "There's something which I want to talk to you about before you go home"; and I wondered what was coming. This was it he said: "Our London office has secured an automobile and a chauffeur for us, and there are seats for two more in the car, and Laura and I want you and 'Peach' to go with us"—the Andrews children always called Jeannette "Peach"; and from that it came that we were known to the family as "The Peaches." No sooner had Jeannette heard the invitation than her mind was made up to accept without question. But I had some hesitations—first I did not know whether I could leave Mother so far away when she so much depended on me; then I did not have the free money necessary for such a journey; then I did not know how the services in the Church could be cared for; and to top the pyramid of questionings, I had a church wedding coming off in a few weeks and I did not want to disappoint Abby Alden; all these problems I brought out for discussion; then "home and to bed" (as Pepys says). I heard the telephone buzzing before I went to sleep, but I paid no attention to it; but in the morning it rang while we were at breakfast and Jeannette answered the call. When she came back to the table she said, "'That was from your mother; Western Union Telegram; it said, 'Go by all means.'" Jeannette had sent Mother a message before we went to sleep the night before; the tide seemed to be setting Eastward. About ten o'clock in the morning came a telephone call; it was Mr. Andrews who said, "I wish that you would stop at my office when you come down town this morning"; and I stopped. He had news for me. "Mr. Crouse (the senior warden) will attend to the church matters while you are in England with us; in half an hour I will have the White Star Line on the long distance, and I think that you can get a cabin on the same deck with us; the bank will loan you the money for the trip; the assistant can take care of the church; and as for Abby's wedding, you can dismiss that from your mind; she will miss you, perhaps, for a moment on the joyous day; but soon she will forget all about it and forgive you." So that was that. We took the train on Thursday, we sailed on Saturday, and in a week's time we landed in Liverpool.

It is vivid with me still, the keen delight which Mr. Andrews took in sharing with us the sights which thrilled him. We must let the unpacking go; we must be out on deck to see the ship pull out from her dock and watch the waving crowd; steamer letters and state room arrangings could well wait for a time when there was nothing better to do; and we must stay on deck till we had passed Liberty—that statue of which the Frenchman said, "You have the statue; we have the liberty." The joy of sharing! the privilege of rich natures! I learned to know more fully what that meant during all my association with Jim and Laura Andrews and their family. From Liverpool we went up to London, and on one jubilant morning we started from the Savoy Hotel in what would look to us now as a funny little car on our way to see what was "on the other side of the Looking Glass." We lunched with John Bunyan at Bedford; we slept at Peterborough; we lunched at the White Hart at Lincoln; we slept at The Swan at Mansfield; and on the way we saw cathedrals at Peterborough and at Lincoln; at Southwell we saw Southwell Abbey and the carvings of its Misereres, and the sculptured capitals in the Chapter House; and J.H.A. was very patient with our lingering longings after old churches. At Mansfield we could not find our way at first into the Swan Inn; one enters from a courtyard which is hidden away at the end of a narrow passage between old buildings. It was well for us that this was so, for it gave us another chance to taste some old-fashioned British humour (being British I must spell it with a "u"). Just across the street from where we halted our car was what we call a butcher shop—there it was called a flesher's—and all in front of the shop there was a grand display of pink and white hindquarters and forequarters and backs and breasts of plump animals (a sight resembling in some ways a bathing beach in this sunny clime); and in the show-window there was a beauteous bowl of mint bearing this sign on a little placard, "Will the party who stole the shoulder of lamb last Wednesday kindly come back for the mint." From Mansfield we coached it through the Dukeries, and we saw Robin Hood's Oak in Lincoln Forest; and toward evening we came to York. As soon as I was dusted off I set out from Harker's York Hotel, all by my lonesome, and made my way without asking directions to Marygate, the street where Father was born. There was a pageant going on in York that weekend; it represented the old York of the days when it was a Roman Colony; and in the doorway of one of the houses stood a tall figure wearing Roman armour and a helmet and carrying a great sword over his shoulder: an irreverent passer-by, who knew who was inside the armour said, " 'Ello, Tom; I suppose you think you're Damocles": "Ah doant knaw who Damocles be," said the ancient Roman. "But Ah kno-ah Ah'm damn 'ot."

From York we motored over to Ripon and to that faery place, Fountains Abbey; then we went to Durham where

Jeannette paid her filial tribute to her forebears in the little Chapel of the Cathedral which is called The Neville Chantry. From Durham we went northward by way of Newcastle intending to be at Otterbourne for luncheon. Otterbourne meant something to me for it was at the Battle of Otterbourne that Sir Hugh Montgomery was killed; but we were delayed by the weather, and it was a weary lot of travellers who came into the little Inn at Otterbourne after a cold raw morning on the moors. We sat ourselves down in the living room about a little fireplace which was doing its struggling best to seem cheerful, and then Mr. Andrews and I went in search of refreshment. There was a promise of tea to be had, and tea is most useful in the chill of the longtime unopened living room of a British hostelry in the country (some one has irreverently said that the reason why the English take so to tea is that it is their sole idea of central-heating). But feeling that *the ladies* had immediate need of something more recuperative than a promise of tea in the distance, Mr. Andrews and I went in search of the landlady and were told by a maid that she was in "the buttery," and that the buttery was down that passage to the left; so down the passage we went, stone-arched with uneven stone floors, and in a little stone cave just off the passage itself we found the good lady, bunch of keys at her belt, occupied in getting some of the necessaries for the luncheon; and when we asked where we could find THE NECESSARY which we came for she reached under a shelf and handed us six bottles—Club Soda, the kind of bottles which have a plunger held up to the neck of the bottle by the gas in the bottle. "There," she said, "is the soda; and its thrippence a bottle; and as for the whiskey, it's in that little keg on the cross-trees there, and you can turn the spigot and help yourself"; and that we held to be true British hospitality. From Otterbourne we drove to Melrose by way of Jedburgh, and then on up to Edinburgh, and from there up to Callander. The evening that we were at Callander we drove in the long twilight to Balquhidder to stand by Rob Roy's grave; and all along our road there grew in the shade such glorious tall foxgloves as I have never seen elsewhere. The next day it was to Balloch by way of the Trossachs and Loch Katrine and Loch Lomond; and the same evening down to Glasgow. From Glasgow we went down to Troon for over the week-end; and such a rainy time it was! It is not slander to say that it rains in Troon 367 days out of the year, for it was a Scotchman, although a Highlandman, who told it to me. Jeannette and I went to the Kirk on the Sunday morning, and on coming out we went to a near-by "Mews" to try and get a hansom to take us back to the hotel. While we were waiting, our luck comes in a tall dignified looking gentleman in top hat and spats, whom we had seen at the Kirk; he was evidently a personality, and all was apologies on the part of the liveryman because they had not sent him a cab; but when Top hat and Spats sputtered and stormed he got this reply, "I'm doin' the best I can, My Lord, you shall have a cab as soon as I can get one in; but there's none in now, and I can't make them up like scones, you know."

Glasgow means the Clyde; and they are inordinately proud of it too, are the Glasgow folk. It is told of some aldermen from Minneapolis who were on a visit to Glasgow, that as they were being shown about by some of the city's bailies they were taken to see the Clyde among other sights. "Well," said one of the Americans, "I don't call that much of a river: you should see the Mississippi." "Ye hae nae reason to be prood o' that," said one of the Scotsmen, "God A'Mighty med the Mississippi, but we med the Clyde oorsels." Glasgow and the Clyde bring me memories of another and a later trip which we made abroad. We were in London, Jeannette and 'Rilla and I; we had arrived there about six in the evening, tired and dusty; and the one thing that I wanted most was a bath. We drove to one after another of the four hostelries which I liked the best without being able to find an apartment with bath at any of them; so I said, "Here's where I'll waste no more time; we'll go to the Carlton"; which we did. On the way up to "room and bath," the others said to me, "Did you see that notice in the lift that you must dress for dinner; we don't want to 'doll up,' do we?" "No," I said, "we'll simply walk over to Simpson's and eat there this evening"; which we did. It was the good old Simpson's of the days before it had been Savoy-ised; and, if you did not know it then, you missed something. Gerald Stanley Lee who wrote things both witty and sober (and if you have not read his book, *The Shadow Christ,* I beg you do it; my copy is all worn with frequent thumbings) once wrote of the restaurant in question, "I love to go to Simpson's in the Strand where for three shillings I get a dinner which it costs me three dollars in New York *not to get.*" Simpson's used to have nice little cosy Pullman car sections all around the sides of the big room with a table with places for four in between the berths; and then in the main portion of the room there were larger tables. By the time we got there all Pullman car sections were occupied, and we were perforce obliged to content ourselves as best we could with seats at one of tables which was arranged for six guests—and we were but three. But contentment was not hard to come at as we watched those white-robed priests hovering near with flaming altars bearing great loins of the roast beef of Old England, (and for a six pence quietly slipped over and a whispered "a slice of the under-cut, if you please," you dined as Royalty might).

Shortly after we were seated there came in two people, a man and a woman; looked around as we had done for one of the little sanctums, and not finding any free, picked on us as looking inoffensive at least, and asked for a place at our board, which was cheerfully accorded them. It was at the time of The International Horticultural Exhibit in the Chelsea Hospital Gardens, and our new-come friends asked if we had been to the Flower Show. We had not been to it for the good reason that this was the opening day; the Prince of Wales was to open the Show, and the entrance was three guineas the ticket, and we had planned to go when the price dropped to six shillings—all of which we did, and it is a wonder just to remember. Our new acquaintances said that they had been to the Opening, and we looked at them with suddenly increased interest for twice three guineas meant thirty dollars for the two of them, and we wondered a little where such nice plain looking people like ourselves got all that money. It turned out afterward that our friend was a

Seedsman from Glasgow, and that he had "Complimentaries." After a bit he asked us if we knew Glasgow, and I said that we did. "Then you've seen the Clyde?" "Yes," I said, "at Erskine Ferry"—I did not add on a rickety old ferry-boat which I feared would any moment turn turtle and dump us, car and all, into the dubious looking stream; and it was well that I hazarded no such comment, for if I had I might have ruffled up his dignity, and perhaps have missed a good story; and so would you. No sooner had I said Erskine Ferry than my Glasgow man looked on me as a friend and a brother. "Erskine Ferry," he said, "well, that reminds me of a story: I was comin' up to Lunnon one night; it was Christmas Eve; and I was sorry for the Pullman mon on the train, and I said to him, 'I hope you had your Xmas dinner before you started'; 'I did, thenk you,' said he. 'Goose and sausage?' I said. 'Goose,' he said, 'but no sausage.' 'What's the matter wi' the sausage?' I asked. 'Well, that's a story,' said he. 'It was this way: I was fishin' once at Erskine Ferry; and there was a mon oot in the reever in a bo-at; and he o'er-set the bo-at and he went into the reever; and when I saw he could no' swim, I went in and pulled him oot; and when I got him ashore he went doon in his claes and got out six shillin's and wanted to gie 'em to me. "No," I said, "I wont tak yer dirty money; I did na get masel' all wet for six shillin's; I did it to be decent." "Ye wont tak me money," said the mon, "then I'll gie ye somethin' better: I'll gie ye some good advice: Ah'm a bootcher; don't ever eat sausage!" ' "

From Glasgow we set out again, this time on a visit to Eglinton Castle in Ayrshire. The Earl and the Countess, hearing from the Countess' brother that I, a long-lost and long-distance cousin, was in Scotland, sent us an invitation to come to luncheon at the Castle. It was a lovely day and we drove down by way of Irvine and received a most cordial welcome and a most engaging luncheon which was served in the big dining room of the castle, a room whose upper wainscotting was hung with painted portraits of all the long line of Earls of Eglinton. My neighbour at table pointed out one dour looking chap and said to me, "He's the ancestor of your branch of the family; we don't care for him much; he's the one who gave the Eglinton Tournament which bankrupted all the rest of us ever since."

After luncheon we made our way southward driving through the Park of Eglinton Castle for miles with rabbits and pheasants popping out along the way from under the trees. It was our intention to spend the night at Dumfries; and in motoring it was our habit to hunt up possible hotels in our guide books before arriving at a projected stopping place. J.H.A. put his dependence on a new red Baedeker; and I, who for some reason do not like Baedekers, put my money on a good old Murray. We had followed this formula on coming near to Dumfries: Baedeker said Station Hotel (locally pronounced 'Stytion 'Otel); and Murray said Woodbank Mansion. As we pulled into the town it turned from a drizzle into a real rain—no longer "a Scotch mist"; and that rain settled the hotel question, for of a sudden I announced, "There is Woodbank Mansion just at the right." The chorus was unanimous: "Don't let's go any farther in this rain; let's stop here!" and so we did. It was a lucky rain, for Woodbank Mansion was an old-fashioned gentlefolk's manor house now adapted to hotel use. Fortunately again they had two large double rooms free; and, as usual, Jim insisted on giving us the larger one. It was a beauteous room, and had been once, I take it, milady's boudoir and dressing room; it was now provided with two beds, each of them the size of a half-acre lot; but the thing which I did not notice at first was the mirrors, seven of them, each of them the size of a cheval glass, let into walls and panels. Bedtime came and my tired Lady was half asleep when I came up. I prepared myself for retiring and was just midway between "undies" and pajamas when I chanced to look up and around. I think that the historic fig leaves must have been a merciful provision for even the untainted natures of the Garden of Eden; my surgical experience has convinced me that almost any one who is past "the age of Innocence" looks better with some clothes on; and my familiarity with men's locker-rooms in golf clubs makes me doubly sure of what needs no assurance that the male animal of the human species is a sight to be avoided when he is wholly undressed; and here was I, reflected in seven full-sized mirrors with a "birth-day suit" as my whole adornment; and I am sure that the neighbours on the corridor must have heard my cry, "For mercy's sake, please shut off the light!"; the switch was on the other side of the other big bed.

From Dumfries we went by way of Carlisle and Penrith to Windermere for a week in the English Lake Country; and then on south to Chester. On another visit to Chester we were walking on The Walls and I had been telling my complaisant family some stories of the building of The Walls when a group of tourists came along, and one of them came over to me and asked me questions of an historical import, which I was most glad to answer for I was all primed with archaeological lore; that led to more questions and more answers, until finally I caught on to the situation—they took me for an official guide. Just before they left one of them quietly slipped me a shilling. Did I give it back? I did not. I make it a rule never to interfere with a good deed: and then, beside that, I knew that she had had much more than a shilling's worth of information at current prices. From Chester we went by way of Rhuddlan and Llandudno, (and I learned that "ll" is pronounced "th" in the Prince of Wales Country), on to Bettws-y-coed and then to Llangollen. The street of Bettws-y-coed was thronged and packed with holiday makers; and we viewed the sight with small enthusiasm, for it was Bank Holiday and we had just been in such a jam at Greenock; only there two bobbies had halted us and told us that they would see us through; each of them put a hand on a headlight of the car and asked us through, after saying, "Drive careful, please; if you touch so much as a tail of one of their dogs it will be more than your life's worth." But here in Bettws-y-coed there were no bobbies in sight; and we did not need any; at Greenock the crowd was a mixed lot of men off the ships—Lascars, stevedores, and "what have you?"—and in Bettws-y-coed it was nice good happy Welsh folk out for their holiday in that lovely country, and their quiet courtesy and their readiness to let the car pass made me a convert to Lloyd George.

At Llangollen we stood on the terrace of the Hand Hotel and watched the hotel fisherman catch a lordly salmon for our dinner from the tumbling waters of the Dee; and the next day we went by way of Shrewsbury where there is a castle built by some one of my ancestors (when they came to New Jersey they called the country road which is at the foot of one of the lanes which leads up to the Big House the Shrewsbury Road), then on past Montgomery (where there are the ruins of a castle which they built when they came Northward after their castle in Cornwall had been burned) to Hereford. On the way we drove through a beautiful park on the outskirts of Welshpool passing for some distance beside a high wall, and then, without knowing that we had taken the wrong turn, we swung with the road sharply to the left and found ourselves to our amazement in the courtyard of Powyss Castle. Before we could re-orientate ourselves and determine how to retire with dignity out rushed a butler in livery and some pages and proceeded to unload our luggage. We sat in dumb amaze. J.H.A., (with his customary aplomb), whispered: "Say nothing at all; leave this to me." Then he disappeared into the Castle in the wake of the lackeys and the bags; to return soon, followed by a smiling butler who explained that we had been mistaken for some guests who were expected to lunch there, and that while the Castle was not open to visitors that day owing to the fact that the family was in residence, yet he would be glad to show us the Art gallery and some of the State apartments. This was partly "Andrews' luck," and partly (so we heard afterward) due to a bit of British gold which passed, hands unknown, to the astute old butler. All went "merry as a marriage bell"; we alighted, walked through a wonderfully interesting gallery where in place of portraits in oils there were fine pieces of sculptured marble on pedestals; and on coming down a stairway to find the car again we met in a lower hallway some of the family. They did not ask us to stay for luncheon, but gave us courteous recognition consequent on the butler's explanation that we were from the

U.S.A. and were motoring through and would be missing all chance to see the beauty of Powyss if we did not see it that day.

At Hereford we put up for the night at The Green Dragon Inn. (I would like to know why there are so many Green Dragons in Wales, and just who that particular old devil was.) We were lulled to sleep by the mellifluous perfume of hops wafted in our open windows; it was the hop harvest, and one might have thought oneself in St. Louis and in the neighbourhood of the Anheuser-Busch Palace.

From Hereford we went on to Broadway and Top Farm, where we had a lovely welcome from the Wells, the owners. It was to this lovely Worcestershire village that Mary Anderson (Navarro) retired after her American triumphs. Mr. Wells grew up as a boy in the neighbourhood and always used to dream of the day when he might own Top Farm, and when his fortune came to him his dream came true. We were interested at luncheon in being served a drink that was new to us and were told that it was "perry," English for pear cider; it was light amber in colour, gently sparkling, delightfully cool; and when the maid brought it in in a pitcher we were told that she had been to the cistern for it; that the neighbours put their common stock of perry in a cistern on the Green, and drew on it as they had need. In the afternoon we wandered about the gardens, picking fruit as impulse moved us, the most wonderful gooseberries I ever saw, more than an inch in length, hanging down from branches of bushes trained like trees, and honey sweet; then after tea in a garden house where we had crumpets of a delicious tenderness spread with golden country butter which dripped up my sleeve, we were taken for a drive to a hilltop from which we saw three Counties, all of England's fairest, glowing gold and green and scarlet; and it was through that beauty of landscape that we made our way in the twilight to Oxford. It was dusk as we wandered through the colleges, which fact accounts for the joyous amazement of an elderly factotum at the fee which came to him; Jim being short of change, asked Laura for her purse from which to tip the guide; it was a half-sovereign that came out of it in the dusk instead of the smaller recompense which was intended. The next day it was back to London; and for the first time in our weeks of motoring we were held up by a bobby; we were given a ticket for "speeding"; it was in Bushey Park, and we were going fifteen miles an hour: the limit there is twelve. "Americans Beware!"

We stayed on after the Jimmies sailed for home; and we went to Bath, one of our dream cities; and also to Cambridge where lived a gentleman who interested me much; he provided me with my "ecclesiastical millinery." One day when I went to visit him at his place on Sidney Street I found him just back from his holiday across the North Sea and he had in his pocket a volume of the Classics in the original, which was his summertime reading.

When in London I was asked to lunch at Lambeth Palace by the Primate, Archbishop Davidson. He asked me all about our travels; all about myself and my father and my grandfather, (in fact a truly Philadelphian enquiry); and then he said to me, "With your English blood and ancestry, would it not appeal to you, Doctor, to take up work with us in the Church of England; we would be most glad to make a place for you?" "I certainly thank Your Grace for the suggestion," I replied, "and if you will make Canon Boyd a bishop and make me rector of Bath Abbey, I will come." Canon Boyd was Rector of Bath Abbey at the time. I never heard that my suggestion was accepted; but for all that, I found in Archbishop Davidson a most charming host as well as a statesman of large vision; and his reasons for not being willing to see the Church of England disestablished won me completely. It is to Bath Abbey that my good friend John Penton may go on an ancestral pilgrimage to see the marble tablets to his ancestors which find honoured place on its walls.

Back in London after the motoring I wanted to escape the cosmopolitan Hotel, so I asked a longtime friend at the American Embassy where in London I could find a really British hotel without continental frills. He named one which he recommended; and being a little cautious from experience I asked him if we would find this hotel of his thoroughly comfortable. John's reply was: "Well, Sam, Archbishop Maclagan goes there when he is in town; and Charlemagne Tower always stays there, and I really think that it would do for you." So we went to Garland's in Suffolk Street. We had an apartment there which looked out on the little narrow street; and the story is told that the old butler (who bore a marked resemblance to Abraham Lincoln) was pouring what in England is called coffee for an American guest, who was seated in front of the big window reading the morning paper while at his breakfast. The butler was looking out of the window as he served. "It looks like *rine,* Sir," said the butler. "Yes" said the gentleman at the table, glancing down at what was going into his cup, "it looks like *rine;* smells like coffee."

Next we came back to America, and Akron, sailing on an Atlantic Transport, in company with a circus and a stock farm as fellow passengers. The sea was as smooth as glass all the way; and it was like being on "'Grandfather's Farm" to be wakened in the morning by the mooing of the cows and the neighing of the horses; but for all that it was one of the best crossings that we ever made.

That first trip abroad seemed to make another one necessary, so in 1910 we went again, taking passage for England; but on the boat we met friends who were going to France and they persuaded us that having seen England it was now France's turn; so instead of landing at Plymouth, as we had originally intended, we went on to Cherbourg. That summer in France included a "cure" at Vichy; which was such a success that in 1911 we went to Vichy again; and this time we took 'Rilla with us, and I realised to the full what Mr. Andrews so much enjoyed, the delight of seeing the joys of travel in Europe as reflected in the fact of a young companion. The year 1911 was "the hot year"; wonderful for the grapes, but not so good for travellers by rail. After Docteur Jardet had given me my ticket of leave from *les Eaux de Vichy,* and after we had thrown roses and violets at the carriages which paced by us in the seasonal *Battaille de*

Fleurs, we went to Lucerne which we reached on the *Quatorze Juillet,* in time to see the water carnival with its procession of illuminated boats on the lake, in celebration of the FETE NATIONALE of France. As Lucerne was very hot and as we did not want to stay there over the Sunday, we asked the Concierge if he could not recommend us a place somewhere on the Lake, which we could reach by boat in the few hours of Saturday which were left to us and which would be an "out-of-doors'y" sort of place. He certainly could; and he said that Kussnacht was just the place which we wanted; so after déjeuner we took the boat and went to Kussnacht, which, we were told, was famed as a water cure.

On landing from the boat we looked at the hotel which was near the dock and soon decided that that was not what we were looking for; however we had them serve us *un petit gouter* which consisted of rye bread, and some delicate Swiss white wine, and some Gruyère cheese with big holes in it. (The French call those holes in the cheese, "eyes," and they say that Gruyère is not good until it has "tears in its eyes," which means that when the cheese is fully ripe the whey condenses in the little holes which are air-bubbles made in kneading the cheese.) Then I went off in search of the water cure place, leaving the others to rest themselves on the dock; and I soon found the place; it was called *"Mon-Séjour";* so far as equipment hydropathically was concerned it left much to be desired; but the garden looked most attractive. On asking for an apartment with a bath, the landlord said, "Why have an apartment with bath when one could take one's bath in the 'Cure' "; and then also "there was the Lake"; however, if we did not mind a small *supplément* in the matter of price, there was just the sort of apartment we were looking for over the Casino; so we went to see it. It was most attractive; just full up with Swiss cleanliness; downy beds, great furry *déscentes de lit* to step your feet into when you got up; fluffy white curtains at the windows; and trailing purple wistaria in fragrant wreaths up the outside stairway by which we mounted, and over all the windows. At seven o'clock *le patron* came to say, *Mesdames, Monsieur; le diner est servi;* and we set forth, expecting to go to the rather stuffy dining room in the main body of the hotel which I had seen on first looking the place over; but instead we found a crimson velvet carpet stretched from the path across the grass to an open space by the Lake; and there the table was set with snowy linen and shining silver; and *la patronne* and her daughter in lovely Swiss costumes waiting to seat us. It was a long late summer twilight, and it took us more than an hour to enjoy the good things in unending courses which were set before us, and *le patron* kept running back and forth to superintend the kitchen doings, and coming occasionally with a long slender bottle of the golden products of the Swiss hillsides. By nine o' the clock we retired, well pleased with ourselves and with the world in general, thinking, too, that here was a good place to stay and stay on. But in the early morning hours we were awakened by—I cannot say unearthly squealing, for it was very mudane—but by squealing which banished slumbers, and for a time we wondered what it could be; soon the curtains waving inward let in the breeze which in the early evening was from the Lake, and which now in the morning hours was from the other direction, and it wafted to our offended nostrils a most earthly smell. Evidently there was a serpent there in our Swiss Eden. A hundred yards away was the pigpen where the thrifty landlord was making ready the bacon for the coming winter months.

I hope that when you go there the pigs will have been removed, for it is a lovely spot; but we could not move the pigs, so the next morning we moved ourselves instead. There was no boat which touched at Kussnacht of a Sunday, and the only exit from that tiny part of the world was by conveyance to Arth-Goldau, and there to take the train for Zurich. The conveyance was one of great elegance, but not having been ordered a long time in advance it took an hour to get it ready; finally at 11 o'clock it was driven majestically up to the door, a great landau with royal blue broadcloth upholsteries, drawn by two enormous black horses; it was the Coach of State of the village used by the *Maire*, and by bridal parties; and in it we set forth. It was the last word in luxurious comfort, albeit slow and ponderous;

and we travelled by a marvellous road skirting a lake and bordered by great black cherry trees in full fruit. These trees were the property of the State, and they were leased to the peasants for the fruit, and no one would think of touching the fruit on a tree which was not his. And now again trouble dogged our steps. A few miles out of Kussnacht horseflies descended in swarms; the horses were protected by flapping white lace nets, and the coachman seemed hardened, but we were fair game for the pestiferous little beasts until we remembered that these insects detest the odor of lavender. Jeannette had a bottel of lavender water in her bag, and we began flapping handkerchiefs saturated with the precious stuff in every direction, and in a short time the flies fled our company. So in time we came to the Railway, and in the afternoon to Zurich and the cool and comfortable Hotel Baur au Lac.

After a few days of rest there we went to Ragaz; firstly for the Baths; and secondly because we hoped that in the direction of the Engadine we might find cooler weather; but the Baths were a disappointment, and so was the weather. Then in a moment of inspiration we decided on a long flight Northward; we went to Bale, and from there to Paris all in one day: we stayed over night at the familiar Hotel Ste Anne in the Rue Ste Anne, which was where we first met Gabriel (of whom more later), and the following morning we were in London, and the next day in the North of England. It was a bright moonlight night when we arrived in York, and our apartment looked out over the ruins of St. Mary's Abbey shining white in the night glory; and far off in the distance were the towers of the Minster. We were still on the hunt for an out-of-doors place where it might be cool, and I knew that it must be cool on the North Sea; so 'Rilla and I started out by motor to find the place, and we found it. We went all up and down the coast from Whitby to Bridlington without finding anything, and on the way back from Bridlington, on passing through Filey, there beside the sea was the most attractive looking cottage, pansies all about the edges of the walk which led through the green turf up to the house, and a sign on it "To Let Furnished"; but again our hopes were dashed for the agent told us that the owner had withdrawn it from the market, and was coming the next day to occupy it himself. Nothing left but to make our way back to York again. In returning we went by way of the South Parade in Scarborough, and there we settled; we took "lodgings" in a house on the South Parade overlooking the sea with lovely views of the old Harbour and of the old abandoned Fort out on the Headland. Our landlord had enough old silver of the Queen Anne period all marked with "W" to set our table; and we found an old Yorkshireman who talked a very broad Northern dialect, who owned a beautiful big black mare and an open victoria, and he drove us at a leisurely pace over country roads in the lovely East Riding of Yorkshire. One day we chanced on a village church which had the history of England written in the very building itself. The foundations of the choir were of Roman brick, laid "herring-bone fashion"; the font was unmistakeably Saxon; the carvings about the entrance door were of the most beautiful early-dog-tooth ornamentation of the Norman period; the chantry was floriated Gothic; and the choir was Tudor. The Senior Warden had been told that strangers were looking at the Church, and he came over to greet us, red waistcoat, green coat, knickers, a crop and a fox-terrier; and I found that he had once lived in Sowerby Bridge where was the former home of most of our Akron choir men. Speaking of broad Yorkshire, there is a tale told of the Cattle Fair which is an annual event at Preston, Lancashire; a Yorkshire farmer who was exhibiting there was being shown some cattle and some chickens by a Lancashire farmer, and his comment was, "Yer cocks craw a' richt, and yer coos moo a' richt; but ah canna mak ye oot, mon"; which same is real English, as she is spoke, in parts. This same Cattle Fair at Preston had elected a teetotaller for their President one year; and when luncheon time came and they were all preparing each one his drink before sitting down to table, one of them said, "What will we do wi' Geordie? he will na touch it?" "Leave Geordie to me," said the other. "Ah 'll fix Geordie." So he went out and mixed a beautiful milk punch, fragrant and foaming, and brought it to the President, and said, "Geordie, mon; we're all o'us fixing oorsels a bit o' drink before we eat. How would ye like a fine glass o' milk for yours; ah brought one for ye?" "Ah 'll tak it gladly, mon; an' thenk ye," said Geordie; and he took the glass and emptied it at one long pull; then he set down the glass, wiped his lips, heaved a sigh and said, " 'Eavin's what a coo!"

It was in 1912 that we went to see England in the springtime. We landed at Fishguard—in those days it was a port-of-call for Cunarders—and during the late afternoon we went on up through the Welsh country while the setting sun was filling the hedge-rows with beauty, a golden glory of gorse;—

Grâce aux éclairs de la lune
Argent brille dans la bruyère;
Grâce aux éclairs du soleil
Or orne les demeures de misère.

Then for two weeks we lived in Bath and saw the silver candlesticks of the chestnuts light up the rolling downs of Victoria Park, and the golden rain of the laburnums shower itself on the grass. We wandered around the old streets and found ourselves a place in one of the Crescents where we should one day live when we retired—a dream which lacked fulfilment. We went to a cricket match which began at two in the afternoon, stopped for tea, went on again the next day, and "further deponent sayeth not"; we did not stay for the finish. We drove by the Vale of Cheddar: we stood spellbound before the west front of Wells Cathedral; saw the swans in the moat pull the bell to call some one to feed them; at evensong we heard a most lovely choir sing, and saw the old images up aloft kick out the hours on the bells; it was a lovely dream, which all too soon came to an end.

Next we went to Châtel-Guyon, in the Auvergne, in France, so that I might take the "cure." There we met Monsieur and Madame Jean Linzeler and their lovely little Simone; and so began a friendship which lasted many years. Then we went to Germany for another beautiful experience.

It was late when we reached Heidelberg, hot and tired; it was just the hour for the closing of the doors of the dining room to latecomers; so I said to the headwaiter, "What will we do for something to eat?" He said that he was very sorry that he could not give us a table at that hour but that they were obliged to limit the hours for serving; then he added, "What is the number of your apartment, Sir?" I told him. "It is an apartment with a terrace balcony; I know it," he said. "If you will leave it to me, I will have a good supper sent up to you." The moon was shining at its full; the Königstuhl was a pyramid of white horse chestnut blossoms stretching out their beauty to the sky; the nightingales were an orchestra; and soon came two waiters who set our table on our own balcony terrace just outside our windows. There was rye bread and crusty rolls and toast; sandwiches with ham, and sandwiches with little smoky fishes in them; dill pickles and mustard; and three kinds of cheese; then there were tall pitchers with beads of coolness on the outside, some light amber fluid in one of them, and some dark reddy brown fluid in the other; and I have heard that these fluids are called Pilsner, and Munchener-Brau; and for dessert we had all kinds of kuchen, and preserves made of big sweet black cherries. Did we come home from there? We did, for work was calling. We came back by way of Holland where we stayed for a time at Domburg in a Hotel which is called the "Bad-Hotel," and where the bathing beach is guarded by a functionary called the "Bad-Man," who wears a suit of red flannel nighties and a red nightcap with a long tassel, and he blows a brass horn in stentorian tones whenever any bather ventures beyond the barrel which marks the safety line. Domburg is on the island of Walcheren in Zeeland; it was almost swept away by the sea in 1808, as was Veere which is a fascinating village on the N.E. coast. Veere is now a silent and a half abandoned city where was once a prosperous place; it has a great church which would hold twice the present number of inhabitants; and its stadthuis is a beautiful piece of architecture with its rows of peaked dormer windows and statues between the windows of the upper floors.

We drove to Middelburg where there is a fascinating butter and cheese market, and where one may see the charming costumes of a dozen near-by villages; and there in the Abbey Church, founded in the twelfth century we heard a glorious carrillon which would play a Beethoven Sonata complete. Before leaving Holland we went to Scheveningen, and heard the most ravishing music by the Lamoureux Orchestra which was playing there that summer; and also to The Hague where in the Picture Gallery we watched Paul Potter's Bull turn his head and follow us with his eyes wherever we went; and then it was across to England from Vlissingen—and back to Akron, and the world of work.

On February 11, 1912 the then Presiding Bishop, Bishop Tuttle, was my guest in Akron, and preached in St. Paul's. One evening while we were sitting before the fire he said, "Watson, the Church in Paris is looking for a Rector; according to its Charter a nomination must be made by the Presiding Bishop to fill the vacancy; they are not obliged to take my suggestion; but equally they may. Would you go there if the place were offered to you?" I asked for twenty-four hours to think it over; and the next evening I told the Bishop that Jeannette and I had decided that, if the Church in Paris were offered on terms which were possible, I would take it. The Bishop said, "That pleases me very much; I will send in your name as my nominee; the rest is in the hands of God; you and I have no further concern in the matter; let us kneel here and ask God to guide us aright." And that was our good-night prayer, the good old Bishop praying with that deep voice of his, and with the same simplicity with which he said his, "Now I Lay Me," before he went to bed.

On the 6th of October of 1912 St. Paul's Church was consecrated by Bishop Leonard, and my dear old friend Bishop Vincent preached the Consecration sermon.

BOOK II

X

THE AMERICAN CHURCH OF THE HOLY TRINITY, PARIS

1913-1918

IN DECEMBER 1912 I had a letter from General Winslow who was one of the vestrymen of the Church in Paris and who was in this country as Chairman of the Committee for filling the Paris vacancy, asking me if I could go to Paris. As the letter was somewhat indefinite in its terms, I took the letter to Bishop Leonard in Cleveland and asked his advice as to what it was best for me to do about it. He said, "I think that you ought to go; you know Europe; you are familiar with France and with French; I would suggest that you telegraph General Winslow, as he wants to return very shortly, and tell him that you will meet him in New York to talk the question over." As a result of this advice I went to New York, and on the 10th of December I met General Winslow at the house of his old friend, General Porter, former American Ambassador to France. After an hour's talk I accepted his proposition, conditionally, on the following terms, that I would come over in the following February and take the work provisionally until the meeting of the General Convention in the following autumn. General Winslow sailed immediately for Paris, and shortly after he landed I had a cablegram from him urging my coming to take up the work immediately, as Bishop Jaggar who had been in charge of the church had broken in health and was not able to continue the work longer. The result of this was that we sailed from New York on Christmas Eve of 1912 on the *Lusitania*, in company with Myron Herrick our Ambassador to France; and it was from him, on shipboard, that we got our first welcome to our new post of duty. On reaching Paris we went to the Hotel Lotti for a few days, and then went down to

Hyères in the South of France for a breathing space, as we were both fatigued by the parting and the journey. After a short rest there we returned to Paris, and my first official act in the ministry there was to take the services on Sunday, January 12, 1913.

The American Church of the Holy Trinity in Paris was in reality a one-man creation, a creation of a man who had loved it, who had given for it and to it all that he was and all that he had. He was my immediate predecessor, the Rev. Dr. John B. Morgan, for more than forty years Rector of the Church in Paris. It was one of my privileges to dedicate to his memory the beautiful Cross which we erected in the garden between the church and the rectory, as also the Tablet which is set in the wall at the street end of the cloister.

Dr. Morgan was a man of wealth when he came to Paris to live and work. He personally saw to the raising of the money for the building of the church and of the spire; the lovely Te Deum windows were his thought, as was also the Tryptych over the altar, which was Edwin Abbey's last great work; the rectory which Mr. Ferris Thompson gave in memory of his mother was meant for Dr. Morgan's occupancy; and the Mortuary Chapel, which has been such a blessing to so many hundreds of Americans bereaved in a foreign land, grew out of Dr. Morgan's personal experience of the pathetic need for such a shelter. When there was lack of money to carry on construction work in the material fabric of the plant, Dr. Morgan either saw that it was provided or else gave it himself. He paid the deficits for current expenses when the income was lacking for carrying on the church—which often happened; and at the time of his passing from earth he left little in the way of money; he had used it all for the church; and in that church this thought must always be present in the minds of those who knew him or knew of him, *"Si monumentum requiris, circumspice."*

To follow a man like that, and above all to succeed to a ministry like that—forty years of ties between minister and people, and often people of two generations; forty years of filling all the church's needs from the gifts of personal friends or from an ample personal purse—it was a task not lightly to be undertaken. And it is no wonder that I hesitated to commit myself to it permanently, and that I asked to make a trial of it first. So, when I came to Paris it was with the understanding that I might be free to return to America in October 1913, should I so deem it best. In the spring of 1913 I asked General Winslow, who was my closest friend on the Vestry, what arrangements were being made to carry on the work when I should leave in the autumn. His reply was that the Vestry desired me to stay; and on my still saying that it was my intention to return to America, he asked my reasons. My reply was that the financial situation of the Church was impossible from my point of view; that if I were to undertake the work it would mean taking on an accumulating indebtedness, in face of the fact that there was an annual deficit constantly being incurred, the necessary expenses exceeding any possible income by many thousands of francs annually; that while I would not shrink from a task just because it was hard, yet I was not willing to pre-pay failure which was bound to come through no fault of mine; and that I could plainly foresee that I could not carry the financial burden as Dr. Morgan had done—I had no such private fortune as he had, and I had no rich friends who could be interested in maintaining the Church in Paris. General Winslow's response was to ask if I would be willing to keep on with the work if a guarantee were arranged for covering all financial deficits for a period of two years. "By that time," he said, "you will be firmly in the saddle, and the future will take care of itself." To this proposition I agreed: and the following letters tell the story:

General Winslow to Mr. Henry White, New York:

"Reverend Dr. Watson having been chosen Rector by the unanimous vote of the Vestry of Holy Trinity, Paris, will occupy the Clergy House in June."

General Winslow to the Bishop of New York:

"When Dr. Watson had been here four months the Vestry with unanimity and pleasure chose to elect him as Rector. The members had then, and have now no doubt of the wisdom of their choice. . . .

"Dr. Watson has an excellent knowledge of the routine and details of Church matters, and is an able administrator. He has a fluent command of French. His conduct of the services is dignified and most satisfactory. He can be called an excellent preacher, and he is a well equipped, cultivated, cultured man and scholar. . . . He is in the opinion of his friends at home and of those who really know him here a deeply religious man. In social life and outside the duties of his place he is a pleasant and agreeable companion. . . . Within a period, short and rapidly passing, nearly all of those who constitute the class contemporary with Dr. Morgan (some of them his admiring friends) will have followed him into a future existence. In other words, the congregation is now and will be composed of men and women almost if not quite new to this Church. . . .

"When Dr. Watson came to Paris he *inherited* a number of things or affairs which had been troubling the late Rector. Dr. Watson, coming here without having associations here, has had the courage of his convictions, happily for the progress of the church in Paris. Several of these questions or affairs have already been satisfactorily disposed of by Dr. Watson; in all of which he has had the sympathy and co-operation of the Vestry."

I want here to pay a tribute of gratitude and affection to General Edward F. Winslow. His keen intelligence, his wide experience in administrative work, his intimate acquaintance with the American Colony, together with his generous devotion to the Church and its interests made him an invaluable aid and counsellor to a newcomer like myself; while his personal devotion to me and mine have made me his grateful debtor. Whatever of worth I was able to do in Paris was made possible by the co-operation and guidance which General Winslow so spontaneously brought to me. The day that we heard in Paris of his death in America we shadowed his onetime seat in the church with gifts of flowers which were but a faint tribute to the honour which we paid him in our hearts.

The following record should also find a place here; it is dated the 18th of April, 1913:

"Whereas; It is our earnest desire that the relations now existing between the Reverend S. N. Watson, D.D. as Rector of Holy Trinity Church, and the Vestry and Congregation of the Church, be made permanent:

"Therefore; Resolved that we do hereby request Dr. Watson to withdraw the reference to a termination of the Rectorship on October first, as it appears in our agreement now on record: and that we ask him to continue to hold permanently the Office of Rector of Holy Trinity Church, and to discharge the duties of this Office; pledging him at the same time, our hearty co-operation in the advancement of such plans as we may mutually decide are for the best interests of the Church and its work.

"(signed by the Clerk of the Vestry)"

The Clergy House referred to in General Winslow's letter to Mr. Henry White was in process of erection when we arrived in Paris. It was designed by the same architect who built the church, and he was a wonderful builder of churches; but, in building the rectory he had this idea primarily in mind that the house should correspond architecturally and exteriorly with the church itself; and secondarily his idea was that the house should be what the name Clergy House implies, a residence for a clerical staff, rather than a home for a family. The house was constructed in England, so far as its materials were concerned, and was brought over to France to be set up; it was English and all the fittings were English, even to the kitchen range which was not a French *fourneau de cuisine* but a massive British affair designed for Cardiff coal to be bought at less than half the price one would have to pay in France for the local kitchen fuel. Our preliminary experience with this kitchen range had its amusing as well as its embarrassing side. Madeleine, our *cuisinière,* and a wonderful one too, was a little widow from the Côte d'Or country, and in all the Decalogue there was no commandment which weighed so heavy in her life as, "Waste not; Want not." On finding that oven things would always come to the table insufficiently cooked, I was deputed to interview Madeleine on the subject; who told me that the trouble was the *fourneau de cuisine;* that it simply would not *marche.* I then hunted up the *entrepreneur* who had installed it and told him of our difficulties and appealed to him, for the Honour of Old England, to find out what was the trouble. After a brief investigation he let me know that the trouble was the cook's economy; that she simply would not use coal enough to heat up a big heavy range like that; it would be *folie, gaspillage,* she said to use such an amount of coal. He was an Englishman by birth but had lived in France some time and spoke fluent French, and so he explained to Madeleine all the why's and the how's, and the in's and the out's of an English range. Then after time enough had elapsed for a normal cooling off of the cook's disturbed prejudices, I went to the kitchen again, and said, "Well, Madeleine, the man has told you all about the range, I suppose; how it works; why it is built as it is; and all its differences from the ones you have been accustomed to." *"Oui, Monsieur."* "Well, it's all satisfactory now, isn't it?" *"Peut-être, Monsieur. Cette affaire-là est bien construite, sans doute; elle durera longtemps, on verra; mais, pour le moment, Monsieur, évidemment elle n'est pas pratique."*—("Perhaps, Monsieur, that affair there is well made, without doubt; it will last a long time; we shall see; but, Monsieur, it is plain to see that for our present use it is simply not practical.") *Pratique,* practical—What a keynote to much of the French character Madeleine struck in that word *pratique!* Above all else the Frenchman is *practical;* you may advance all the pretty theories you please, and he'll give them no credence in advance; you must show him that they will work French-fashion, and if he cannot see that they will *work* he will have nothing to do with them. Much of the present failure of other peoples to understand the attitude of France in the present condition of world affairs is due to a total lack of understanding of her (what the French call) *préoccupations,* the racial background of her thinking; what she means and why. Madeleine was a real Frenchwoman when she said in the name of her country as well as for herself, *"mais, pour le moment, évidemment ce n'est pas pratique."*

The rectory being some months from completion we took advantage of the gracious offer of Mrs. Stannard Wood and

Miss Margaret Gordon to let us have their apartment at 10 Avenue d'Eylau for a time during their stay on the Riviera. They left with us their maitre-d'hôtel Baptiste and his staff to take care of us. One evening I heard a great crying of "Extra" on the street, and I sent Baptiste out to get a paper; he brought it in a few minutes and handed it to me saying, *"C'est rien du tout, Monsieur; C'est chute du ministère."* This was my first introduction to French politics—fall of the Government; that was nothing unusual, and nothing to get excited about. One hears frequent unfavourable comment in America on what is called the "instability of the French Government"; an opinion based on the oftentimes rapid changes in the Ministeries. This is simply a misunderstanding of the rôle which the Cabinet, called the *"Conseil"* plays in governmental affairs in France. The permanent element in the French Government is the President of the Republic on the one hand and the Directors of the various Ministries on the other; the President is the essential element, he maintains the continuity; Ministries may come and go, sometimes in rapid succession, and it looks to the uninformed like disintegration; but it is nothing of the kind; it is simply a striking evidence of the responsiveness of the Government to the will of the people. The Parlement is the expression of that will, and if the Government of the moment does not satisfy that will, why, *Chute du Ministère.* It arrives in this way: a question comes up on an appropriation; or a deputy announces that at a certain time he will *interpeller* the Government on some matter, and these questions are often not of great importance; the Government demands a "vote of confidence"; it is refused; and "out they go"; the Government resigns, which means that the *Président du Conseil* (something like Prime Minister) calls together the Council of Ministers, and they go to the Elysée and present their resignations to the President of the Republic. "But if all these Ministers, Foreign Affairs, Finance, War, Interior, Public Instruction, and all the rest quit all at once, does not that entail some cessation of continuous direction in these departments?" is the American query. Not at all:

there is a permanent *Directeur du Contrôle,* or some other similar permanent official who has probably been at the head of the practical functioning of his department for years, and who has every detail of its business at his fingers' ends, and who knows so much about it that when a new Minister steps in, the first thing he must do is to go to this seasoned official to learn "what it is all about." When such a *chute du Ministère* occurs, the President gets in touch with the leaders of the dominant parties and after consultation with them he commissions one of them to form a Government, which means that as Prime Minister, or *Président du Conseil* as he is called, he tries to get together a Cabinet who will be competent, in his opinion, to swing a majority vote in the Parlement. He then presents this Cabinet to the President, who, as a matter of form, accepts them; they then prepare what we would call "a Platform"; and with this Platform they go before Parlement seeking a vote of approval. If they fail in obtaining Parlement's approval the same procedure must be repeated until a ministry is consolidated which will stand. Frequently it is the same Premier who tries to form a new ministry, and often the new Cabinet contains many of the men which were part of the old one which was rejected; which gives point to the proverb often repeated, *Plus ça change, plus c'est la même chose.* Each department of the Government is a self-contained machine running by itself; and the change of the Minister, who is really simply the Government's representative in what concerns his Bureau before the people, does not retard the functioning of the office in any serious way. *Chute du Ministère* then simply means warning given to the Cabinet that the people are not satisfied; that there is something which is not right and that it must be made right. The Cabinet in France is wholly different from what is called by that name in our American method of government—or lack of government. In Paris while the President theoretically appoints the Cabinet, it is actually the Parlement which appoints them; the Cabinet represents the people and not the President. In France they say of us here in America, "You are a republic in name, but in fact you are an oligarchy; you give your President full and uncontrolled power in the appointment of the men who form the Cabinet, and you turn yourselves over to that group and to a Congress over which you have almost as little control for a period of four years, without recourse; and while the ballot gives you an ultimate control, within the limitations of politics, of another Congress than the one which you have, yet until the four years limitation expires, you are tied, you can do nothing; our Government in France," they say, "is immediately responsive to the people's will; it is really and in actuality what you call your American Government, a 'government of the people, by the people, for the people.' "

It was at 10 Avenue d'Eylau that we gave our first official dinner. The guests were Ambassador and Mrs. Herrick; General and Mrs. Winslow; Mr. Mather of Cleveland and his daughter, Constance; and Mrs. Richard Crane and her mother, Mrs. Hutchinson. Mrs. Stannard Wood's apartment was a treasure house of most beautiful glass and china and plate; and we had instructed Baptiste to put it all away carefully and to lock the doors of the cabinets in which it was kept, as we did not wish that any possible breakage of these beautiful things should take place during our occupancy. But when the evening of this ceremonial dinner arrived the table was royally decked with all this glory; and when we reminded Baptiste (with due compliments for his thoughtfulness) that our instructions had been not to use all those glories, the good old French *serviteur*—and proud he was to be a *serviteur*—replied: "I did it for the honour of my *patronne,* Monsieur; I knew what she would have wanted me to do; she put all her treasures in my charge, so I, alone, am responsible."

That fact of the pride which a Frenchman takes in his work explains a great deal in their life; and it also contributed much to the ease of life in France for us when we first went there to live. A good butler desires nothing more than to be the best kind of a butler; and if he has a son, he desires nothing better for his boy than that he may do the same. There are classes in France, but there are no envies as between class and class, no desire to imitate, no striving for a change of place or position. To do one's work well and then learn how to do it better is the Frenchman's ideal. There is no restless dissatisfaction on the part of Jacques until he can have all that Monsieur Millefrancs has—radio, electric washer, one automobile and then a more expensive one; all of contentment for him is not based on an imitation in things and the ownership of things; and black gloom does not settle on the household because Suzette cannot go to the Cinéma whenever she gets it into her little head that she wants to, or as often as Mademoiselle de l'Avocat does. I am often asked how France could come back after the War as she did; where that wealth came from which gave her a store of gold, second only to that held in America; her provinces to the North and the East devasted and their towns and villages destroyed and the trade of that which was her chief industrial section wholly ruined—where, in a word, did she get all that money? And my reply is that that wealth came from the only source from which wealth can never come in reality, from INDUSTRY and from ECONOMY; from hard and unintermittent work and from constant joyous saving. Wealth is natural product enhanced and multiplied in value by human labour, and it is the returns of that labour and of that product of industry saved, and not spent as fast as it comes in, or faster. It has been said to me: "You would not want the working man and the working woman in America to work as do French men and women, and to cut themselves down to the scale of living of the French *paysan* or *ouvrier?"* My reply has been: "That is not the question at issue; it is wholly beside the point; you asked how it was possible that a country invaded and a third of whose most productive territory had been the battle ground of contending armies which she had been compelled to support, a support which took the very bread of life out of the mouths of her women and children, how it was possible that the forty millions of French people could have to-day more gold per capita than the one hundred and twenty-five millions of an uninvaded America?" And I have given the answer which is, WORK, and then more WORK, and economy, and patience, and the being willing to put up with less of things and less of luxuries. I am not saying what Americans should do; I am only making it clear that they make their choices, these two peoples; and that each has what it is willing, or unwilling to pay the price for. The French have a proverb, *on ne peut pas être et avoir été;* which is another way of saying, You cannot eat your cake and have it too.

It was at that dinner at Avenue d'Eylau that the Ambassador said to me: "Doctor, Washington's Birthday falls on a Sunday this year: is it your plan to mark the Day especially at the American Church?" I told him that we had planned some special music, that the Colours would be massed in the chancel, and I asked him if the Embassy would be willing to have a part in the Celebration. To this he most readily agreed; and then he added, "I would like to have all the diplomatic representatives of the South and Central American countries present in the Church on that Day, if you will invite them." I said that I would be glad to arrange for it and that I would provide seats of honour for them, as was customary, and then I asked him how would be the most fitting way for me to invite them to come. Mr. Herrick replied: "I have thought of that; it is my custom to give a Diplomatic Breakfast on Washington's Birthday, and the Day falling on a Sunday this year, the Breakfast will be on the previous day. I will invite you to be one of the guests, and then after I have made my address of welcome, and the Dean of the Diplomatic Corps has made his reply, I will give you an opportunity to explain the meaning which the Day has for all of us as Americans, why we are celebrating it in the Church, and you can then invite these representatives of larger America to be present." I replied, "That is very thoughtful on your part, Sir; but my difficulty would be that I do not speak either Spanish or Portuguese, and most of these gentlemen do not speak English." "Well," said the Ambassador, "talk to them in French; they all understand French." "But I never made a speech in French," I said, "I can speak enough French to get by socially; and I can speak hotel French, and travel French, but to make a public address of importance is a horse of another colour, or at least of another shade." "Oh, well"; said Mr. Herrick, "you can do it; just prepare a speech in advance." Which I did in this way; I put in six weeks in intensive study of French and in preparing that speech; for I was really more concerned about doing the Ambassador credit than I was about the speech, for I knew that I would "get by" with that somehow. There was in Paris at that time a teacher of French, Mademoiselle Alice Blum, whose book, *Oral French Method,* is just what she describes it to be, "a system for rapidly acquiring facility in the speaking of French," (and as far as that may be had from a book, this is the best book of the kind that I know of). I have a copy of her book in which she has written, *"A Monsieur le Docteur Watson; hommage de respectueuse admiration."* In six weeks Alice Blum taught me to make that speech, and a lot beside about the use of a language not my own; for facility in public speaking means not so much knowledge as it means confidence; it is not the knowing how, it is knowing that you *can do it.* And many times in after years when I had to speak in French in public, I realised that my debut as *orateur* in France on that 22nd of February 1913 was the door to much in the way of privilege which came to me then.

When we left the Avenue d'Eylau it was to go to the apartment which was kindly placed at our disposal by Mrs. Jaffray in the Rue de Longchamps. I am told that the Avenue d'Eylau is no more; like Rue Pierre Charron, and Cours la Reine, and Quai de Billy, and saddest of all for me, Avenue de l'Alma, it has been re-named. Once, when the fashion was for trying to get rid of saints in France, they changed the name of St. Germain en Laye to Mont de Bon Air; but descriptively good as that name was, the old name came back. And I am wondering if perhaps the passage of the years will not show the impulsive Parisians that there is history and charm and romance and treasure in the old names of their streets; and that it is taking away the children's heritage to throw in the discard such names as *Bac* and *Cherche Midi* and *Faisanderie* and *Vieux Colombier,* to replace them with names of moderns soon to have neither interest nor historic meaning. Mrs. Jaffray's apartment was a most hospitable home for us until the rectory was ready for our occupancy; and it was there that Marion Andrews came to make us a visit.

It was in June 1913 that we moved to Avenue de l'Alma as the first occupants of the rectory which had been built on the narrow bit of ground beside the church. The gift of this rectory was wise, thoughtful and generous. During his lifetime Mr. Thompson had paid many of the bills for the construction of the building, and in his will he had made ample provision for the completion of the building; with the result that when his estate came to be distributed there was a considerable sum of money remaining of this bequest after the rectory had been paid for; and this money his family placed at the disposal of the church for the furnishing of the rectory, thus obviating the necessity for a rector who must come from America of bringing his household goods with him: an almost impossible proposition for more reasons than one: for the rectory was a most *éxigeante* house as to furnishings; and this we found out when we came to the choosing of the furniture. "But, what fun!" you will say; "to be in Paris to live; to have an empty house given you, and with it thousands of dollars at your disposal to buy furniture with!" It sounds like it; doesn't it? and we would have liked nothing better than to have taken all that money, and browsed around the different *Quartiers,* finding a bit here and a bit there which we would love to live with, and having a year or two of artistic delight in matching and acquiring treasures. But, why didn't we do just that? For two reasons: the house was needed for immediate use, the work of the Church needed it, we needed it, and the Vestry urged its occupancy at the earliest possible moment; and in the second place, one could not have found in all Paris period furniture to harmonise with that demandful house; and, even if that could have been done, the amount of money to be expended had its limits, for all that the gift was so generous. In all this matter of the furnishing of the rectory we had the counsel and aid of General and Mrs. Winslow. We had the house studied by artists, and sketches made of the furniture needed to correspond to the lines of the architecture of the building and the rooms; these designs were sent to the Saint Antoine Quarter where the furniture was built by skilled artisans; even the clocks were built for the house, the old *Maison Charles Hours* sent designers who copied the leadings of the windows for the frames of one of the clocks; the carpet for the *salle à manger* and the tapestry above its wainscotting were made and dyed in reproduction of an old piece of sixteenth century stuff; with the result that we were at home and receiving far sooner than could otherwise have been possible. The advantage of this is easily seen. We were newcomers, and we had to make a social place for ourselves, and for that a residential background was needed; next, the rectory of the Church in Paris was a sort of little Embassy where hospitality must be offered to constantly coming visitors; and, as the Church was in large measure dependent on the casual gifts of American visitors to Paris, the hospitality of the rectory was an important element of the work. Before the War there would often pass weeks when we would rarely sit down to a meal in the *salle à manger* by ourselves; for *le petit déjeuner* was never served as a meal, but was brought up to us on a tray.

As I look over the records of those first years in Paris, I am amazed at the way in which baptisms, marriages, burials followed each other in quick succession, and chiefly burials; I officiated at the last rites for so many of that old Colony of Americans in Paris, so fine in meaning, and now almost all gone. The first funeral ceremony at which I officiated was that of the Comtesse de Montsaulnin who was of the line of my Morris family, and whose daughters, the Comtesse du Luart and the Comtesse de Gourcuff, were friends of the after days; there was Madame Sorchan, of whose family was Mr. Horace Binney who came from the line of the descendants of William Montgomerie of Upper Freehold; there was Madame d'Hauteville, and the Grand d'Hautevilles were of the Morris line of my family—the list is a long one. The old American Colony had already begun to pass on when I began my work in Paris; there are but few of them left now. It was the second time that I had been part of the going of an older culture and a witness of the coming of a new. That old American Colony in Paris, which I knew, were men and women of distinction, of culture, and above all of ideals; they held themselves as each of them standing in an ambassadorial relation on behalf of America to the people of another race and country; they had traditions, national traditions and traditions of family and of breeding; they upheld those traditions with dignity and with firmness; and I would here render them a tribute of honour and respect.

On April 14, 1913 I delivered the Commerorative Address at the Memorial Service which was held in Holy Trinity for Mr. Pierpont Morgan. There were three of these services, one in New York, one in Westminster Abbey in London, and the other in our Church in Paris. I have a most beautiful silver plaque which was the gift of the Morgan family, and which had been struck in commemoration of the head of the family, his life, and his achievements. On July 7, 1913 I officiated at the funeral of Mr. Henry Ridgway. There was a wonderful dignity about Mr. Ridgway's passing, about the last rites, and all the attendant events. On the evening of the 2nd of July I was just about to enter the rectory on my return from Moret-sur-Loing, where I had officiated at the interment of Miss Grace Lee Hess, when the young Comte de Ganay came to ask me to come at once to his uncle's bedside; at the entrance to the house I was met by the dignified and gracious courtesy of Mrs. Ridgway (née Munroe). The Princess d'Hénin came in while I was still there; she was a strikingly beautiful picture, in dinner dress, with a strand of white hair laid back over her dark hair (she was née de Ganay). And on the 7th of July the final rites were said: at the house in a *chapelle ardente* erected in the entrance to the courtyard, in order that all the *personnel* might pay their tribute there; and at the church where the tower entrance was vaulted with black draperies lit by a great silver lustre with candles; the whole picture is full of reverent memory. As I let recollections of those years enter, I remember the funeral of Mr. Iselin; of Mr. Moorhouse who was one of our vestrymen; of Mrs. Bertha Barnes Clinch-Smith; of Mrs. Le Roy, one of the older members of the Colony and a woman of strong personality; of Mrs. Sanderson, the mother of Sybil Sanderson; of Mr. Stellwag; and of General Macdougal. Especially marked in memory is the funeral service for Mr. John H. Harjes. Mr. Harjes had written me a beautiful letter of appreciation of the Morgan Memorial Service and of the address which I had made commemorative of his former partner in the banking business, a letter written with his own hand in days when failing eyesight made it most difficult for him to write, which made his courtesy all the more touching. Then there was the funeral of Mrs. Theodore Evans, a remarkable type of the old Colony; her figure as she came to church with her long velvet cloak was most striking; she was of the family who aided the Empress Eugénie to escape from the Tuileries. On July 29, 1914 I officiated at the funeral of a very dear friend, a noble gentlewoman, Mrs. Augusta Hunt Gray; she and her daughter Alice Hubbard were amongst our dearest friends. On June 20, 1914 was laid to rest in the cemetery of Saint Germain-en-Laye the body of Mr. Charles Singer, whose daughter was the Princess Ghika. The rain was falling heavily when we left the church for the long drive to the cemetery on the hill at St. Germain, a spot hallowed as the resting place of the bodies of so many Americans, that it was spoken of as the American Cemetery. While we were on the road between Chatou and Le Pecq, travelling as rapidly as possible to get ahead of an approaching thunderstorm, a bolt of lightning struck a telegraph pole and threw it in blazing bits across one side of the road. The *fourgon* carrying the body was the first car in the procession, and it just escaped being struck by the pole. My car was next, and my chauffeur Gabriel, seeing the thing coming, put on both foot and emergency brakes, and we skidded sideways, stopping just alongside the burning fragments of the pole. There was

of July, 1915; this I did; it was printed in the Paris edition and cabled over for the New York edition. I have Mr. Bennett's office proof of this article marked with his characteristic blue pencillings. Later Mr. Bennett asked me to take on the Sunday morning editorial for the *New York Herald* as a regular duty; but, much as I would have liked to do this, I had to tell him that I could not accept his offer; that I was already overworked, and that I could not in justice to the tasks already on hand accept any new responsibilities which were avoidable. His offer was a personal courtesy from a friend to a friend; and it was also a tribute from a great editor which said more than the words in which the offer was couched. It was on the 14th of September, 1914 that we went to déjeuner at Mr. Bennett's house, 37 Avenue d'Iéna; the other guests were the Ambassador and Mrs. Herrick; the German offensive of September was on, and Paris was very tense. Just before we rose from the table Mr. Bennett pushed back his chair and gave the clearest definition of the issue that was on, which was ever made by any one, to my knowledge; he talked for a quarter of an hour. This War, he said, is not a fight of men and arms, nor will its issue be decided by material forces; it is a combat of spirituals, a struggle for the saving of ideals; and the meaning of the struggle is to be found in what has been the motive force of civilisation's rise. Mrs. Bennett and I are the only two who remain of that company which was so thrilled by Bennett's words.

When I left Paris in 1918, too worn to carry on any longer, Mr. Bennett was in the Midi; he passed away before I could see him again; but on the Sunday morning after my leaving Paris there was an editorial from his pen in *The Herald* entitled "Au Revoir; but not Good-Bye," in which he paid his tribute to me and to my work. Shortly after my reaching America, while I was at White Sulphur Springs for treatment for a weakened heart, I received a telegram from the editor of *The Herald* of New York, asking me to come to New York to make the address at the Commemorative Service for Mr. Bennett which was to be held there, and which took place in Grace Church, where it was my privilege to pay my homage to the memory and the work of a great American.

One day when we were lunching at his house in Paris, Mr. Bennett said that he was seriously considering abandoning, at least for a time, the issuing of the Paris edition of *The Herald.* Jeannette urged him most strongly not to do this because of what the paper stood for in Europe. She stressed the fact that it was vital to the courage and the spirit of Americans abroad for it stood for what no other print in Europe did; that it was an encouragement to France and to the Allies to see the brave front which *The Herald* displayed; that it was his own personal organ and his means of sharing his vision and his convictions with the world; and then she naively added, "And, Mr. Bennett, if you stop *The Herald* now, you will break the continuity of my Wartime files; I have every copy of *The Herald* since the War began but one, and I am still hunting everywhere for a copy of that issue." Mr. Bennett's surprise and pleasure at this were marked. "What is the date of the missing number?" he asked; "I'll see if I can find a spare copy at the office"; we knew that he could not do so, for we had already tried to get one there. Some days afterward came a note from Mr. Bennett, "Here is the copy of *The Herald* that you need"; he had had the entire paper reset and the copy run off especially. The complete file is now in THE WATSON COLLECTION at Stanford University; —and *The Herald* did not suspend publication.

And now for more marriages. In 1913 I officiated at the marriage of Mrs. Emily H. Crane and Francis T. A. Junkin; the wedding reception, which was held at Hotel Crillon was a notable gathering of Chicago folk. In the same year occurred the marriage of Miss Helen McLean and Major Herbert V. Ravenscroft of the British Army. In 1914 I performed the marriage of Jeanne Rosen to Jean Pierre Maurice Magre. Mademoiselle Rosen's brother was a prominent New York banker; and Monsieur Magre was an author and playwright well known in France in those days, and who has since won fame in his profession.

Maurice Magre once gave us the manuscript of one of his poems, of which one of the verses reads:

AUX MORTS

"Vous vivez sous la terre anonyme toujours,
O Morts! vous aurez chaud durant les nuit glacées:
Nous avons fait avec la trame des pensées
*Des Lits de souvenirs et des berceaux d'amour."**

One of the loveliest of the weddings of Paris days was that of Marion Deering to Chauncey McCormick, which took place at the house of Mr. James Deering; Mr. Charles Deering, the bride's father, coming to Paris from his Château en Espagne to be present.

An international marriage which interested me much was that of a Swiss girl, who came to Paris bringing me a note from Mrs. Herman Duryea—the Duryeas had won The Derby a short time before—and in the note Mrs. Duryea said: "This note will be brought to you by my Swiss maid Mademoiselle ———; she speaks no English; she is to be married to one of the grooms of my racing farm in France; he is an Englishman and speaks no French. I will count it a personal favour if you will facilitate this marriage in any way possible." I explained to the girl the ceremony and its wording; she had already filed their notice at the Mairie, according to the Laws of France, and was provided with the *Certificat de Mariage* duly attested, without which no marriage may take place. I then said to her, "Do you wish the service to be said in French or in English, Mademoiselle?" "In French, of course, Monsieur." "But the groom, does he know French?" I asked. "Oh, I'll teach him enough so that he can say, 'Yes,' at the right place"—and she did just that. Trust the canny Swiss for rising to an emergency, especially a lingual one! It was a little group that came to that marriage; most of the men were *poilus* or British soldiers on leave of absence. The

* Nameless beneath the sod, you live on,
Our Dead! You shall be warm the cold nights through;
With woof and warp of tender throughts we've made
Cradles of love for you, and couches of remembrance."

nave of the church was too vast, so I had the sacristans seat them all in the choir stalls; and I remember few marriages which appealed to me more than that one.

Frequently Americans would come to Paris and expect to have a marriage performed as is done in America—get a license and run around the corner and find a minister, and the operation is all over in one day. When they found that that could not be done in France, there was an explosion of righteous indignation: "But, why not? we are Americans; this is the American Church!" And I would have the task of trying to explain the French laws regarding marriage; sometimes with poor results so far as satisfying my unsympathetic countrymen was concerned; and often with the characteristic comment on their part: "Hang such a country! Why can't they do things as we do them in America!" For my part, I think that the French way as to marriage ceremonies is the better one. France considers a marriage an affair of the State; it is a matter where property is involved; wherein protection for the woman and for possible children must be provided in advance; and where the whole underlying structure of society is at stake: it is not "easy come, easy go," as it is so often here. Furthermore, in France the Church may not usurp the rights of the State, as it does in America. From the standpoint of Society—and the Family is the foundation of Society, and hence of the State itself—marriage is a contract, involving rights upon which the State may one day have to pass judgment. Neither the State nor the Church makes a marriage; the State authorises the marriage and registers the contract; the Church may ask God's blessing on this new venture of life; but, so far as the man and the woman are concerned it is neither the State nor the Church which marries them; they marry themselves. Marriage is primarily, essentially, a spiritual fact, a union of more than bodies and more than material values; it is a union of life motives and life principles; and if it is not considered and treated as such by the contracting parties, it is a "house built upon the sand." I never say "I married so-and-so"; for I did not; and when asked, "Will you marry us?" my only rightful reply should be, "I will ask God's blessing on your marriage." This may seem like an over-nicety in details; but it is just our sloppiness about such important details, which is one of the lethal defects of our American Society and State. It is a condition which has lasted on as a "hang-over" from pioneer days, when there was no settled Society, when a minister of any name or kind or a Justice of the Peace over the corner grocery was the only factor available for the regularising of a life union of man and woman; and that same loose point of view with regard to the marriage contract and relation is with us to-day.

Here in this country we have a mixed civil and ecclesiastical arrangement in marriage matters, which I think is bad: the Church assumes the prerogative of saying whether or no a marriage may be entered into, whereas the Church has no possible right to interfere in what belongs to the State as the civil authority and the legal guardian of constituted Society. As a result of this muddled manner of acting, a judge may celebrate a marriage, a Police Court officer may celebrate a marriage, or the parties concerned may have recourse to the services of a minister who may never have seen either party before; and that is held to be all the validation of a marriage which is needed; and it is poor protection for all the interests of Society which are involved. It is my judgment that every marriage, as a contract between man and woman involving the most vital meanings of human Society, should be entered into by a civil ceremony duly registered and sanctioned in a Court of Law; and that it should be definitely decided and recognised that it is the State and the State alone which decides who are qualified to enter the marriage relation. Then, if the contracting parties desire that the marriage shall be celebrated ecclesiastically and religiously, either as a vitally necessary sacrament, or as a benediction of lives in God's name, the man and wife may ask for that sacrament or benediction—which is just that, a sacrament or a benediction and not a marriage—the marriage is made by the consent of the man and the woman. The State authorises and registers it and the contract involved; it is then for the Church, in

God's Name, to say, "May the Eternal bless and keep you!"

It is dangerous for the institution of marriage as a function of human Society, this American custom of running into the first minister's house which may be handy, and known or unknown to him, having a few words said out of hand and calling it a marriage, and having it accepted by Society as not only valid but as all that is worth-while. And this usurping by ministers of religion of the rightful functions of the State weakens the whole stabilising influence of the Civil Government in this most essential of Society's foundations. It also detracts enormously from the esteem in which the function of the minister with regard to marriage should be held. The minister who officiates at such a ceremony is often considered, just as the justice of the peace on the corner is held, as simply an unavoidable intermediary for the securing of legal sanction for what the participants intend to do, without any regard to what the invoking of the Name of God means and without any intention of carrying into life what the benediction asked for implies. The only remedy for this situation is that the churches and their ministers shall demand that a civil ceremony before a recognised Court shall precede any religious ceremony at which they consent to officiate. It is so in France. The contracting parties must make declaration of their intention at the Mairie of their *Arrondissement* in writing; such papers are posted on the doors of the Mairie for ten days before the ceremony; they set forth the names of the parties to the proposed contract together with the names of their witnesses; before the ceremony at the Mairie, papers must have been signed by the parties to what is called a *Contrat de Mariage,* and these papers provide for either community of goods, separation of goods, or a mixed relationship financial; they also provide for the protection of children and for the disposition of property in the case of a death of either party or in the case of a divorce. Then on the day set for the ceremony, the parties appear before the Maire with their witnesses, and the Maire wearing his Scarf of Office addresses the couple who are seated in two gold and scarlet chairs in front of him, and legally declares the State satisfied as to the marriage; he then gives them a *Certificat de Mariage* which they may take to any church or minister which they may choose. I have known a marriage ceremony to be performed for the same couple at two different churches on the same day, at our Church in the morning and at the Greek Church in the afternoon: it is not being married twice, as an American would say; it is simply having the marriage twice blessed.

One other marriage calls itself to my memory especially—the marriage of Suzanne Lalique to Paul Haviland of Limoges. Suzanne Lalique was as exquisite in her beauty as the lovely things which her father, René Lalique does in metal and in glass; Monsieur Lalique's house on the Cours la Reine has a façade of his designing which is a fairy dream. And as I remember Suzanne on the day of her wedding, she was the most charmingly pretty daughter of France whom I ever knew.

On May 15, 1913 was held at Geneva in Switzerland, the Convocation of the American Churches in Europe; and at this meeting I was elected President of the Council of Advice of the Jurisdiction. It was a position of some importance in times like those of the Great War. It was impossible to have frequent meetings of the Convocation; and there being no direct episcopal supervision of the American European Churches, and, as during the War, no official Visitation by a Bishop for a long period of time, many questions would have to be settled by the President of the Council. For instance, there came to me at one time the representatives of four congregations in France, who were using for their public worship the official translation of our Prayer Book in the French language, and who were calling themselves *l'Eglise Episcopale Française;* and they desired some sort of official recognition on our part, either by federation or otherwise. One of these congregations was ministered to by a former Lutheran pastor, and two others were cared for by men who had been at one time French Catholic priests. My decision on this question was given in accordance with a principle which I had established for myself early in my work in France. It was this: Our American Churches in Europe are *foreign* churches, established and maintained for service to Americans living abroad; they are in no sense indigenous to the country where they exist, and they have no normal relationship to the people of that country; they are there by courtesy, to minister to American visitors or to Americans who, for some reason, are residing abroad. This decision was taken in line with the established policy of the Church of England, our sister Church, which began Prayer Book Services on the Continent of Europe long before we began any work there. The Church of England, for example, has no bishop resident in Northern or Central Europe, thus recognising the fact that these are Christian countries with bishops of their own; their Churches in Europe are called chaplaincies, their ministrants are chaplains, and the "assistant bishop for North and Central Europe" is a suffragan to the Bishop of London, on the accepted theory of the English Church that the Bishop of London has all travellers in his charge: he is at present the Bishop Suffragan of Fulham. In my time it was Bishop Bury who ministered Confirmation for me during the War and who rendered me many other gracious services. There is a bishop of the Church of England for the South of Europe, the Bishop of Gibraltar; for Gibraltar is British-owned. The Church of England has abstained, with the wisdom of years, from ever making any semblance of intrusion or claiming a See or a Jurisdiction where its rightful setting-up might fairly be questioned; and hence has limited its episcopates to British owned territory, or to what would be called "heathen lands," lands with no Christian Church or Bishop of their own. In line with this established policy of the Church of England, it seemed to me right and wise to make clear both by word and act that our Church in France was not there as a Mission; that we gratefully recognised that the people of France were a Christian folk and that for the greater majority of them the French Catholic Church with its bishops in every large centre of population was the Church of the people; and must therefore be for me the representative of the Catholic Episcopate.

I made this clear in an article entitled *"IL VA NAITRE,"* which was published in *LA REVUE HEBDOMADAIRE.* Further, it was perfectly in accord with ecclesiastical usage and comity, and met the fullest approval of the Catholic authorities abroad that we should minister to our own people, Americans, wherever they might be, with fullest sacramental and ceremonial ministrations as being a foreign Church without any claim to jurisdiction in France, which was a Christian country with a Church and bishops of its own, and with an intelligent Christianity, and not one of a degraded type, such as has been set up as an excuse for our intrusion into the field of other Catholic Churches in other countries. Therefore for me the Cardinal Archbishop of Paris was the Bishop in all that pertained to France and the Christianity of her people; and the American Church of the Holy Trinity never gave the Church of the people of France cause to think that we, as the American Church in France, made claim to place of title, which might be considered by any one as the setting up of dual régime. Many a time French Catholics and French Protestants who were attracted by the beauty of our services, who felt the bareness of the Protestant forms of worship, or who were impatient of the rigidity of dogma in their own Catholic Church, have come to me to ask about being received as members of our Church in Paris. My reply was always the same, namely, that it would be an unwise step for them to take; that they were French people and should remain with a French Church; that ours was an American Church solely for Americans as foreigners in a foreign land; that in the event of a War between France and the United States, their position as members of such a Church would not only be anomalous but would be hopeless. If they were Catholics, I made the matter stronger by telling them that in such a case they might be altogether cut off from a bishop; that our American Churches in Europe are under the jurisdiction of an American Archbishop whom we call Presiding Bishop; that the Bishop who came abroad occasionally for Confirmations and for general supervision was not a Bishop in France nor for France, and could not be such, and made no claim to be such, as he could have neither title nor See in Europe, where the United States possessed no territorial jurisdiction. My position in this matter, both as to proselyting and as to the place which I accorded to the Cardinal Archbishop of Paris, made my relations with the Cardinal himself as well as with the French Catholic Church in general most cordial; and my attitude was fully appreciated. Mr. Robert H. Gardiner, Secretary of "The World Conference on Faith and Order" wrote me:

> "Bishop Brent tells me that it is to you that we are indebted to a great extent for the attention which the French Cardinal has given to the World Conference on Faith and Order. I am very greatly obliged to you."

When questions like that of *l'Eglise Episcopale Française* came up, I thought it was wise to communicate the facts to the Cardinal Archbishop, and the method of communication would be this: a French Catholic friend of mine would invite me to luncheon and would have as another guest a Benedictine Abbot who was *persona grata* at the *Archevèché;* the matter in question would be brought up and talked over, and in due time I would receive a reply if any were needed; and communications would come to me in the same manner; in other words the diplomatic procedure of use would be observed. I had the deepest reverence and personal regard for Cardinal Amette; I have a charming letter of thanks from him; he was a great Frenchman and a noble, large-visioned, large-hearted Churchman. In the first occasion when the French Catholic friend, of whom I have spoken, invited me to luncheon with the Benedictine Abbot, my host asked me if I would consider it entirely courteous if he should ask the Abbot to say the Grace; this was done, and the Abbot with due regard to my supposedly militant Protestant proclivities prayed a long extempore prayer in French. When it was over and we had a chance to begin the convivialities, I said to the Abbot that I was both surprised and disappointed. "At what, *Monsieur le Recteur?"* he asked. "That you did not use the conventual Benedictine formula, *Benedictus Benedicat, Amen!*" "Then," I added, "we would have been spared that long Protestant exordium which you evidently would have willingly escaped; and we could have gotten to meat the sooner." The Abbot roared with laughter, as did the company at the table; and the way to diplomatic procedure was much abbreviated and softened by that interchange of amenities.

I was once asked by a witty French lady, "Monsieur l'Abbe, just what Religion do you belong to?" "I call myself a Catholic, Madame," was my reply. "Is it so?" she said. "Yes, Madame," I replied, "I have sat beside Monseigneur Amette in the choir of his Cathedral of Nôtre Dame on the occasion of a solemn vespers for the commemoration of the birthday of King Albert, when Père Janvier was the preacher; I have sat in the bema of the Protestant Temple of the Rue de l'Oratoire at a service of the Culte more than once; I have sat beside the Grand Rabbin in the seats of the Elders in the Synagogue of the Rue de la Victoire on an eve of a Sabbath, when a congregation of some thousands of Jews were assembled there to pray for the souls of their young men who had fallen in battle; and for several years I have had an office amongst the *Libres Penseurs* at the *Ministère de l'Instruction Publique*. I think that the record entitles me to be called a Catholic in the largest sense of the word." They asked some clever questions at times, those witty French ladies. One day a French girl, whose family were friends of mine, asked if she might bring one of her girl friends, the daughter of a French General, to see the church at some time, when I would be free to show them about. So I made an appointment for a Friday morning after Litany, when I would be sure to be there. On the day set the two girls came to Litany, then after the service was ended they came to the sacristy and I showed them all the treasures—that sacristy is a veritable *Musée d'objets d'Art anciens,* I had Narcisse open the vestment cases and show them the embroideries; then I opened the safe and took out that glorious chalice all encrusted with jewels; then we walked about the church to study its beauties and to look at the altar from a distance and to get the perspective of the triptych above the altar; and when they had seen it all and admired it all, the General's daughter said to me with a naive smile: *"Eh bien, Monsieur l'Abbé, quelle espèce de religion est celle-ci,—Est-ce un mélange?"*—("Please, Monsieur l'Abbe, what kind of a religion is this? is it a medley?")

Of all my relations with Latin Catholics none was a truer index of what we made our own Church to mean to them, and none is a more gracious memory to me than a visit which I had from a high dignitary from Rome, who came to see me one day. The Princesse Caraman-Chimay, who was my next door neighbour on the Avenue de l'Alma, sent me word saying that her uncle, the Prince Giovanni di Borghèse, would like the pleasure of an interview with me. He came in that afternoon and stayed two hours; then came the next day and stayed as long. He said that we might talk in either Italian or French; I chose French; and it was fascinating to listen to his masterful use of that precise and wonderful medium for definition and discussion; at times it was fencing between us, at times it was an exchange of confidences. He said that they had heard in Rome of this American Church which ministered to all needs, regardless of creeds ecclesiastical; which gave to the Cardinal's especial Charity, to the Sisters of St. Vincent de Paul, to *Les Filles de la Sagesse* in Brittany, to the Deaconess Houses maintained by both French Protestants and Lutherans; which sent portable altars to *aumoniers* at the Front, and harvesting machines to the *maires* of country villages; which helped maintain *crèches* under the direction of Jewish ladies; and which furnished shoes for the needy children who were shepherded by the Grand Rabbi of France. They wanted to know the point of view of this type of American Christianity, which had been said to be a species of propaganda but which they well knew was not; and he would be glad if he might be considered courteous if he asked me many and plain questions; to which I willingly agreed with the request that I might be free also to be as frank as he. At the close of the second interview, the Prince stood, a tall slender figure in frock coat, thanked me, then with his long graceful hands he took my hands in his, his face radiant with sympathetic understanding, and said: "*Monsieur le Recteur, entre vous et moi les mots Catholique et Protestant n'existe plus; nous ne sommes que des frères.*"—("Monsieur le Recteur, between you and me the words Catholic or Protestant no longer exist; we are just brothers.")

Among my memories of friends made in France, which I hold dear, is that of my acquaintance with Bishop George Kinsolving, "Texas George" as he humorously called himself. Among my books there is a volume of Kinsolving Sermons entitled *Memorials of Special Events,* and on the flyleaf is this inscription, "'For the Rev'd Dr. Watson, in memory of May 28th, 1913." This was the date of the ordination of the Bishop's son, the Rev. W. O. Kinsolving. I received a telegram one day from Rome from Mr. Kinsolving, asking if he might be ordained to the priesthood in Holy Trinity, Paris; and that his father was coming to Europe for the express purpose. It was so agreed, and the Bishop came. There were some canonical provisions to be arranged, (and dis-arranged), but Europe is a sort of extra-canonical region; so I officiated as examining chaplain, and presenter, and associate in the laying on of hands at the ordination, which was a most solemn and affecting service, the father in the flesh saying the words of the Great Commission, as Father in God, above the bowed head of his son. He was a great man and a great Bishop, was George Kinsolving.

On the Fourth of July of 1913 I pronounced the Annual Commemorative Address at the tomb of Lafayette in the *Cimitière Picpus;* that little burying ground hidden away behind an old Convent near the Place de la Nation. The man in Paris, to whom the memory of Layafette meant most among all the Americans who lived there, was Mr. Cleveland Coxe, a son of a former Bishop of Western New York. He was a lawyer and an ardent American; and I am indebted to him for many courtesies not the least of which was the bringing to me the privilege of welcoming the Marquis de Lafayette at my house.

In the spring of 1913 Aurilla Brigham came to France again to brighten the house with her presence, and she was our companion when we went to Châtel-Guyon for the baths and for the waters. Châtel-Guyon was a lovely place that summer. From our apartment we could look up a deep valley lined with firs, so blue that they looked black in the dusk; and the nightingales began their songs and ended them with such regularity that one could set one's watch by them. La Fête Dieu occurred while we were there, and a French girl who lived in the village asked us to come to the apartment of a friend to witness the procession from its balcony which overhung the main street through which the procession must pass. As far as one could see in either direction the street was a carpet of green; the people had gone to the woods and had brought in cart-loads of moss which they had spread on the cobbles of the roadway; the walls of the houses which were all of them flush with the street were hung with their choicest embroidered linens and decked with flowers and religious emblems; along the way of the procession there were altars built (*reposoirs*) at intervals, and these all bore candles ready to light. Afar in the distance there was the sound of singing; then the head of the procession appeared; first a guard of *Suisses;* then the Master of Ceremonies; then a group of acolytes with censers and baskets of rose petals which they scattered in the pathway of the Holy Sacrament; then a choir of men, most of them wearing old, old vestments, copes so stiff with embroideries of gold that they would stand alone, and singing from old horn-books; then some priests; then the Bishop under a canopy borne by four men, and four more holding cords attached to the four corners of it. The Bishop carried a Monstrance in which was the Host, and when he reached one of the *Reposoirs* he mounted the steps of the altar, the candles were lit, and he placed the Sacrament on the Altar, said the ritual prayers, and then turned with the Host in his hands and blessed the people who were all of them kneeling in the street; as far as one could see, long, long lines of kneeling people. To a devout soul it mattered little whether one were a Catholic or not, the thrill of sharing a tremendous emotional experience when the souls of a people were upborne to God in moments of mystic reverence beckoned the soul of the silent witness of the scene: one felt the unearthly power of the heart of all religion. I wrote these words once about Religion in France:

"C'était dans une grande église ou les ombres allaient et venaient; je l'ai vu entrer un jour, lui, un homme du peuple. Il portait sur son dos une hotte pleine de laitues et de chicorée; et il alla droit s'agénouiller devant la statue de Jeanne d'Arc, et il cacha sa figure dans ses mains. Longtemps il resta la absorbé dans ses méditations, et quand il sortit il y avait une sorte de rayonnement sur son visage. Que faisait-il la? Priait-il la statue? Revait-il de Dieu? Peu importe. Le fait essentiel est que seul ou dans une foule c'est l'ame du peuple en contact avec Dieu. Car l'univers entier n'est qu'un temple; et tout ce qui existe n'est qu'un symbole; et le spirituel est le fait essentiel qui explique tout; et les églises et les images et les autels et les lumières et les cérémoonies et les mots des rites ne sont rien que la suggestion d'un 'Il y avait une Fois' dans la communion de notre coeur avec Dieu; et la fondation de tout dans notre vie humaine est ceci: 'Un seul Dieu, le Père, de qui procèedent toutes chose, et nous sommes pour Lui'; et la religion de ce peuple francais n'est que le coeur enfantin de l'homme auprès du grand coeur paternel de Dieu leur Père. Comme la Pucelle à Domremy qui parlait aux anges parmi les arbres de son jardin, ils parlent à Dieu comme un homme parle à ses familiers. Et ils connaissent bien d'autres qui connaissent Dieu: les Saints sont leurs amis, et les Saints sont les amis de Dieu: et Dieu, c'est un homme qui souffrait, et qui avait une mère humaine qui l'aimait; et ils lui parlent, à elle aussi.*

*(It was in a great Church where the shadows came and went that I saw him come in one day—a man of the people. He had on his back a tall basket full of salads, chicory and lettuces; and he went straight to the statue of Jeanne d'Arc and knelt before it, his face hidden in his hands. A long time he stayed there wrapped in meditation; and when he rose and went out I saw a clear radiance shining from his face. What was he doing there? Was he praying to the statue? Was he dreaming of God? It matters little one way or the other: the essential fact is that alone or in a crowd it is the soul of the people in living contact with God. For the whole world is nothing but a temple; and all that exists is but a shadow of the real; and the spiritual is the essential fact which alone explains it all; and churches and images and altars and lights and ceremonies and ritual words are nothing but a suggestion of a "Once upon a Time" in the communion of our hearts with God: and the underlying fact in this

This mystic element in the religion of a simple people is to me Religion at its highest; so that I have often longed to be like them. Its fruiting is an abiding reverence for some Infinite which is all that they can dream of love and care and beauty and power; a childlike trust in the Spirit of Life; a reverence for old age and for child life which will not permit that they should go uncared for; a glad willingness to help the helpless; a simple honesty in all that pertains to a trust or to a word once given. These are qualities which I have seen so many times in the simple folk of France. What more can life mean of nearness to the Divine?

From Châtel-Guyon we went to Bex in Switzerland, and from our balcony terrasse at the Grand Hotel des Salines we saw a morning and an evening miracle, the majestic Dent du Midi painted in all the colours of the Aurora by the rising and the setting sun. Soon a telegram recalled me hurriedly to Paris and I left Jeannette and Aurilla at Bex. On their way back to Paris, Jeannette was taken very ill and had to leave the train and remain in Lausanne until well enough to travel again. In the meantime Aurilla came up to Paris for school days were at hand; and I arranged that she should follow a course of regular French schooling at the Cours Victor Hugo in the Rue Benjamin-Godard.

On leaving Paris for the cure at Châtel we left the house in charge of a Swiss couple who had been butler and housemaid; but on my return I found it necessary to make a change of personnel, and with masculine helplessness I turned to a woman for help. Miss Mary Montana was an American girl who had lived in France for a long time; she had been of great assistance to us in finding the furnishings for the house; she knew where to find everything needed,

human life of ours is this: "One only God, the Father, from whom come all things, and we are his"; and the religion of this people of France is but the child heart in men reaching out to the great Father heart of God. Like the Maid of Domremy who spoke with angels through the branches of the trees of her garden, so this people speaks to God as a man talks to his near friends. And they know well others too who know God: the Saints are their friends, and the Saints are God's friends: and God—He is a man who suffered once as man; and he had a human mother who loved him;—and they talk to Her also.)

and was expert in making *le meilleur marché*. So to her house I went, and we looked through the morning papers till we found a *menage* who seemed desirable; the next day I met the two at Miss Montana's; then and there I engaged Alexis Jacquin and Louise his wife, Alexis to be *maitre d'hôtel,* and Louise to be *bonne;* and I "called it a day," and a great day it proved to have been, for their devotion was *hors du prix*. Later in the summer Jeannette came back to Paris, health restored; and life took on its normal.

Among Aurilla's friends of whom we saw much were Alice Marre, a niece of our Akron friend Mr. Saalfield; and Laddie Eaton, a San Francisco girl and a niece of Mrs. Morton whose collection of carved elephants was unique. In the spring of 1914 America called Aurilla back; it was a call which made it possible for her to return before the War broke upon us.

On June 11, 1914 I was in Spain. The American Ambassador to Spain, Mr. Joseph E. Willard, had asked me to come to Madrid to officiate at the marriage of his daughter, Belle Wyatt Willard, to Kermit Roosevelt. The Spanish Ambassador in Paris had most kindly given me a Laissez Passer, to make the crossing of the frontier from France into Spain easy and to free me from all annoyance and complications at the Douane, and so to facilitate the transfer of my trunk containing my ecclesiastical paraphernalia; a like courtesy was extended to me by the French Ambassador in Madrid for my return to France. The marriage took place in the Chapel of the British Embassy in Madrid, which was most courteously offered by the British Ambassador, Lord Harding. The Chapel was a quaint old building of stone at the rear of the garden; its ceiling was of beams of age old oak; and its walls were hung with precious old rose damasks; on the side of the altar there were great six foot flambeaux of wood gilded and carved. The official witnesses to the marriage were Theodore Roosevelt and Joseph E. Willard. In order that official record might be made of this marriage—there being no possibility of such record being made in Spain—I had cut from the Register of Marriages which was kept in the safe in the sacristy of the church in Paris the page necessary and had taken it with me to Madrid, where the President, the Ambassador, and the other members of the bridal party signed it in due form, and I then took it back with me to Paris and inserted it in its proper order in the Register. At the ceremony I wore the hood of my Doctorate of Divinity degree, the colours of which are scarlet and gold. At the reception which followed the ceremony, two Spanish Grands came to me, and said, "You are from Paris, Monsieur; are you not?" On my saying that I was, they said, "We thought that you must be, for we had remarked your thoughtful courtesy in wearing the colours of Spain on your vestments."

On the way back to Paris I had expected to have a compartment in the Wagon-Lit, which I had been told would be arranged for me by the Embassy; but on reaching the train I found that the compartment which my ticket evidently called for was not available, and I was shown to another which I shared with a very friendly young gentleman, whom I found to be one of the secretaries of the American Embassy in London. On the long day ride from Madrid to Paris, President Roosevelt asked me to his compartment and I was deeply impressed with the scope and the depth of his thinking, with his largeness of views on world affairs; and his genial comradeship lightened in large measure the tedium of a dusty journey. At Angoulème we left the train for a walk on the station platform; which gave an opportunity for the reporter for the *Excelsior,* an illustrated Paris daily paper, to take photographs of the President and myself in company; *Excelsior* published the photograph the next morning, and I still have a copy of it. Before we reached Paris, one of the newspaper writers who was on the train—I think it was Mr. Wile—said, "Doctor, it will interest you to know why the reservation made for you on this train at Madrid did not hold good. You had been assigned one of the compartments next to Mr. Roosevelt's; but just before leaving both the compartments next to his were ordered occupied by Secret Service men; this arrangement was made by the Spanish Government too late to change your assignment; I think that it is a courtesy to all concerned for me to tell you just how it happened; no one neglected anything; but the change simply could not be helped."

On July 2, 1914, I officiated at the interment at St. Germain of the body of my valued friend the Rev. Harry W. G. Mesny, who had been the assistant of my predecessor, the Rev. Dr. Morgan, and who was of inestimable aid to me, a newcomer, when I came to Paris to take the Church there. The highest tribute that I can pay him would be none too much; he was always forgetful of self; always ready to serve others. His long association with the Church in Paris had placed him *au courant* with all the details of the administration, and with all the relations of the Church to individuals in that most individualistic of congregations. All this he shared with me, and more. He had married a Miss Atterbury; and it is to her and to her family that the splendid work of "Concordia" in Paris is due. When Mr. Mesny's strength began to fail, the Vestry offered him a leave of absence; he went to Leysin, Switzerland, where he passed away.

The Rev. Dr. Isaac Van Winkle was at this time the devoted pastor of St. Luke's, the Chapel in the Latin Quarter for American students living on the Left Bank; he remained at this post until the War came on, and the income for supporting the work there vanished so that St. Luke's had to be closed temporarily. Dr. Van Winkle then returned to New York, to which Diocese he was canonically attached; and his going was deeply regretted by many friends in France.

Two necessities were upon us before Mr. Mesny's death; both of them correlated. One was the finding of a Head for the Choir School, and, if possible one who should be at the same time assistant minister at the Church. The Choir School was a unique institution. In order to provide music fitting the services in that great Gothic Church, it had been thought necessary to have a choir of men and boys, the tones of whose voices would be harmonic with the massive dignity of the building. But boys who could sing the services in English, (there were no services in the French language except the occasional offices) meant American boys, and there were none; or else it meant bringing boys over from England. In order that English boys might be allowed to come to France, it was necessary that provision be made that they should have the equivalent of an English Board School education, so that when they should go back to England after their voices began to break, they would not be handicapped educationally. This all meant the establishing of a choir school in Paris; which Dr. Morgan established, and I inherited. Positions in this school were eagerly sought for, for they meant free scholarships and the chance to learn French; and the filling of vacancies as they arose was made dependent on the outcome of competitive examinations which were held in England. For a long time the school had its quarters in an old building on the Rue de la Tour; the Head of the school was an old fashioned English schoolmaster; and the school itself was a refined edition of Dotheboys Hall. When the old Master who had been head of the school was retired, advertisements were put in the *Church Times* and in the *Guardian,* stating that it was desired to find a man in Holy Orders, who would be qualified to direct both the educational work and supervise the boys' musical education, and who would also take a place as assistant minister of Holy Trinity. Applications came in by the score in answer to these advertisements; we thinned them down to two; and these two were asked to come to Paris to see me. Of the two, one was an outstanding man, and he was chosen. He was the Rev. E. H. Williams-Ashman, now Canon of St. Paul's Cathedral, London. Mr. Ashman was born in Detroit, Michigan, the son of a Church of England clergyman. When his family returned to England, he was placed in an English choir school; and from that school he was one of the boys who gained one of the competitive places in Holy Trinity Choir School in Paris; hence he knew French, and he knew the school. One might say, How fortunate! I would say, Another guiding of Providence. After having decided in my own mind that Mr. Ashman was the man for the place, I told him that I wanted him to be fully satisfied that he would find working with me wholly satisfactory; that it was my custom to give a colleague free scope in his own allotted field, only asking of him that the work be done; that if he had any pet notions as to ritual or other similar matters which were essential to him, it was better that all such questions were discussed in advance. Then I asked him as to St. Peter's, Paddington, which was the church to which he was at the time attached: and his reply was, "Well, Rector, I can answer all your questions by telling you a story. At one time the Bishop of London, who was then Bishop Creighton, sent a letter to all the London churches, saying that in his opinion incense should not be used at the regular morning service. With this request most of the churches complied, St. Peter's, Paddington among them, as incense had never been used there at any time. A few of the churches however held out; so the Bishop sent for the rectors of these recalcitrants and laid the case before them as a matter of counsel from the Ordinary, to whose opinion they might be expected to defer. "But, my Lord," said one of them, "with me, this is a matter of conscience." "Agreed," said the Bishop, "but you may well, I think, subordinate your individual conscience in such a minor matter to the corporate conscience of the Bishop and the Diocese." "But, my Lord," said another, "'I must insist that I have a cure of souls." "Yes," said the Bishop, "and I have often noticed that gentlemen of your opinions seem to think that souls, like herrings, cannot be cured without smoke." A man with as ready a sense of humour as that story evidenced must have, I thought, the capacity of adaptiveness, which would be most valuable in our Paris work. So Mr. Ashman came; did wonderful work; and was with me all the time of my stay in France, and often at the price of real hardship for himself. His devotion to the work and to me personally knew no limits. When I left France, he returned to England and was a master at Rugby for a time; then he was made Chaplain of the British Embassy Church in Brussels,—what was known as the Edith Cavell Church; and he left that attractive post at the call of his University (Cambridge) to become Warden of the Universities Mission in London Docks and Vicar of Christ Church, Rotherhithe.

Next, by appointment of the Lord Mayor and Council of London, he became Vicar of St. Peter's Church, Bethnal Green; and his work there has won him such recognition that he was made Canon of St. Paul's Cathedral, London. He has a devoted wife and two children, and his boy Guy is my godson.

XI

THE WORLD WAR

IN JULY 1914 we went to England, thinking to get some much needed rest. Our destination was Cromer on the Norfolk Coast, and there I took up golf again for the first time since leaving America; and as my clubs were in storage in Akron with my household goods, I got the "Pro" at the Royal Golf Links Club House to fit me out with a bag of clubs. One thing which we noticed at this hotel which was perched up on the cliffs overlooking the North Sea was the fact that the personnel of the house were mostly Germans, with the exception of the head porter; and that the manager was a German gentleman, evidently a person of distinction. One morning when I was out on the Links digging away with my niblick in a sand-trap, a ball whizzed perilously near my ear, and after a short wait the owner of the ball came over the crest and proved to be a German gentleman who suggested, as I was alone, that we might do the round together; which we did. That same evening in the lounge before the fire, we talked on various subjects and I improved the occasion to refresh my German which was very rusty. We made an appointment to play golf again on a succeeding morning; but on coming down to breakfast on the day appointed I found a note on crested paper by my plate from my acquaintance (a German nobleman and officer), regretting having to break the appointment to play, and saying that he had been suddenly recalled to the Continent, but that he hoped we might meet again in *happier times*. Just what "happier times" indicated I did not then realise, although we had plainly noticed that the service in the hotel was becoming disorganised apparently, and that things were not running smoothly. The world had so long refused to take trouble in the Balkans as meaning any general European danger, that it seemed difficult to believe that this War talk on the Continent might possibly develop anything definitely serious. However as the situation did not quiet down, we packed up and went up to London.

There rumours were so disquieting that we decided on an immediate return to Paris and the post of duty. To facilitate travel I went to the Morgan Bank in London, to which I had been accredited, and asked to exchange some English money for French money, only to be told that they could not let me have any French money, as they had no idea what it was worth, face or nothing; but they gave me the address of a broker to whom they had telephoned on my behalf and who said that he would let me have some French money. I went to his office and got the money, at a considerable premium, and mostly in large bills, while what I wanted was small money for local expense and travelling tips. However, I had a little French gold in reserve and I kept some English gold, knowing that gold was good money whatever happened. Then I went to the shipping offices to arrange for our passage to France; there I was told that they would sell me the tickets but that I must take my chances on getting any kind of a place on the boat, as crowds were hurrying back to France while it was still possible to go. I then took up the matter with the Travel Bureau in the lobby of the hotel where we were staying and asked to have a cabin reserved for me. The man in charge said that he would do his best but that he was doubtful of results. Knowing what the Channel boats would be like in case of a crowd, I told him that if he succeeded in getting me the accommodations I had asked for, there would be a half a sovereign for him, and that he could tell the agent at the Folkestone pier that there would be a guinea for him if I got a room. On coming down stairs on the morning of my proposed departure for France, I was met by the agreeable information that the cabin on the boat had been arranged, and as evidence the man handed me a slip of paper which was a copy of the telegram which he had received from Folkestone. So, we started for Paris leaving behind us a London boiling with uncertainty, and with hotels crowded with Americans in a panic, all trying to get accommodations for a homeward sailing. "Mobilisation" had been ordered in France; War seemed imminent. On our way down to Folkestone in the Pullman car, Jeannette called my attention to a gentleman and a lady who were seated opposite to us, and said, "Those people are Americans; they are going to Paris, I heard them say. Don't you think that you should tell them what they are going into; they do not seem at all to realise what is going on." Despite the fact that I had personally met the man who had made his fortune by attending to his own business (there was once one such person), I let good nature overmaster discretion, and I made the acquaintance of our vis-à-vis. They were very attractive people, from Cincinnati; they had that American idea of aloofness from all world concerns in general which seems characteristic of us; their tickets called for a trip from New York to Paris and return; and they could see no reason why those tickets should be invalidated by what might be going on in Europe. So we all reached Folkestone. On going aboard the boat which was already crowded, I gave my name to the steward who came to take our bags and told him that I had a reservation of a private cabin. He consulted the list which was posted beside the entrance to the saloon; then said that he was very sorry but that there must have been some mistake somewhere, as my name did not appear on the list of cabin reservations. Well, I thought, we are here, and we'll make it somehow; and if my half-sovereign to the chap in London is gone, at least I have saved the guinea to the purser. In a short time, however, back comes the steward followed by the purser who most politely asked us to follow him, and we were shown to a large cabin with settees on two sides, and two large windows looking out on the deck. In the mirror above the lavabo there was a card which read "This Cabin is Reserved for the Duchess of Westminster." At once I called the purser's attention to it and said, "Have you not made an error in the number of the room, Purser? this cabin is evidently meant for some one else." "No, Sir; No, Sir; not at all, Sir" said the purser: "You are the Duchess of Westminster, Sir: it was the only way that we could put the reservation through, Sir." So, the Duchess of Westminster set sail for France; and, for what seemed to be war.

When we had pulled out from the dock I set out to find our friends from Cincinnati, and after a time I found the gentleman and asked him where his wife was, and had she found a comfortable place. She was up forward sitting on a pile of rope and almost in collapse from faintness due to the press of the crowd. She was too overcome to walk, so he and I made a chair by crossing hands over wrists, and with difficulty we got her down to my cabin, literally over the the heads of the crowd which was one close packed mass of wretched humanity, already overcome by the tossing of the Channel. On reaching Boulogne I took the two ladies to the gate which closed the entrance to the train sheds, and by the judicious manipulation of a Five Franc silver dollar, I secured an entrance for them to the waiting cars where they might sit in some comfort until we could get the bags past the Douane. On the train they told me that they were going to the Grand Hotel in Paris; by this time I knew that it would be useless to ask them why it must be the Grand Hotel; so I did my best to help them on their downward path. At the station in Paris my good Gabriel met us with the car; I told him who our companions were, and asked him to go out and get them a taxi. "But, there are no taxis, Monsieur," he said. "There is no one to drive them; this is the eve of mobilisation, and all the men have gone to their depots." Mobolisation in France means that every man of military age must report at his depot which is usually the *chef-lieu* of his Department of origin; he may be living in Lyons but if his depot is Lille, then to Lille he must go to get his equipment and report for service at the Front. "But, Gabriel," I said, "I've seen several taxis go by; get one for these friends of mine; they must have one even if you have to buy it; these people are not well, and they must get to the Grand Hotel where they have their rooms engaged." Gabriel still objected: "It is not safe, Monsieur; these taxis which you have seen are not driven by Frenchmen; the Company is taking any kind of a foreigner whom they can get." But our friends were equally insistent, and in the course of time a taxi came and they were put in it with strict injunctions to pay nothing to the driver but to wait till they came to the Grand Hotel, and even then to assure themselves that it really was the Grand Hotel; then to leave the matter of payment to the man in royal livery who would come to the door to meet them. A few days later the two wanderers came to the rectory, looking the very picture of despair. They told me that the cooks and waiters at the Hotel had all vanished; that they had divided one soft boiled egg between them for breakfast; and they ended by saying: "You were good enough to get us here: now, for heavens' sake help us to get out!"

After having seen our American acquaintances off from the station—destination unknown—it was time to look after our trunks and have them strapped on the back of the car and to make our way to Avenue de l'Alma. So leaving Jeannette in the car, Gabriel and I went back to the gate leading to the platform where we had landed from the train, only to find it locked, and a sentry standing there who refused us admission to where the trunks should be, saying most politely but most insistently, *"Consigne formelle, Messieurs!"* And in reply to our questions where we might find the trunks in the morning, if we did not get them that evening, he admitted that he did not know any more about that than we did. What to do? Gabriel, always resourceful as to methods for peacefully avoiding the oftentimes disturbing regulations of police and military, suggested seeing the Chef de Gare. So to the far end of the station I went; climbed up a circular iron stairway, and found myself in the sleepy but august presence. He was a tired but complaisant man, this Monsieur Ronde-de-Cuir, and he asked me drowsily what he could do for me. I had expected politeness, but I was wondering all the way up the stairs how I would manage it to get something more; and all of a sudden I bethought me of some papers which I had in my pocket. I always carried with me in travelling a case of soft leather, which was the gift of Mr. William Hogan, a friend who did me many favours, and which held my miscellaneous assortment of papers, official and semi-official. In response to the query of the Chef de Gare, and to his tacit enquiry by look as to why I was coming up there disturbing his well-earned repose, I handed him the diplomatic papers which the Spanish authorities had given me for easing my crossing of the frontier on my recent trip to Madrid. Spanish "was all Greek" to him. A blank look came over his face, "And what are these, Monsieur?" In as lofty a tone as I could command my weary voice to assume, I replied: "They are credentials from the Government of Spain, Monsieur le Chef de Gare." Instant awakening; in what way could he serve me? The answer was easy; "Would he please write an order to the *planton* at the gate down there, instructing him to go with my chauffeur to get my trunks." No sooner said than done; and in due course we were on our way to what we hoped would be supper, and what we knew would be bed.

It is now time to introduce to the honourable company a typical Frenchman, one of the truest of friends and one of the most faithful of companions, who went everywhere with me in all my wanderings in France and in and around the capital—Monsieur Gabriel de la Houplière. I first made his acquaintance in 1910 when he was driving a car which was kept at the disposal of the guests of the Hotel Ste. Anne, on the Rue Ste. Anne in Paris, and he was my conductor, guide, and interpreter in my first year of explorations in and about Paris. In 1911 and 1912 the acquaintance ripened, so that by the time I needed a car for my work it was to Gabriel that I turned naturally. At the beginning of my work in Paris I had the use of a fine landau and horses which were put at my disposal by the kindness of Mrs. Johnson; but time soon came when an automobile was necessary, and I made arrangements with the garage where Gabriel was employed that I should have him as driver with a car which they would furnish. Our first car was a Delahaye; and the next one was a Delaunay-Belleville; but always with Gabriel as chauffeur. Then came the War; all cars in the garages in Paris were requisitioned, which meant that I would have to buy a car. Through the courtesy of Mr. William Hogan I was able to get a 20/30 Renault Phaeton which had belonged to Mrs. Rutherford Stuyvesant, and Gabriel came with me then as chauffeur. Technically, perhaps, Gabriel was a *servant* as so regarded in France and as the word means in French usage; but to me he was helper, companion, counsellor and friend; and that relation of affection and friendship still exists between us, as witness the fact that I have regularly letters from him which show that I am still part of his life. *"Monsieur, où allons-nous aujourd'hui?"* The day before had been a hard day's run, and I had found my bed at the Hotel de la Poste at Beaune so attractive that it was now 11:00 o'clock in the morning, and I had just come downstairs and had stepped into the courtyard to look at the weather, and there I found Gabriel telling two *petits garçons* some of the virtues of our Renault 20/30,—("which could easily run 70 kilométres the hour, but we did not usually go over 50 as we did not wish to hurt the roads.") That "Monsieur, where are *we* going to-day?" which was Gabriel's question, is a commentary on our relationship; that *allon-nous,* that "we" associated him with my interests; it was meant to tell me confidentially that my interests were his; that we were working together; that life was a co-operation; that it made no difference in essentials that one might be master and one might be servant, if so be that it was good master and good servant, for the work of each was necessary in order that the other should do good work. Again also there was in the familiar form of his question that sort of half-affectionate comprehension expressed, which is a charming reality in the intimate relation which is created between oneself and a French servant of the good old type. I was *le patron,* it is true, and officially I was several kinds of *Monsieur le Président;* but, for all that, Gabriel felt himself a very real part of all that I was doing, officially or otherwise. His attitude was like that of the little nephew of the *curé* who was running home from the Church one morning when some one hailed him: *"Jacques, Où est Monsieur l'Abbe?" "Il est à l'Eglise, Madame; nous venons de célébrer la messe";* said the boy: (WE have just celebrated Mass). My work took me very often, sometimes daily, to the various government offices, and Gabriel came thus to know all their concièrges and to hear all the gossip that was passing in the outskirts of officialdom; which made him feel all the more a part of public affairs. One morning coming out of my house I found Gabriel waiting for me with the car; and I noticed that he had a sort of apologetic air as if not quite certain whether he had committted sacrilege or not. I saw several persons just going away from where he was standing, and I said, "Who were those people? did they come to see me?" Gabriel explained to me it was a *curé* from the village of Montdidier, who had come with several of the villagers to express their thanks for an American harvester-binder which I had sent up there to help in getting in the grain from the fields of the widows just back of the Front; and he said that he hoped that he had not exceeded what was proper in the matter, but knowing that I had an appointment at the Ministry of the Interior, he had said to them, "I beg of you to excuse us this morning, Messieurs; *mais nous sommes dans les ministères ces jours-ci jusqu'au cou.* (We are up to our necks these days in work at the ministries.) And he made his refusal courteous by including himself in the excuse. I could write a book on *Les bons mots de Gabriel.*

I wrote an article in French at the request of a French diplomat which was published in *LA REVUE HEBDOMADAIRE* under the title *"IL VA NAITRE."* It appeared in the issue of May 22, 1915; and its purpose was to give my impressions of the spiritual and religious attitude of France in time of war; it was later translated into Spanish and was used in Spain by the Foreign Affairs as favourable evidence for a France which had been maligned as an irreligious nation; and a preface to the article speaks of it as "a tribute rendered spontaneously to the religious idealism" of France. On the evening of the day of the appearance of this article in print, I drove to Rue Garancière and brought home with me a number of copies of the *Revue,* and on dismissing the car for the day I gave a copy to Gabriel. When I came out of the house in the morning following I found him reading it. With a quizzical air he said, "Monsieur, Who wrote this preface to your article in the *Revue Hebdomadaire?"* I replied, "It was written by Monsieur Alfred Dumaine, the

Ambassador of France at Vienna, when the War broke out." *"Ah, c'est ça,"* said Gabriel, *"j'ai cru reconnaitre le style chatié du Quai d'Orsay."* (I thought I recognised the meticulous style of the Ministry of Foreign Affairs.) I received countless letters soliciting money, and one of them ended by saying, "You ought to grant my prayer, Monsieur, for I too, am a saint." I took this letter out and showed it to my counsellor, and said "Gabriel, just what does one mean in France by 'a saint'?" "Why, for my part, Monsieur," he said, "the saints are all dead, I think." He had unlimited confidence in my ability to do the impossible, had Gabriel.

One day on starting for my work in the City with a leather briefcase, (what Gabriel called *"votre serviette de servitude"*) stuffed with papers under my arm, I found him talking with a wounded soldier whom he introduced to me by name. The soldier asked me to get him some word from his wife and daughters, whom he had not seen since the War began; they were all in a village in the North when mobilisation called him to his Depot in the Midi; the battle line had swept between; his village had been in the hands of the enemy; and he was terribly anxious to know that no harm had come to his family there. I told him that I would do what I could; although I had not the faintest idea what that would be; but it turned out that I succeeded well. One day at the Château de Pontault Combault where I was at luncheon, the daughter of the house, Mlle. Leon, brought in to see us a little girl who had been separated from her family for three years and had been cared for all that time by the enemy who occupied their village; the attack came hurriedly; she was at school and her home was on the other side of the village from the school; the family ran one way and she ran another, and she was left alone, hiding in a cellar. They were good to her, those rough soldier men; she was but a little thing; and in those three years she had forgotten all her French; she spoke only German; she had even forgotten her family name: but, in the end, Mlle. Leon found the family. She was occupied with a fine work in Geneva, the interchange of postal cards between people in the North of France behind the German Front and their relatives in

France; and she also did the same service for those who were in concentration camps in Germany. I told her what the wounded soldier had asked of me, and she said that she would try and get the word desired; and some weeks later she sent me a post card signed by the soldier's wife and daughter, saying that all was well with them. I had Gabriel bring the man to see me, and when I gave him the card, his pent up emotion broke bounds, and he fell on his knees and kissed my hand. I said to him, "But tell me, my friend, why did you ask such an apparently impossible service of a foreigner?" "Oh! Monsieur, it was your chauffeur, Monsieur Gabriel, who told me to do it; he said, 'You just ask my patron to do it for you; asking him is like asking the good God himself.'" Gabriel de la Houplière is now in the employ of the Hôtel Ambassador, Boulevard Haussmann.

On reaching Paris on the eve of mobilisation I found that my assistant, Mr. Ashman, was not there; he was off on holiday, as he thought. So little idea did one have in Paris that war was so imminent that he left Paris the last week in July to go to Hamburg to visit his sister. On crossing the frontier of France he saw every evidence of military preparation on the German side of the line, and on reaching Cologne where he left the train and tried to return to Paris, he was told that the frontier was closed and that there was no possibility of going back; so he continued his journey to his sister and her family. And here is one of those tragedies which war brings. His sister, an English girl, had married a graduate of the University of Cambridge who was manager of the London-Shanghai Bank in Hamburg; he was born in Germany but he went to England as a boy; was educated there; grew up in English life; married there; his children said their prayers in English; and now, just overnight as it were, the whole family becomes German in Hamburg because of the father's parentage. Mr. Ashman tried to get to England by sea, going aboard a small steamer in the Hamburg harbour which was freighted for Hull; but the steamer was seized and he was arrested as an enemy subject. After some months of waiting he was exchanged and came back to Paris.

Three serious situations faced me when War broke out in Europe. The first and the most pressing was the condition of American travellers who were stranded there. Most of them arrived in Paris without baggage or even a change of clothing; many of them were without money; a moratorium was on at all the banks, and drafts and letters of credit were valueless; cultured, well-dressed women were without money to pay a taxi fare, and often I saw them sitting on a bench beside the street holding their shoes in their hands, too lame and tired to walk farther: and it was so that they often came to the Rectory. The next question was as to how to house and feed these waifs together with quantities of other Americans, in case of a sudden swift enemy advance on the City, or a possible siege. For the housing I arranged for beds to be placed in the Parish House and in the nave of the Church if they should be needed; but the question of food was a more serious one; for hoarding of food on any one's part was strongly protested by the citizens. I went to see the manager of a large provision shop on the Left Bank; it was difficult to get entry to the store; the iron grilles at the front were open but a foot or two and were guarded by police so that the store could not be rushed, and but a few people were allowed in the store at a time. (Those who remembered what the siege of '70 was like and what food conditions were then could easily become desperate on the slightest sign of shortage.) When I finally reached the manager, presented my card, and made myself known, I told him that what I wanted was to make a food provision in case of an emergency for stranded Americans, and that I was prepared to pay cash. He offered me anything which he had in stock, and gave me an order to the police to pass my car into the area at the rear of the store. We then filled the car with all the dry provisions which the balance of my vacation money would buy—some $200 worth—and under cover of the dusk, with the aid of Jean and Narcisse, our two sacristans on duty at the time, Gabriel supervised the storing of the supply in the downstairs hall closet at the rectory.

Later on, after the rush of the Marne was past, these provisions were given as need might arise to hungry people who came to the Ouvroir at the Parish House.

Next in urgency came the outfitting of travellers who reached Paris having lost their baggage on the way. The sister of one of our Bishops reached us without hat or even a handbag; her head wrapped in a black lace scarf. She took with her on leaving for England a steamer trunk well supplied with just the things she needed; it had belonged to a lady who could not take it with her in the rush of departure and who had sent trunk and contents to us. That was what often happened; Americans with a plentiful supply of belongings and strictly limited as to what they could take on trains simply sent trunks and all to us, and we distributed the contents and gave away the trunks as need arose.

The Ambassador soon made arrangements by which the Morgan Bank would cash personal checks of Americans, who carried letters of credit or who possessed other evidence of financial responsibility; and I was told that less than 5% of the obligations so created were defaulted.

Having a car, and being known in Paris, made it possible for me to render many services to my compatriots who were eager to get away to America. Most grateful letters came from many of them after they had gotten away. One of them reads: "God bless you for the help given. We have our passports and are off for England." Bishop Lines wrote: "It was our good fortune to come home on the *S.S. Celtic*. —You, dear Dr. Watson, have filled out the ideal of a great public servant at this time." Dr. Milo Gates, now Dean of the Cathedral in New York, wrote in a printed article: "The Rector of our Church in Paris has performed a service as remarkable as that of any man in the field." As this is history, no apology need be made here for what might, otherwise, seem to be self-laudation.

The most urgent and serious situation which the breaking out of War presented for solution to me, as Rector of Holy Trinity, was the maintenance of the Church and of its services, for all guarantees expired with the outbreak of hostilities; and if the financial situation of the Church was precarious in ordinary times it became infinitely more so now. Normally, in those days, and as I found it, the maintenance of that great Church in a foreign city was a three-legged stool; one leg was pew rentals, and before the War was on many months a large proportion of the pews had been given up; another leg was the offerings at the Sunday services, and by 1915 these had diminished tremendously—75 to 100 people was a large congregation by the time that June 1915 arrived; the third leg was the gifts of generous Americans who once were there as travellers and who were there no more; European travel had ceased. When it became a question as to whether it would be financially possible to keep the Church open for the services, the Duchesse de Talleyrand offered me the use of the building in the Rue Pierre Charron, which was known as The Miller-Gould Foundation which could easily have been arranged for our use; and in addition to the use of the building she offered to provide all costs of maintenance, such as heat, light, and caretaker. But soon money enough began to come in for the use of the Church, specifically, and I saw that we would not have to close the Church's doors. I have by me a pile of receipts which I have kept, which cover amounts sent in in those War days by friends in America for the support of the Church in Paris, and I am amazed as I read the figures. Here are some of them: "Ten Thousand Francs for Church Maintenance—One Thousand Francs—Twenty-six Thousand Nine Hundred Francs—Ten Thousand Francs—Twenty Thousand Francs—Eight Thousand and Ninety Francs—Two Thousand and Fifty Dollars—One Hundred and Fifty-five Dollars—Five Hundred Dollars—Four Hundred and Eighty-four Dollars—Ten Thousand Francs;—and then I find this one—Five Thousand Dollars for the shortage in Church Receipts for 1918. These and similar gifts made my task of keeping the Church's doors open possible of accomplishment. All these receipts—with the exception of a few which were signed by H. H. Harjes or by Mr. James or Mr. Laurence as Treasurer of the Church—were signed, "G. Schlatter, Ass't Treasurer"; and as I write that name a wave of gratitude comes over me, for Georges Schlatter meant everything to me in all this financial work which came upon me, both for the Church and for Charity and Relief. Georges Schlatter was a man of Swiss birth; he was one of the tellers of the Morgan Bank, and while Mr. Harjes was the Treasurer of the Vestry, it was Mr. Schlatter who paid the bills and saw to the general financing. There was nothing too much for him to do for me. Every gift for the Church itself and every contribution for Relief or Charity which came to me passed through Mr. Schlatter's hands; every sum which I received for these purposes was paid over to him and by him deposited in the Bank to an account marked, "Special"; and all sums drawn from this account were drawn through his intermediary; and I owe his name and his memory this tribute of gratitude.

The possibility of my personally remaining in Paris to carry on the work became a serious financial issue for me. The necessary expenses of the Rector's office were large, too large for me to cover from any income which I had. In this emergency there were generous friends who came to the rescue; and chief among them were Mr. Edward Tuck, the Duchesse de Talleyrand, Mr. James Stillman, Sr. and Mrs. Herman Frasch. But for them this story would not be written.

The enforced absence of Mr. Ashman, while a prisoner in Hamburg in the early weeks of the War, created a need for immediate additional help in the Church, and for a time this need was wonderfully met by the presence in Paris of the Bishop of Tennessee. Bishop Gailor had known me from my student days when I was in his classes at Sewanee. He was in Paris with his family when War broke out, and he found all of a sudden that the little hotel where he had been staying was about to close its doors, and they were setting out his trunks for removal. The Rectory most gladly opened its doors to him, and the Bishop, and Mrs. Gailor, their two daughters, and Frank Hoyt Gailor their son were all our guests for a time. The Bishop said to me, "You can leave the routine work at the Church all to me; I will take the daily services, see all callers, and I will preach for you on

Sundays." And for the three weeks of their stay with us the Bishop was a strong right arm of power, both physical and spiritual. In an article which he wrote for publication, the Bishop said: "I am profoundly impressed with the variety of the Rector's responsibilities here, and with the exceptional wisdom and ability of his administration; in this time of peril he has given the Church a recognised leadership in the work of relief and comfort. Two of the leading business men said to me the other day, 'We find your Rector a tower of strength to us all. It takes high courage for there are no available funds, and the Church's charities and its offices of mercy are freely distributed to all classes of society and to all who have need.' "

On the morning of the third of August Bishop Gailor and Gabriel and I took Alexis, our maitre d'hôtel, to the train on his way to his Depot. Alexis belonged to the famous Regiment of the *Cent-Trente-Trois;* and I think that his going was harder for him—apart from his parting with Louise—because of his thought of who would look after us, and who would do his work. I had told him that as long as we remained we would look after his wife, and that he could feel that Louise was in our care; that he would be my representative at the Front for I would pay Louise his regular wage monthly and that she could keep it for him until he returned. When we came opposite to the Railway Station Gabriel stopped the car; we all got out and stood for a brief moment of parting; then Alexis kneeled on the pavement and Bishop Gailor laid his hand on Alexis' head in blessing; then the Bishop took off his hat and waving it called out to the watching crowd, *"Vive la France!"* then we went back again to our waiting tasks. After some days longer the Bishop and his family left for their homeward voyage; and from London the Bishop wrote: "We shall never forget the gracious hospitality of the Rectory, and the loving kindness of Mrs. Watson and yourself; it will be a lasting and a gracious memory."

Alexis was gone fourteen months before he had his first *permission,* and could come back to the house for a rest. I asked him what was the first duty of his day as a soldier, and he said: "It is I, Monsieur, who serve the men with their *petit verre.*" (Each soldier has the right to a little glass of brandy the first thing in the morning.) "Well, you are in luck," I said. "How is that, Monsieur?" "Why, you have the bottle." "But Monsieur knows that I never touch the stuff." "But what do you do with your portion? you do not throw it on the ground, I suppose." "No, Monsieur, I friction my hair with it." And it was perfectly evident that something had worked a change: when Alexis went to the Front he had very little hair on top; and now a fine soft black thatch was making its appearance. As soon as Alexis had been to a Turkish bath after arriving from the Front, he came to see me in the salon. I told him that I had made arrangements that he should have the day off with the car, and that Gabriel would take him and Louise wherever they might want to go. "But, Monsieur, I do not want to go anywhere, I want to stay here. And, Monsieur, just look at the stair carpet; it is getting all worn on the edges of the stair treads with the way Monsieur has soldiers and everybody coming up here to see him; I must change that carpet before I go back. And then my silverware; has Monsieur looked at it? It too needs my care; I must polish it." Again I urged that he take a rest and go out; but he insisted that the streets of Paris would be no treat to him; what would rest him most and help him best to put out of mind for a time what he had been through would be his familiar occupations, the little duties of the household—*mon service, Monsieur.* I love to think of it and of the fine spirit of the man. It is so characteristic of the Frenchman; his joy in little things, and his love of doing them all well.

I had invited the Minister of War to dinner on one of the evenings while Alexis was at home, not knowing at all in advance that Alexis was coming; and I had told Louise to engage one of the concièrges of the neighbourhood to come in and help her with the table service at the dinner. Most of these neighbourhood concièrges were former butlers, who had graduated into that enviable position, the throne from which a concièrge rules both the *immeuble* and its *locataires.*

"Monsieur," said Alexis, "Louise tells me that you are having distinguished company to dinner, and that you have asked her to get *un maitre d'hôtel provisoire* to help her with the dinner service; but, Monsieur, now that I am here, it will be permitted me to take my service as usual, will it not?" Again I suggested that he take a rest from work while he was *en permission;* but his reply was that his work in the house would be the best kind of rest for him; and then he added: "If it is on account of my moustache that Monsieur hesitates to let me serve the dinner, I will cut it off, if Monsieur wishes."—He had grown a moustache while he was at the Front, and he had the well trained butler's thought that it was not good form for a butler to wear a moustache; in fact, he said to me at one time, "Monsieur, is it possible that the War has done this to us, that the butlers in Paris wear moustaches?" It goes without saying that Alexis served the dinner, and several times I caught a look in the eye of the Minister of War which seemed to ask why this man was not at the Front; so I told Monsieur Painlevé, who Alexis was, and what was the number of his Regiment, and how long he had been at the Front before he had his first *permission.* The Minister then asked if I would have Alexis come in at the close of the dinner and serve him personally a liqueur; and when this was done he stood and put his arm about Alexis' shoulders and with a winning smile like that of a frank good-natured boy, which was one of Paul Painlevé's greatest charms, he asked us all to lift our glasses to this *enfant de France;* then he lifted his own glass to his lips and then passed it to Alexis that he might share it with him. It is that *camaraderie* between the great and the small, which is the bond of union between Frenchmen, especially in the Army. There, your Captain may have been your coiffeur in civil life, but you are both *enfants de la Patrie;* and the Colonel will take the arm of a *petit poilu* (a private soldier in the ranks) and will call him *mon vieux;* and there will be neither breach of etiquette nor any risk to the formality of other occasions in his doing so. Alexis was mobilised on the 3rd of August, 1914; he received the *Croix de Guerre* in September, 1915, his Citation reading: "a man of rare courage; as Agent de Liaison on the 12th and 13th of September despite an intense bombardment and violent machine-gun fire he traversed the barrage three times to carry important messages"; and his Colonel certifies also that "the Lions of the 133rd" won the right to wear the *fourragère* by their heroism. When we came home from France, Alexis was still with the Army of Occupation in the North along the Belgian Line, and from there he wrote: "If Monsieur and Madame can find a place for Louise and me in their country, we will go to the ends of the earth to serve them."

While I feel an especial tenderness for Alexis and Louise, that does not mean that I appreciate any the less the personal devotion of Gabriel and Madeleine and Corinne and Jean and Narcisse. And I write their names here in this page as a part of the Roll of Honour of those who served the American Church so well, and in doing so served France also.

In time it seemed necessary for reasons of forced economy to close the Choir School and to send the boys back to their homes in England. That move hurt us deeply for it meant the disbanding of a wonderfully fine choir and one which was peculiarly fitted to the architectural meaning of the great church itself. With the sole exception of the choir in the Temple Church in London, I have never heard a church choir which was its equal. There were two occasions when the Choir did work which was memorable. One was the welcome which the boys gave to the King and Queen of England when they came to Paris to open an Exhibition of Textiles in the Pavillon Marsan in the Louvre. I had had a note from the Minister of Fine Arts, saying that they planned to have the British National Anthem sung as a welcome, just as the King and Queen came under the great arch which was the entrance to the Pavillon, but that the French pronunciation of "God Save the King" was an insurmountable barrier, so far as French singers were concerned; and would I come to the rescue of the Government and have our Choir Boys there to greet their Majesties royally and nationally. This was most gladly arranged; and after the entrance ceremony and the singing, the boys, with Mr. Ashman, came down to the farthest alcove in the Pavillon where I was waiting for them. When their Majesties reached the alcove on the opposite side from where we were standing, the Queen looked across and recognised the British look of the Eton jackets which the boys wore, with their bowler hats tucked under their arms; then she came straight across and asked me who the boys were. I told her that they were English boys from the Choir of our American Church in Paris, and that they were the ones who sang the welcome when their Majesties came in. Without further ceremony the Queen called to the King and asked him to come and see the English boys. There was but one comment from them both, which was that they thought that the exquisite music which they heard on entering was just one glorious mezzo voice. You could have knighted those boys and they would not have been happier than they were over the friendly courtesy of their Sovereigns; who had asked each boy individually what his name was, where in England he came from, and had a personal word for each one of them. British Royalty, as exemplified in King George and Queen Mary, is an admirable and lovable rulership, and "God Save Our Gracious King" is tribute which comes well from the hearts of their people.

Another time when the Choir Boys did lovely work was on Christmas Eve of 1917. The French Government had arranged a Ceremony of Gratitude at the Sorbonne, in recognition of the help which had come from abroad for the relief of the Orphans of the Great War, and our Choir was asked to take part, and the touching way in which they rendered with exquisite enunciation and musical feeling, *Ceux Qui pieusement Sont Morts Pour la Patrie,* left but few dry eyes in that great amphitheatre of the Sorbonne, which was packed with thousands of the people of the city, in those days when there was hardly a family which did not mourn some one of their own who had died at the Front.

This last remembrance means that the Choir Boys were back in Paris again. After the enemy retreat at the Marne and the dangers of the first wild rush on Paris was past, my good friend Mr. Edward Tuck, asked me if it would be possible to have the boys back at the Church again; and on my expressing an earnest wish that that might be brought about, he said that he would send a cheque each month to supply the difference between the cost of the Choir School and the indifferent mixed Choir which we had installed as a temporary measure. So the boys came back, and they stayed on until the increasing bombardments at night broke their nervous equilibrium down and sleep and digestion began to be affected; and then their parents urged their coming home. So back across the Channel they went again; and the doors of that fine school closed definitely. The records made by many of the boys of the Choir School are an honour and credit to the School's meaning and purpose. Many of the old boys are in positions of responsibility in England and in the Colonies; more than forty of them were in the Great War; one of them was on *The Black Prince* when she went down; one of them was killed at Ypres; and another of the boys, who was originally in the Merchant Marine on one of the Atlantic Transport ships which was converted into a cruiser for war service, had his ship torpedoed under him twice, and was in a third ship of this Line when she went on the rocks off the shores of Crete.

This is emphatically and purposedly not a War Book; and wherever in the book mention of the War is made, it is solely for the purpose of picturing individuals and happenings as the War revealed them. As to War itself I shall speak positively, and from the standpoint of one who was a participant as well as an onlooker. I saw it all in the very beginning, both in France and in England. I saw the utter and absolute unpreparedness of England, and I saw the peasants coming in from their fields in France, scythes on their shoulders, and wearing the old red trousers and the familiar *képi* of other days. Armaments and Preparedness did not cause the War. That nations so unprepared for war, as were France and England in 1914, should have purposely or willingly brought on that War is beyond any possibility of imagining; it was not armaments or preparedness, on the part of France or England, which did it. In any event armaments are not the inciting cause of strife: two boys may stand making faces at each other and shaking their fists at each other (the boys are the newspapers), but there will be no fighting until the first overt act of violence occurs. War is caused by the nation which strikes the first blow. And again Treaties of Peace have no influence in determining whether there shall be war or no. Never was there a treaty with terms more plainly defined than was the Treaty which guaranteed the Neutrality of Belgium and which was signed by all the Great Powers; but that Treaty went the way that all treaties will go IF a seeming military necessity calls for their violation.

I have no faith in the League of Nations, *as originally constituted,* as being essentially a Peace move; the very name League is a confession of its inherent weakness. A League is but another name for a Balance of Powers; and whenever any one nation or any group of nations in a League considers itself sufficiently strong or sufficiently justified to break the conventions of the League for purposes of its own, then those conventions will be broken; and the further weakness of the League is shown in this that in such a case there is no remedy which the League can apply except that of Force, either open force by arms, or disguised force in the form of a boycott, material or diplomatic. A *Family* of Nations I emphatically believe in, but I have no faith in Leagues. On the Fourth of July, 1915, in Paris, I made open appeal for a Family of Nations; for that is the divine ideal. I consider the League of Nations to be a worth-while experiment; another praiseworthy gesture was the Pact of Paris, so-called; but no League and no Pact nor any other Treaty agreement will ever prevent war, if war is in the hearts of peoples. Peace is not secured by treaties, nor is war caused by armaments. Peace is a matter of good will between nations; and disarmament is essentially and compellingly an economic question, whose ethical relation is secondary in result though primary in initial motive. Between the United States and Canada lies an undefended frontier; no treaty could make peace between our peoples more secure than it is; no armaments on either side would incite us to war one upon the other BECAUSE WE HAVE A WILL TO PEACE. I believe absolutely in Disarmament as an economic move, and one necessary to prevent and stop a wholly unproductive waste. I believe in the Pact of Paris and in every other like gesture of good will, as being a token of what we want to create in the hearts of human kind; but I consider the faith which is placed by many in such moves to be misplaced confidence.

XII

INDIVIDUALS AND EVENTS

FROM now on in my story, the War will be only a backdrop to throw in relief events of interest which I witnessed or people of note with whom I was associated.

Foremost the personalities who come into the picture is Myron T. Herrick who was our Ambassador to France in 1914. I count my intimate association with him as one of the great privileges of my life. Myron Herrick was more than a traditional holder of a diplomatic post by gift of Washington; he was essentially a statesman with a great vision, while being at the same time a diplomat of ready tact and remarkable wisdom. In the preface written by Raymond Poincaré, former President of France, to Colonel Bentley Mott's *Souvenirs de Myron T. Herrick,* Monsieur Poincaré says, *"Il n'était point diplomate de carrière . . . nous ne fussions pas nous-même habitués à placer nos banquiers dans nos ambassades."* (He was not a traditional diplomat . . . we ourselves have never been accustomed to the placing of bankers in our ambassadorial posts.) This comment brings into sharp relief the difference between the diplomacy of politics and the diplomacy of a statesman like Myron Herrick. There is an English *bon mot,* which says that, "an ambassador is a man who lives abroad for the good of his Country," which is paralleled by another, which said of a noted Prime Minister, "He lies in Westminster living, that he may lie in Westminster dead"; all of which means that Diplomacy in Europe is a game in which the play of the game transcends any normal moralities of life in the ordinary. The game played by the Chanceries is a contest of wits played all apart from the living life of peoples; the winning of the game is the sole end in view, and it is being played on a field delimited by inherited traditions and shadowed by monarchical *pré-occupations.* For the training of adepts in this game Schools of Diplomacy are maintained, and *la Carrière* (diplomacy) as a profession becomes the sole aim of those who enter on this pursuit, to such an extent that its followers live in a world of thought often isolated from the vital course of human movements or of normal human ethics; history and precedent are the bases of the rules of the game, and success in the battles of the Chanceries is the objective and the spur to action. Now the background of American political thinking is totally different both in principle and in fact from that of Europe, whose diplomatic mentality is either subtly or openly compelled by the inherited traditions of struggling and closely contacted States which once were monarchies; and the same may be said of the contrast between our American ideals of procedure and those of other nations non-European, which have an inherited monarchial tradition, with specific reference to all nations of Latin origin. Monsieur Poincaré's comment on the placing of "bankers" in ambassadorial posts is illustrative of this. The *banquier* is thought of in the old world as a man with a delimited mind; a man with a closed vision; it is the same picture as is often drawn of what we call "the small town banker—a village product sitting behind a closed wicket to keep the people from getting any of the bank's money; whereas a real banker is a man whose vision takes in the constructive needs of the life of community or nation, and who sees the bank and its trust of money as but a means to that end and its accomplishment. Myron Herrick was a *banquier* of this large-visioned mould, and he carried into his work as an American Ambassador that same dominating thought of the largest interests of humanity as his inspiration. Always courteously complaisant toward the traditions of diplomatic procedure, he used diplomatic methods as necessary tools of the trade while quietly but persistently refusing to be shackled by them. An instance in point is an occasion when a secretary urged him most strongly to submit a certain issue to the State Department before making his decision known, on the ground that his acting on his own initiative would be out of line with customary procedure. It was the statesman in Myron Herrick which replied, "Your comment is perfectly to the point, but I have already acted." There is a world of difference between a statesman and an international politician; and Myron Herrick was a Statesman; and so was Morrow, and so was Dawes, and so was Mellon: "bankers" all of them, but men of large vision, whose reality often found itself in collision with the artificialities of the Foreign Offices abroad.

Among the letters which I received from Mr. Herrick are these:

"Paris, April 15, 1913

"Just a line to tell you that I think the Memorial Service for Mr. Morgan was the most impressive of any that I have ever attended. Your remarks were exceptionally good and appropriate. I should very much like to have you send me a copy of them before Friday, that I may send them to Mrs. Morgan."

"Paris, May 19, 1913

"This extract from Colonel Satterlee's letter I am sure will interest you: 'I read to Mrs. Satterlee and her sister Mrs. Hamilton the remarks made by the Rev. Dr. Watson at the Memorial Service, and we all think they are very appropriate and dignified. More than that they are very eloquent. His English is really very beautiful. I am having copies made for Mrs. Morgan and the rest of the family.' "

"Paris, December 28, 1913

"It has been a great comfort to both Mrs. Herrick and myself to have you and Dr. Watson here. . . . I am sure that Dr. Watson does not in the least comprehend the big place that he is making for himself here. It is a great thing to be *good* and *true*, but when those admirable qualities are accompanied by unusual intellectual power, it is then that one becomes effective; and Dr. Watson has won such a place here that his good work will continue effective long after he has gone." (To Mrs. Watson.)

In the spring before Mr. Herrick's official return to Paris on his second tour of duty as Ambassador, I wrote him of my great satisfaction on hearing of it, and of my feeling that he could do in Europe at that time that which no one else could accomplish; and I had this reply:

"Beau Manor Farm, May 27, 1921

"I was both touched and charmed by your fine letter; touched by your evidence of real friendship, and charmed because you have been around the world, and comprehend its need in this hour of peril.

"I want you to have a larger place in the re-organisation. Let the meadow-moles make their little channels as they always have done without the knowledge of the sunshine which can be seen if only they were to push up their noses: but they always will and always must push on making the straight and narrow groove just beneath the light of day.

"How I would like to make you Bishop-at-large, and then let you select the place to preach the Gospel that the re-organised world will demand in order to mobilise the spiritual force that won the War, . . . for preserving for mankind that which was so dearly won.

"I'd like to have your reaction on Harvey's speech. Think you that America has no sentiment, no idealism?

"I sail July 7th, and shall be obliged to make several speeches in the two or three months after my arrival—

One, American Chamber of Commerce
One, Laying of Cornerstone at Rheims
One, Cornerstone at Louvain
One, Dedication Statue Aisne to Marne
One, Dedication Statue presented American Legion by Lorraine. . . .

"I wonder would I be asking too much to have you suggest a few paragraphs for each occasion: I am driven to the limit with work, and shall be until I sail: . . . your letter is so fine and so broad that it will help me in my work just ahead. I must stop now, but hope that you will help me start.

"I am really enlisting, because I have the hope that I can aid countries that I love, and thus help the entire situation."

"Paris, July 10th, 1924

"It was with the greatest pleasure that I received your most interesting letter, for it awakened some of the dearest memories of my life; in which we were associated.

"I shall be delighted to have the copy of Mrs. Watson's latest book which you are so kind as to send me, and I will transmit the copy to Monsieur Poincaré with much pleasure.

"I am enclosing, confidentially, a copy of a cable which I sent to the Department with regard to Monsieur Herriot a week before his election as Prime Minister. I thought this would interest you as the prophecy, thus far does not seem to have been a bad one.

"I am deeply interested in what you say about making Santa Barbara your home. It is my hope that I may also own a home there later; and it would be most agreeable if in the afternoon of our rather eventful lives we might have the pleasure of 'sitting in the shade' together from time to time.

"With affectionate regards to both you and Mrs. Watson, I am as always,

"Your faithful and devoted friend,
"Myron T. Herrick."

Mr. Herrick knew of my admiration for Monsieur Herriot, and also of Monsieur Herriot's courtesies to me; and what he had to say about Monsieur Herriot's fine idealism as a man with relation to his work as Prime Minister might well be repeated at this later date.

On October 17, 1924 Mr. Herrick made a most telling speech on affairs in Europe at a luncheon which was tendered him by The National Security League in New York, a speech which was replete with a vision of broadest statesmanship; and on reading the printed quotations from this speech I wrote him my most enthusiastic comments. He replied to my letter, as follows:

"Cleveland, November 4th, 1924

"I have just received your letter in time to thank you for your kind expressions on my views in relation to the day's affairs, and I am greatly impressed by the ideas which you express. The speech in question was gotten up very hastily, but since you approve of my ideas I am enclosing herewith a copy for you.

"I am sailing on the 12th.

"With affectionate regards to you both, I am as always,

"Your devoted and admiring friend,
"Myron T. Herrick."

My association with Mr. Herrick in all that pertained to my work in the Paris Church was a source of constant strength to me; he was always ready to listen to my problems, and always sure to give wise counsel. All that an Ambassador could do for the work of the Church he did, as well as all that he could do for me personally. It has been said that one attentive and sympathetic hearer is audience enough for any speaker; and I remember with sincere appreciation how the presence of Mr. Herrick in the Ambassador's seat on a Sunday morning always gave me a feeling of uplift.

The two outstanding movements of American Relief during the War were both of them due to Mr. Herrick's initiative; they were the American Relief Clearing House, and the American Ambulance Hospital, which latter was the parent of the American Ambulance Field Service. The word *ambulance* in French has as its primary meaning a military hospital, a mobile unit of hospitalisation which follows the army; and from that came the secondary use of the word as meaning any military hospital, as also the vehicles used for the transport of the wounded. The permanent American Hospital at Neuilly-sur-Seine with which so many Americans are gratefully familiar, with its fine buildings and beautiful gardens, was chartered by the French Government in 1906; and in 1913 it was chartered by Act of Congress of the United States. In August 1914 there was opened that great American gift to France which was announced as, "A large Hospital for the wounded of every nation"; it was the work of Ambassador Herrick at its start, and the first gifts toward it were made by Mrs. Herrick. At the outset it was under the aegis of the Board of Governors of The American Hospital, and the direct control of the Hospital was placed by them in the hands of a governing body to be known as The Ambulance Committee. This Board of Management as originally named were H. H. Harjes, L. V. Benet, Chas. Carroll, F. W. Monahan, L. V. Twyeffort, and S. N. Watson; and by the mutual agreement of all concerned I was named Chairman of the Ambulance Committee. The French Government assigned for the use of this Hospital the buildings of the Lycée Pasteur at Neuilly; and amongst my papers (now in the Watson Collection at Stanford University) there is a copy of the official acceptance of the Hospital by the Government addressed to me as Chairman of the Ambulance

Committee, and signed by General Février as head of the Service de Santé. The vast buildings of the Lycée Pasteur which surrounded a hollow square were unfinished at the time that we took them over; there were no doors, windows, plumbing, baths, heating, electricity; there were no kitchens, and the floors in general were covered with plaster; such was the condition of the plant on the day that Charlie Carroll and I went there to locate the offices and to plan for the beginning of administrative work. In a wonderfully brief time we completed the buildings for hospital use, and installed our first floor beds. One evening shortly after this was accomplished there came a telephone call; "message of immediate importance from the Chef du Service de Santé for Monsieur le Président of the American Ambulance." "Yes, mon Général."—"You will please make ready to receive 300 wounded to-night."—"But, mon Général, we have but 100 beds as yet." And the reply came back, short and sharp—"Beds! who is talking about beds? it is wounded soldiers I am talking about; if you have not beds put them on straw on the floor." Here was an old campaigner talking, who knew all about war and wounded men who had been lying by the roadside for days, possibly, with no change in their first-aid dressings. (We saw plenty of that in the days which followed.) And we, only civilians as yet with our American ideas of what a Hospital should be, and of sanitary measures in times of peace, we were what the British would have called "a mite fussy" in those days; yet I believe that it was the result of just that attitude that the Ambulance Américaine de Neuilly became a model among the hospitals of the War, so that men and even generals asked to be sent there. I remember leaving the Hospital one evening after a meeting of the Executive Committee, to go home to dinner, when up drove a little red fiacre and out stepped a British General, very exhausted, his right arm in a sling, but still full of decision and pluck. I greeted him, and he asked if the Hospital could take him in and care for him. I told him that he was most welcome, and that if he had let us know we would have been glad to send an ambulance for him to any part of the Front. He said that they had started to evacuate him to some hospital or other, but that he wanted to come to the American Ambulance, so he took matters in his own hands and made his way by train and came to Paris, and then knowing that he needed a barber, he stopped on the way from the Gare to the Hospital and had a shave and a haircut. Think of the nerve of the man—compound comminuted fracture, and stopping at the barber's!

As for General Février's 300 wounded which we were asked to get ready for, we did just that, we got in the 300 beds that night; but they sent us only 80 wounded.

The method of administration of the Ambulance services for the wounded was through a Medical and Surgical Committee, of which I, being a graduate in medicine was a member. The Ambulance Committee met once each day to consider and authorise all new business and was represented during the intervals between sessions of the administrative body by one of its members who was designated Officer of the Day. I was also, by courtesy of the Board of Governors of The American Hospital, made Liaison Officer between the Board and the Ambulance Committee.

It was also my duty to arrange for religious services for the wounded, and for the last rites for the men *in extremis.* We were most fortunate in being able to get the Abbé Klein as Chaplain for the Catholics. He was a man of generous culture, and an author of note; he had travelled in the United States, and his books, *In the Land of the Strenuous Life,* and, *An American Student in France* (this latter book being dedicated "To My Young Friends in Harvard and in the University of Chicago") are interesting reading for one who wishes an intimate insight into the French point of view. I have two of Abbé Klein's books written in French and both of them autographed by him with a personal dedication. One of them is *La Guerre vue d'une Ambulance,* and the other is *Les Douleurs qui espèrent.* In this latter there is inserted a card from Monsieur l'Abbé Klein which reads, "With his thanks and his most sincere congratulations on this Article so generous and so admirably Christian"; he is here referring to *La Transfiguration des Nations,* which I published in *La Revue Hebdomadaire* in its issue of March 24, 1917. For the British wounded we were most glad to obtain the co-operation of the Rev. Mr. Blunt, who was Chaplain of the British Embassy Church; and for the French Protestants and all others who were not Catholics or Church of England we secured the ministrations of the Rev. Merle d'Aubigné, who was Pastor of the French Protestant Church in Neuilly and who spoke English perfectly. With this provision made I thought that our religious needs were fully cared for; but religious needs are more difficult to satisfy than any other. One day on arriving at the Ambulance, I was told that call had been left at the office saying that a soldier in Ward —, Second Floor, desired to speak to the Chairman; and on going up to see him, I found that it was the consolations of "releegion" that he was lacking; he said that he was a Scotchman, and that there was no Scottish minister there as Chaplain. Had he seen Mr. Blunt, who was a fine Britisher? Yes, Mr. Blunt had been to see him, and Mr. Blunt was "a varra nice mon," but he was Church of England. Well, the French Protestant Minister, Monsieur d'Aubigné, was a Presbyterian, and he spoke English. Yes, but he was not Scotch. Scotland was as important as any other part of the Empire, and the Scotch wounded should be permitted to see a "meenister" of their own. Explanations as to the difficulty of arranging additional military passes for entry and exit did not suffice; so, after considerable effort it was arranged that the minister of the Scottish Church in the Rue Bayard would come to the Hospital for periodic visits. After his first ministration there I was told that there was another call to go and see the Scotch soldier again, and I went expecting a visit of smiles and congratulations. Nothing of the kind. The "meenister" of the Scotch Church had been to see him, and he was a "varra nice mon"; but he wouldn't do; he was "Estaiblished," and our soldier was "Wee Free." I gave it up in regret, for short of importing a chaplain from across the Channel there seemed no way of meeting Wee Free's needs for a "meenister o' his ain."

We had arranged that the fine large Chemical Lecture

Room of the Lycée should be the Chapel, and it was admirably adapted for the purpose. At one end of the room everything had been arranged so that Abbé Klein might say Mass regularly; and at the other end of the Chapel the British Embassy Chaplain had prepared an Altar for the rites of the Church of England. At a very early hour the Abbé would say Mass; and an hour later Chaplain Blunt would celebrate the Holy Communion; it was *l'union sacrée* in its most perfect form. On the 24th of September, 1914 the Archbishop of Paris, Cardinal Amette, came to visit the Hospital, and it was my privilege to welcome him and to go with him to inspect the buildings. I had never met His Eminence before, and he asked me where I was stationed in Paris; and when I told him that I was Rector of the American Church in the Avenue de l'Alma, he said, "Ah, I know it well, the Church with the most beautiful spire in all our City." When we came to the Chapel and its two Altars were called to his notice he expressed himself as deeply touched; and then he knelt for devotions at the footpace of each of the two Altars, and gave his benediction to the place. He was in every way a great man, was Cardinal Amette. I have a most gracious letter from him expressing his thanks for American help which had been given him for the maintenance of a farm, to which he sent boys from the streets that they might learn the beginnings of agriculture.

Many were the visitors who came to the Lycée Pasteur to see what an American Hospital for the Wounded was like, and greeting them was always one of the bright spots in my Hospital days. I remember especially the Prince of Monaco, the Duc and the Duchesse de Vendôme, the Duc and the Duchesse de Talleyrand, General Février, l'Amiral Bienaimé, the Marquis de Valtierra Ambassador of Spain, Herr Vedel Jarlsberg Minister of Norway, and Messrs. Aristide Briand, Denys-Cochin, and Charles Benoist.

On the 7th of September 1914 President Poincaré came to the Hospital, accompanied by General Galliéni and Monsieur Viviani. They were received by Ambassador Herrick and the members of the Ambulance Committee; and it was touching to witness the pride which Mr. Herrick took in the work of his compatriots in caring for the wounded of the Allies. The Hospital was very near his heart, and once when its existence seemed momentarily to be imperilled, he took immediate and vigorous action in its defence. I knew nothing of the inner side of the story till years afterward, though I had an active part in the events as they happened. It came about in this way. The Chairman received from the Chief of Orderlies each morning on his arriving at the Hospital a list of the wounded men taken in during the night, classified by nationality. On the 14th of September 1914 I received the following report:

British	25
French	42
Algerian, Tunisian, Moroccan	21
GERMAN	2

That that report meant trouble for some one was the first thought which came to me when I saw it. It was an Auxiliary and not a Military Hospital that we were conducting, and we had had our orders from Headquarters of the Service de Santé that all enemy wounded must be sent to Val de Grâce Hospital; the reason being that though they were wounded men they were none the less prisoners of war to be kept under guard, for which we had no provision; and furthermore they must be kept isolated in order to prevent their communicating with any possible spies and thus revealing the location of troops. The head orderly, on being questioned as to the admission of these German wounded to our Hospital instead of sending them on to Val de Grâce, said that he had had no choice in the matter; that the men were brought in during the night by Mr. Robert Bacon, former Ambassador to France, who was one of the most devoted workers in and for the Hospital; that the Military Attaché of the Embassy came with him; and that the men were brought in the Ambassador's car. Here was a dilemma for the Chairman of the Committee to meet; so I went off post haste to the Chancery in the Rue de Chaillot to find out from the Ambassador just what the situation really was. I found Mr. Herrick most welcoming, as usual, but unusually non-communicative. I explained to him that the Ambulance Committee would be held directly liable for this violation of the orders received from the Service de Santé, and that whatever may have been the accident which brought German wounded to the Ambulance, it was my duty to call his attention to the matter at once. The Ambassador seemed to me to be secretly amused at something, instead of being disturbed as I was over what I had to report to him. He said that I need give the matter no further concern; that he would take all responsibility for the occurrence and for its possible consequences. And when I endeavoured to impress upon him the need that we should be assured by him that we were free to refuse any such unwanted guests, even if they were brought by his Military Aide, he simply put his arm about my shoulders and with that engaging smile of his which was enough to disarm all objection, he eased me out into the reception room and welcomed the incomer who was there waiting for him; and all that I could do was to drive back to the Ambulance and assure my colleagues that the Ambassador had assured me that the incident under discussion would be cared for by him. Those German boys had all the luck; they developed measles, of a very German type, and had to be finely cared for in our isolation ward instead of being packed off to Val de Grâce where they belonged.

In 1919 Mr. Herrick took luncheon with me at a cottage which I had rented in Montecito, on what are now the Biltmore grounds and which were then known as Montecito Park. After luncheon he said to me, "Doctor, I never treated you badly but once, did I? but I did so once, I know, and now that the story can be told I want you to know all about it. The Secretary of State, Mr. Bryan, was much exercised about that Ambulance Hospital of ours at Neuilly; he held that our maintaining and supporting it was an non-neutral act; that inasmuch as it was called a Military Branch of the American Hospital of Paris which latter was chartered by Congress, it was virtually an interference in the War by a recognised creation of the Congress of the United States; that it was therefore within the power of Congress to revoke the Charter of the American Hospital, and that then the Hospital would have to close. Whether this was merely a threat, or whether it had some reality behind it I did not know, but I made up my mind to take no chances on what the demonstrations of an ultra-neutral Administration might result in, so I said to my Military Attaché, 'I would like to have a couple of wounded German soldiers in our Ambulance at Neuilly; can it be managed?' 'Most easily,' he said, 'they are lying all along the road but a few miles away.' 'Good,' I said, 'when it is dark, take my car and go out and get two of them and take them to the Ambulance.' Robert Bacon was in the office at the time, and he said, 'I'll go with him.' They got their prisoners and brought them to the Ambulance and safely installed them there as you know; and when their report came to me that the deed of darkness had been done, I cabled the State Department, "Hospital neutral; have German wounded." That was real diplomacy.

One of the problems of the Ambulance was the care which had to be given to the soldiers who came originally from the French Colonies in Africa. France was a great success at colonisation, and many of the Algerians and the Soudanese and the Moroccans consider themselves as much a part of the Republic as if they dwelt on the mainland, *Moi, français*—, they would say. Now with some of these soldier folk the food to be served them was a matter of great importance, for to send up bacon on the tray of a Mohammedan who might eat it not knowing till later what it was would be a sacrilegious performance, and might well lead to a riot. *Le petit déjeuner* (early morning breakfast) at the Ambulance, as elsewhere in France, consisted of cafe-au-lait with bread and butter; and we found that some of our guests from Africa, not knowing what the little pats of butter were, put the butter in the coffee and drank it up. Comfort-bags had been sent to the Ambulance by rememberful ladies, and each bag had in it beside other articles a toothbrush and a tube of toothpaste—these bags were hung on the foot of each bed; and some of our African guests after rummaging in the bags, found the tubes of toothpaste, opened them, smelled them, liked the perfume, and so proceeded to eat up the nice tasting pink contents with great gusto. (I wonder if I might not sell that story to the publicity department of C ————'s Toothpaste. "Is eaten and relished by Hospital patients: not a Pain in a Tubefull"). One day word came that a patient in Ward— had bitten a nurse; the man was a Soudanese and his name was Mouca. He had a badly fractured leg when he was brought in to the Hospital the evening before and could not be given the ritual bath, but was given temporary treatment by the interne on duty and by the orderly of the ward. In the morning the nurses came in to care for him, and when one of them started to turn down the sheet to change his dressings he resisted vigorously, and when she persisted he seized her arm and bit her. In order to quiet him, another Soudanese was brought in from a nearby ward and was given a bed beside Mouca. Maciga was his name, and Maciga spoke some French as well as some English, and he told his fellow-countryman all about the Hospital, and soon Mouca was like a well behaved baby. Then Maciga explained to the ward attendants what the trouble with Mouca was. It appeared that Mouca came from a tribe where no woman could give a man the personal attentions which bathing and dressing involved without losing caste. Mouca felt that it was a degradation for him to submit to such woman-handlings; so he bit; but within ten days he was sitting up in bed and knitting a scarf.

One more Hospital story is worth telling; it is the story of *Fend-l'air*. At the Gare d'Aubervilliers was a cantine where devoted women were on duty day and night, to give food and drink to soldiers passing through on the trains. Word was brought to the Ambulance Committee in session one evening that the Directrice of this Cantine d'Abervilliers desired to speak to some one in authority; and that she had a dog with her. This was her story—One evening a train of wounded men rolled in and out of a car, and they took a *sergent de Zouaves* who was followed by a dog, a beautiful red and white English setter. As the ambulance men lifted the soldier into one of the service cars attached to the American Ambulance, the soldier called out, "My dog! my dog! I want my dog with me." "But, my boy, we cannot take a dog to the Hospital in the ambulance"; but the soldier kept saying, "My dog! I want my dog!" "Go to the Hospital in peace, boy," said the Directrice of the Cantine; "I will take care of your dog, and when you are well you shall have him again." "Thank you, Madame; only be sure to tie him up securely or he will break away and follow the car." So they put a chain on his collar and kept him well tied; but the dog would not eat or drink; real tears kept running down his muzzle. Finally the ladies at the cantine decided to appeal to the authorities at the Ambulance to let the dog at least see his master. We put the case to the surgeon in charge; and he had the dog taken to the disinfecting room and thoroughly cared for there; then he was taken up to the big ward where his master lay. At the door of the ward the dog stood for a moment as if undecided, his beautiful muzzle pointing up and sniffing the air; then he gave one bound and was running down the ward to the cot where his master lay, and the Zouave and *Fend-l'air* mingled tears of joy. Every morning after that *Fend-l'air* was admitted to the ward, and after he had exchanged ceremonial greetings with his wounded friend, the dog would lie down quietly at the foot of the cot, content so long as he could watch the soldier with his eyes.

This is "The Story of the Dog," as the Zouave told it: "It was in Algeria that I first knew the dog; he belonged to an English gentleman who came to us for the shooting; and when he came over in 1914 he brought his hunting-dog with him, and I used to go with them as a guide. The dog could run so fast that we called him *Fend-l'air,* which means, 'Cleave-the-Air.' Then came the Call to Arms, and my English gentleman had to leave at once for England; and as there was no possibility of taking a dog with him at such a time, he told me to keep the dog for him, and that he would join us for the next season's shooting. Then it was I who must obey the Call to Arms; and when we started on our March to the Sea *Fend-l'air* followed beside the Company.

When we embarked for the Mediterranean crossing I bribed a coal-passer to hide the dog in the Coal-storage; and when we again started for the Front *Fend-l'air* went with me, and was my constant companion in the trenches. It was on the 12th of December that a *marmite*—a big black shell (the French called them *marmites* because of their resemblance to the soup-kettles which are on the hearth in every little home in the country)—burst just in front of the trench where I was standing and killed all my comrades and threw me to the ground unconscious, wounded, and almost buried me in the earth which came from the crumbled walls of the shelter. Alone and helpless, I would have given up but for *Fend-l'air,* who licked my face, scratched the dirt away from me, brought me back to myself again, and helped to recover my morale which was as badly shattered as were my legs; then we painfully crawled back to where some stretcher-bearers picked me up, and finally I came here to this Hospital; so it is no wonder that *Fend-l'air* and I are devoted to each other."

As Chairman of the Ambulance Committee an extraordinary duty devolved on me from the outset, viz., that of providing the current cash for the daily expenses of the Hospital. Large sums had been subscribed in Paris, and larger sums were coming over from America; and the Morgan Bank had been made the Depository. The Bank was accountable for the monies entrusted to it; the daily expenses had to be met day by day. Business was done by cheque in France in ordinary times only in a very limited degree. (Many a time I have seen the head usher of a business establishment come to the Bank and draw 50,000 or 60,000 francs in paper money, stuff the bills in his wallet which he carried by a strap slung over his shoulder, and walk out unconcernedly into the street.) But in time of War, when no one knew where he or any one else might be the next day cash was the only possible payment; as a consequence the money to pay the Hospital expenses in cash had to be provided. But the Bank was not covered by the legal status of the Ambulance Committee; we were not incorporated; the money was subscribed specifically for the American Ambulance and not for the American Hospital of Paris. And here again the diplomacy of the Ambassador came into play, and his influence with the Bank opened up a way for us to pay our bills. The Morgan Bank had decided that while the monies subscribed and deposited with them could not be paid to the Ambulance Committee as not being a person in Law, they would pay such monies as were necessary for the maintenance of the Hospital to me personally, on my personal signature. As a result of this decision, I drew from the Bank in the Boulevard Haussmann, and personally signed for varying sums in the months of August, September, October, and November—the largest amount at any one time being 35,000 francs, and the smallest amount being 10,000 francs. I then put the money in bank notes of varying sizes in my pocket, walked out of the Bank, got in my car, and took the money out to Neuilly, by way of the Porte Maillot through all the crowd which gathered about the Gate in those days, some coming, others going, and all of them delayed and milling about because of the winding way one had to go. Trenches were dug across the street on either side of the Gate and Zouaves were in the trenches; trees were felled across the road with the ends of their branches sharpened to make wooden chevaux-de-frise—and there were steel chevaux-de-frise also; and one had to twist and turn one's car this way and that to make one's way past them and through them. All this because it was by way of the Avenue de la Grande Armee that a rush on Paris would come if it were made. Then there was the Octroi at the Gate which one had to stop for; and when I reached the Ambulance I turned over my pocketfull of money to an unbonded clerk in the Ambulance Office; and was I glad to be rid of it?

For what a crowd, what a mixture of human elements, foam and dregs, one passed through at the *Sortie* of the Porte Maillot in those days—people of all sorts and descriptions, good, bad, and otherwise! Strange sights I saw after the order had been given that all the villages and farms within the radius of the ring-forts about Paris must be evacuated and that all their inhabitants must take refuge inside the Fortifications: men, women, children, horses, donkeys, pigs, cows, and goats; and most pitiful sight of all, the little carts on which and in which the people had jumbled all their movable possessions. One day I saw a donkey-cart coming in, and on top of the load was a feather-bed, and from under the bed the head of the pig was poking out, and on the bed was sitting the grandmother—a little old woman holding in her arms the precious clock and candlesticks; she did not need to read Daudet's *La Pendule de Bougival;* she had a keen memory of her own of the clocks which went across the Rhine in 1870. As to all the money which I convoyed past the Porte Maillot, and as to my personal responsibility for the same, it weighed little on my mind in those days; I was covered, in a way, by the authorisation of Mr. Herrick; and then, more than that, I had in mind a comment which Robert Bacon once made in talking to me of another matter in connection with the Ambulance: "This is not business that we are engaged in; this is War; and war-risks do not follow ordinary rules." However, for the consolation of my "heirs and assigns" I want to note here that after the Ambulance was duly and legally authorised to transact business on its own account and my functions as purveyor of the daily cash had terminated, I obtained from the Morgan Bank a statement of the sums which had passed through my hands in this way, the total sum from August 19 to November 23 being four hundred and fifty thousand francs; and I had this sum verified by the Disbursing Officer at the office of the Ambulance and duly receipted for by him; further recognition of the correctness of the statement being given by the signature of the Teller at the Bank through whom the business was transacted.

I have most vivid and touching memories of some of our volunteer workers at the Ambulance in those days. I think especially of Mrs. W. K. Vanderbilt, Mrs. George Munroe, Mrs. Charles Carroll, Miss Florence Matthews, Mrs. Audenried, and Miss Grace Gassette. Especial mention must be made of two of the men who gave their lives to the service; Vally Blacque and Abe Ranney. Mr. Blacque was a striking figure of a man; a grandson of Dr. Valentine Mott. When the first funeral procession left the Ambulance bearing the body of a soldier who had been the first one within our walls to answer to the last roll call, it was Vally Blacque who took the place of chief mourner and who walked bareheaded just behind the *fourgon* which bore the body through the streets, till the *Cimitière de Neuilly* was reached; for the soldier had no family who could be present, and Vally Blacque took the place of the family. I have a picture of him as he walked behind the hearse; he is carrying a French flag and also the Stars and Stripes; and he said afterward, "I was so proud to be chief mourner at the funeral of that brave boy." Mr. Blacque simply gave his life away until there was no more to give; he passed away on the 9th of January.

Abram Nave Ranney was another "of ours," who freely offered his life in those first days of the great Struggle. His mother and his sisters were among our best of friends; and when he came and said, "Dr. Watson, what can you give me to do?" it was at a moment when he was greatly needed. He became Chief of Orderlies at the Ambulance; it was his hard task to meet the convoys of wounded at the door of the Hospital; to register the names of the men; to receipt for their valuables and papers; to arrange everything for that necessary first bath: it was a herculean task, and it was bravely done. For four months he kept at it; then, at Mr. Herricks' request he placed his knowledge of German at the disposal of the Embassy and took over the work of inspecting the Camps for German Prisoners of War: it was a short mission, for in January he too passed through the door to the beyond.

And I remember Mr. Stuart and Mr. La Chaise, and their ceaseless devotion to our work for the wounded.

Among American doctors who came over to help in this work, I recall especially Dr. Walton Martin and Dr. Richard Derby. And that recollection takes me in memory to a day when they came together to take déjeuner with us at Avenue de l'Alma; it was a day when they had been present at a ceremony at the Mairie which moved them very deeply; and the talk at the table that day revealed the fineness of the spiritual nature of those two men, and made me grateful again for the share which I had in the medical profession, and for the quality of the men whom America was sending over.

Our Service of Motor Ambulances which was attached to the Hospital kept on growing in size and in importance, until it outgrew its original intent and became The Field Service of the American Ambulance. Where so many men were so devoted and so efficient, it is possible only to make especial mention of a few who were the leaders in that work. Our former Ambassador Mr. Robert Bacon, first in every move to help France, was chief official sponsor for the Service; and to Mr. and Mrs. Bacon the Field Service owed a large share of its possibilities of usefulness. Colonel A. Piatt Andrew organised and directed this Field Service with the French Armies, which ultimately consisted of forty-four Ambulance and Transport Sections; and the devotion of the men in the Service to Colonel Andrew knew no bounds. Among the drivers whom we knew best were Lovering Hill, Charlie Baird, Frank Gailor, and Robert Redfield. The Story of the Field Service is all in print, and the copy which I have bears Lovering Hill's signature written in it on the day before he started for Salonica in command of an Ambulance Section. In the Section with him went Charlie Baird: they were under Orders "For the West Coast." This book bears also the signature of Elizabeth D. Hall; she was the mother of Richard Hall who was killed while on his Ambulance on Christmas Eve of 1915; she had come to France and had taken work in our American Ambulance at Neuilly. On May 27, 1917 an interesting ceremony took place in the fine old house at 21 Rue Raynouard which had become the Headquarters of the Field Service. Our Ouvroir at 23 Avenue de l'Alma outfitted this house with eight dozen sheets, eight dozen pillow slips, eight dozen towels, and other like supplies that were needed. On the day of the ceremony at the house, I said some words of benediction over a number of fine American flags which had been given by Mr. Clarence Mackay, and which were presented to the Field Service by our devoted friend Charles Carroll. It had been suggested that at this benediction I read some poem in French which was a tribute to the American Flag; but not finding any which seemed suitable I took my old friend Harry Bennett's "The Flag is Passing By," and put it into French verse. It reads:

LE DRAPEAU PASSE

Chapeaux bas!
Tout le long de la route s'avancent
Son de trompettes, roulement de tambours;
Eclat de couleurs sous l'azur;
Chapeaux bas!
Le drapeau passe!

Bleu et Blanc et Rouge il brille
Au-dessus des rangs serres et bardes de fer;
Chapeaux bas!
Devant nos yeux les Couleurs flottent:
Mais, est-ce le Drapeau seul qui passe?

Combats sur terre, combats sur mer,
Combats féroces, combats suprèmes;
Luttes soutenues pour saver l'Etat;
Etapes tuantes; navires sombrantes;
Hourras de victoire poussés des levres des mourants.

Jours de paix, jours d'abondance;
Croissance rapide d'un peuple fort;
Liberté, Egalité, Fraternité pour tous;
Dignité, Honneur et Révérence:
Chapeaux bas!
C'est ça qui passe!

Emblème d'une nation grande et rude,
Forte contre tout agresseur;
Gloire, Fiérté d'un peuple, Honneur;
C'est le Drapeau qui les maintient.

Chapeaux bas!
Tout le long de la route s'avancent
Son de trompettes, roulement de tambours,

Des coeurs loyaux battent en cadence:
Chapeaux bas!
Le drapeau passe! *

By March 4, 1915, the Hospital had more than a million of francs on deposit in the Bank; more than 500 beds had been installed; the Department of Facial Reparation with Doctor Hayes and Doctor Koenig as specialists was already making history. By that time I was convinced that my services would be equally effective for France, if I were to take some other lines of work which pressed for acceptance, and as a consequence I resigned at that time the position of Chairman of the Ambulance Committee. Captain Frank Mason was the next Chairman of the Ambulance; and that

* Hats off!
Along the street there comes
A blare of bugles, a ruffle of drums,
A flash of colour beneath the sky;
Hats off!
The flag is passing by.
Blue and crimson and white it shines
Over the steel-tipped ordered lines.

Hats off!
The colours before us fly:
But more than the colours are passing by.

Sea-fights and land-fights, grim and great,
Fought to make and to save the State:
Weary marches and sinking ships;
Cheers of victory on dying lips:

Days of plenty and years of peace;
March of a strong land's swift increase;
Equal justice, right and law,
Stately honour and reverend awe;

Sign of a nation great and strong,
To ward her people from foreign wrong;
Pride and glory and honour, all
Live in the colours, to stand or fall.

Hats off!
Along the street there comes
A blare of bugles, a ruffle of drums;
And loyal hearts are beating high:
Hats off!
The flag is passing by!

tour of duty was the last one which that brave old soldier took on; in a few months he laid down the load, and passed from Death into Life; and a few weeks later Mrs. Mason followed him.

While no words of appreciation would be too great in speaking of what the other members of the Committee did to carry on this work—Carroll, Monahan, Twyeffort especially—a place of first importance should be given in this record to Lawrence V. Benet. The Ambulance owed more for its continued efficiency, and the wounded men owed more for the effectiveness of the care rendered them, to Mr. Benet than to any other one man. He had had the experience of a military and a naval environment; he had long training as an executive; he was tireless in work, and unhesitating in his turn of command; and his devotion to the wounded soldier as well as to the Ambulance as a piece of war machinery has won him well merited recognition.

It was my custom on leaving the meetings of the Ambulance Committee to drive to the Chancery in the Rue de Chaillot and there to meet the Ambassador and to give him the news of the day from my end of the line, and to get his advice on the problems which faced me from time to time. Frequently he would propose that we walk together to the Embassy in the Rue François Premier; in which case Gabriel would follow along with the car at a discreet distance, and would then pick me up and take me back home for dinner. In those walks and talks I came to know the heart of this great man, whom a Paris newspaper one day in an Editorial Heading called, *"le Bon Géant"*—(the Good Giant). What his presence in the beleaguered city, his walking the streets of Paris unattended, his brave front and cheery greetings—what all these meant in the way of sustaining the morale of the populace, no words can tell. And when his official tour of duty came to an end and he was recalled from Paris by the exigencies of politics, it was a very hard day for us all. On Thanksgiving Day, 1914, the Ambassador and Mrs. Herrick gathered what they graciously called their official family for dinner at the Embassy; there was the same table, and the same men-servants, wearing a livery which I was next to see when from the Ouvroir at the Church we sent those good coats, minus insignia, to the Hospital at the Casino of La Baule in Brittany. On the following evening we were welcomed to a dinner given by Mr. and Mrs. Robert Woods Bliss at their house; and in the cold grey dawn of the following morning we were on the Quai d'Orsay Station platform, not to say "Good-Bye" but to breathe a lonesome *au revoir,* and to say a "God Bless You." Outstanding among us all were two of our French Wounded, officers of the French Army from the Ambulance; one of them had lost his right arm, and on the other arm he carried a sheaf of roses tied about with the *Bleu, Blanc, Rouge* of France; these he brought to Mrs. Herrick saying, "Madame, I regret that I have but one arm with which to serve you; but all France serves you with her heart."

It was a fortunate thing for France and for us all that Robert Woods Bliss was still at the Chancery of the American Embassy; it was due to him most of all that in the change of Ambassadors there was no break in continuity in French and American relations, and no loss of touch with our American representatives in France on the part of the rest of us. Mr. Bliss was heartily conversant with the ways, the people, and the language of France. I use the word "*heartily*" advisedly; for while Embassy and Consulate were distinctly officially of the politics of the White House and of the Cabinet in Washington, official politics have no control over sentiments and feelings, and both Mr. and Mrs. Bliss were friends of France, and were sympathetic and understanding friends of all of us, who were openly in revolt against a Governmental order which required American citizens to be "neutral in thought and word and deed." If Mr. Herrick had not been with us at the outset, I do not see that the Washington Government could have refrained from taking unpleasant notice of the "thoughts and words and deeds" of some of us; and when Mr. Herrick left us it was a great satisfaction to know that we had a wise and constant friend in Robert Bliss. He carried heavy loads of work, yet he was never too busy to listen and to counsel. His knowledge of the French language, and his familiarity with diplomatic procedure made everything possible for the new Ambassador, Mr. Sharp, who came to France without European or diplomatic experience, at a time when the complications of an Ambassadorial post were most difficult. Mr. Sharp had my fullest sympathy from the outset. He came to France a political appointee, in accord with the Wilson-Bryan philosophy personally and also as a matter of political expediency. He knew the earnest desire of both France and Great Britain that Mr. Herrick be permitted to remain at the Paris post—a desire so plainly expressed that it could hardly be interpreted otherwise than as a wish that he, Mr. Sharp, should not come, at least at that time. Yet, in the light of his relations with the Washington Government, he could not do otherwise than take up the duties of the post which he had assumed. Mr. Sharp was a quiet, unassuming man; friendly and welcoming to all offers of co-operation. That he was not a type of man so perfectly fitted to understand and to be loved by the French people, as was Myron Herrick, cannot be reasonably held against him. In succeeding to an Ambassadorship wherein the love and devotion of a people like the French had been so fully acquired by his predecessor—tributes from the heart of a people which could not be transferred from one man to another like Letters Credential—Mr. Sharp could not but feel the enforced strain of the situation. For all of us Americans abroad loved Myron Herrick also; we hated to see him go; we did not believe that his going was good statecraft nor good international diplomacy. It was rather the effect of routine political procedure, which in "piping times of peace" might sometimes work well, or again might work badly; but which in times of stress was utterly inadequate and hurtful. While I do not believe in the *carrière* method of conducting the business of diplomatic representation; while I believe that under ordinary circumstances a five year period is long enough for an American diplomatic representative—except in the consular service—to be absent from America; and while my opinion is that a longer absence tends to alienate a diplomat's thinking from American thought, and to make of him, perforce, something of a representative of the country to which he is accredited, and that to the detriment of his clearness of vision —(I have lived years abroad, and I speak *en connaissance de cause*); while I am convinced that our representatives in diplomatic service would feel a helpful renewal of spirit from being dipped anew in the vital waters of the natal spring; yet —and it is a very important "yet"—there are men in our Service abroad who are large enough and positive enough in character to invalidate this rule of general procedure, and who could wisely and with great profit to their country remain Ambassadors or Ministers in foreign posts, more especially so if they were changed occasionally from post to post, and from the habitudes of one environment to those of another. And furthermore I am certain that in a time of emergency, when one of our diplomatic representatives has shown his power to be of great service to America as well to the country to which he is our Ambassador or Minister, and when nothing real is to be gained for that international exchange of thought which is the purpose of a diplomatic service by a change of representatives, to insist at such a time on recalling a Minister or an Ambassador and sending another simply to comply with a noxious internal political barter, or to follow an antiquated rule of procedure which would be more honoured in the breach than in the observance, is to kotow to official etiquette to the derogation of American common sense.

The living in a land and amongst people whose habits and methods of thought are divergent from our own, and to whom we must always remain *étrangers* (foreigners), as in the case of all Latin or Oriental peoples, is a wonderful school in political geography. Americans are quick to learn; and Mr. Sharp had every desire to learn that he might be of better service; furthermore he had had long experience as a practical politician, and as a consequence, little by little his new shoes became easier, and he began to find his work a pleasure. It was a hard pull for him when Washington became non-neutral overnight, as it were; because that about-face of the home Government meant the necessity on his part of a complete reversal of attitude and of verbal expression; and Mr. Sharp was so frankly honest a man and so thoroughly consistent in his logical procedure, that the change from a Neutral coat yesterday to an Allied one to-day, simply because his Chief had decided that the Right and the Wrong had been reversed, must have been a real shock to his thoroughgoing consistency. Yet I think that he was relieved to escape from what must have been for him an anomalous situation; he had grown to love France; and at heart he was glad to be with us in her service; and we were glad to have him as an Ally.

I impersonated Mr. Sharp once, unwittingly, to my great amusement. The Conseil Municipal of Paris were giving a great reception, a *champagne d'honneur,* at the Hôtel de Ville (City Hall), in celebration of our new made alliance. First there was a ceremony and speeches at the foot of the Statue in the Place d'Iéna. Pol Plançon sang the Marseilles; the song was better than the speeches, and even the speeches were good. Monsieur Laurent, Préfet de Police of Paris, had sent me each year a *coupe-file.* Now a *coupe-file* is the most valuable document which you can have in the City; it is a little card which says to Police and to Military that you and your car have "right of way." So if you want to get in or out of a theatre or other public place, you do not have to wait until all the other cars in line have had their say, you can just drive up and show your Police Pass, and "but in" or "but-out" as you may please; and when you come to a street which is blocked by a line of Military because the King of Borrio-Boola-Gha is expected to ride down the Avenue shortly, you simply drive up to the line of soldiers and when the nearest specimen of officialdom rushes at you and says, "And How?", you simply wave your little card at him and say, "I am Monsieur Coupe-File, Thank You. Did you say something?", and then go on your way rejoicing. Well, on reaching the Place d'Iéna I said to Gabriel: "Take the coupe-file, and drive through the lines, and get our car as close as you can to that big grey limousine over there; that is the car of the Military and Naval Attachés of the American Embassy. Mr. Carroll and I will get out here and will stand here by the Statue till the shouting is over, and then we will come and get in the car, and as soon as the procession starts you are to follow that grey car as closely as you can, for the Ambassador's cars will have right of way; and so we will get through the jam and to the Hôtel de Ville without waiting all afternoon." All of which happened almost as indicated, but not exactly so. The fact was that the Ambassador's own car was missing, at the time when he was to leave the Embassy to come down to the speech-making at the Statue, and he had come down in a small car. After the ceremony he hurried back to the Embassy to find his own car there, and so missed being in the parade, with the result that when the procession got under way, it was Gabriel and Charlie Carroll and I who were following close after the big grey official car; and we all done up in frock coats and top hats, and the car with little American Colours on the headlights. It was thus that we came down the Cours la Reine, down the Rue de Rivoli, on to the Hôtel de Ville, passing through a narrow lane about thirty feet wide, with thousands and thousands of people on either side. As we passed some one cried, *Vive l'Ambassadeur Américain! Vive l'Amérique! Vive les Etats Unis!;* and then flowers were thrown at us; and Charlie said to me: "The Ambassador's car isn't here; they take us for the Ambassador. We'll have to make good!" So we began to respond, and to wave hands, and to wave top hats, and to smile benignantly like good Allies; and so we made our triumphal procession to the *Champagne d'Honneur.* On our return from the Hôtel de Ville it was the same thing. My big Renault car had been noted as the car which the crowd greeted before, and now the *populo* was more enthusiastic than before; it was *Vive les Etats Unis! Vive l'Ambassadeur Américain! Vive son Excellence!* All over again. As we moved more slowly on account of the crowd closing in more and more, a *jolie petite gamine,* a little street girl of about twelve years old, jumped on the running-board of the car and put her cunning little tousled head in the open window of the car, and called to Gabriel, *"C'est bien l'Ambassadeur Américain que vous avez la, n'est-ce-pas? Eh bien, n'allez pas si vite; laisse' le voir au moins"*—(It's really the American Ambassador that you have there, isn't it? Well, don't go so fast then; let's have a look at him at least.)

At that reception at the Hôtel de Ville, I had an experience which gave me a thrill; it was meeting a man whom I had heard had been badly wounded, possibly crippled, possibly blinded, the *Conseiller Municipal* of the Hopital St. Louis Quarter, Monsieur André Payer. I had come to know him in this way: one day Louise, my *bonne* at the Rectory announced a lady who had asked to see me; the lady came up; she was as pretty as a picture, and as gay as you like, or as I like. She told me that her husband was the representative in the Municipal Council of that poorest of Quarters, the Hopital St. Louis Quarter of the City; that he was at the Front, and that she wanted to try and take his place in caring for the poor of the District; and could American aid be had? I was glad to help; and thus began an acquaintance which I valued. One day I saw in the *Echo de Paris* an account of the severe wounding of the Counsellor Payer; that he had been brought back from the Front, legs shattered with shrapnel, and the sight of one eye gone. He could have taken advantage of his privilege as Municipal Counsellor, but he would not, and insisted on taking his place with the Regiment of Heavy Artillery to which he was attached. Now that he was back from the Front, and wanting to get word of him, I asked Monsieur Ambroise-Rendu, also a member of the Council, what had been heard from our friend André Payer. "Why," he said, "here he is himself!"; and turning around I found myself warmly greeted *à la Française* by a tall man in a blue *imperméable,* bandage over one eye, walking with two canes. After the first word of greeting, I asked him if he and Madame Payer would come to déjeuner or to dinner with us at any time that they were free. His response was that he would be more than glad to do so, but that he was only back from the Front for two days, and that kinfolk of both their families had claimed all his free time. "But," I said, "you are not going back in this condition!" "I must," he said, "there are so few of us who are experienced in handling those heavy guns, and I am needed." "But, your eye, and your legs," I said. He answered, "As for the eye, the doctors tell me that it will come out all right in time; I can see some grey light with it; but the other eye is perfect; and as for the legs, there are a few pieces of bone to come out still, but there is an Ambulance a few miles back of the Front where I can have that attended to." All my pride of service was gone, as I realised what André Payer was doing. In my *Livre d'Or de la Legion d' Honneur,* there is a tribute signed André Payer, which I put in the front rank of those which I value most. It reads:

"La vraie recompense aux actions humaines est celle du droit accompli. Mais quand l'insigne d'honneur est souhaité et voulu par un peuple comme le peuple français pour un homme d'action qui a fait ses preuves de solidarisme et d'abnégation,—quand cette marque exprime les sentiments d'estime d'une nation qui se connait en altruisme, elle s'accorde avec la sanction de la conscience; l'une embellit l'autre. Le bénéficiaire de cette marque est un élu auquel on a le droit de rendre l'hommage du coeur.

André Payer; Conseiller Municipal de Paris;
S. Lt. au 114 Reg't d'Artillérie Lourde" *

André Payer has written, so I have read, a volume of verse called *Poèmes de l'Enfance.* I have tried to get a copy of it but have failed: I trust that he may read this tribute of mine to our friendship, and that he will send me the book.

Here again is an instance of what I have so often noted in connection with men in public life in France. André Payer, Lieutenant of Heavy Artillery, Municipal Counsellor, soldier, politician, writes *Poems of Childhood.* So many Frenchmen in public life are scholars, artists, lovers of the beautiful in some of its many forms, scientists, literary men of note. Their patriotism is a wholly different sentiment

* "The real reward for our deeds is the consciousness of having done what was right. But when the badge of Houour is so decreed and willed by a people like the people of France to a man whose acts have borne witness to his singleness of purpose and his unselfishness,—when this badge expresses the deep feelings of a nation which knows what unselfishness means, it but adds to the approval of the conscience; the one glorifies the other.

The recipient of such a mark of esteem is one of the elect to whom it is right that we render the homage of our hearts."

from that of most of us; their love of France is akin to their love of beauty, just as the peasant's love of France is part of his love for his little corner of her earth which is his France to him. My best of friends in France, Monsieur Manuel Beaudouin, Premier Président de la Cour de Cassation, could write an entire orchestral score of his own composition. Monsieur Raymond Poincaré was not only a jurist of note but was also a writer and commentator of the first rank. Monsieur Herriot, Sénateur, Président du Conseil, Maire de Lyon, is a scholar, a literary man, an educator, and some of his books—I am thinking of one which describes the beauties of the forests of Normandy—are literary treasures. Monsieur Barthou was one of France's most cultivated writers. Monsieur Paul Painlevé, former Président du Conseil, War Minister, Minister of Public Instruction, was an authority in the field of Mathematics, Vice-President of the Academy of Sciences, and Professor of Mathematics in the University of Lille. The way in which the really great men in France give themselves to the service of *la Patrie* strikes one hard, when once one comes to know France intimately; and they do it out of *altruisme.* As André Payer wrote for me of France, it is *une nation qui s'y connait en altruisme.* And when I say that "there's nothing in it" for them, I think of my close association with Emile Ogier who was my Chief at the Ministry of the Interior. I said to him once: "In America a man of your ability would be getting $25,000. a year and more as the head of some great business"; with a quizzical smile he looked at me and said, "Where would he be the gainer?" He was a typical Frenchman, and the Frenchman does not expatriate himself easily; he is not at home where France is not; to him France is life, her *joie de vivre,* her homely pleasures; not forgetting his bottle of *vin rouge,* and the *fromage* which is his especial delectation. When the War broke on us, my friend the Directeur du Contrôle du Ministère de l'Intérieur was about to write a book on *The Romance of Cheese.* Once when I was about to start in the car for a long journey, he wrote out for me *un itinéraire gastronomique.* Here it is; it is probably as valuable to-day as the day it was written; try it on your next motor-trip in France:

ORLEANS (Loiret) Restaurant Jeanne d'Arc
ST. AVERTIN (près Tours) Restaurant Fouqueux (ne pas y aller le dimanche)
CHABLIS (Yonne) Hôtel de l'Etoile
SAULIEU (Côte d'Or) Hôtel Picard
TOURNUS (Saone-et-Loire) Hôtel du Sauvage (voir à l'Hopital le Musée Greuze)
SAINT VALLIER (Drôme) Hôtel Terminus
GRENOBLE Restaurant du Vautour
LA SAINTE-BAUME (Var), par St-Zacharie Hôtel fondé par le Pére Lacordaire; très bon.

As the War grew longer, and the fish grew scarcer, and the meat grew "worse-r," we came to depend more and more on cheese. One day Monsieur Ogier said to me, "How are you getting on for food?" "Well enough," I told him, "except for bread and cheese, (the bread was a fright at times). "What cheese do you use?" he said. I told him that we used Gruyère often in place of meat or fish; but that our Crémérie could no longer supply us with it. "No," he said, "Gruyère has all gone to the Front; it must be ripened many months, and the supply of old Gruyère in the cellars is all exhausted, and there are no longer any men left in the Gruyère country to make any more; it will be some time before we get any good Gruyère again." The French have a saying that Gruyère is not good until "it has tears in its eyes"; the holes in the cheese they call "eyes," and the little drop of whey which collects in them during the ripening process is called a "tear." "But," said my friend, "have you tried Cantal? It is much like Gruyère in taste, and it is ripened in the same way." So we took to Cantal, and found it very good; but after a time Cantal joined its comrade Gruyère at the Front; and I said to Monsieur Ogier one day: "Well, Cantal is gone now." "At your Crémérie, perhaps," he said, "but I will tell you where to get it. Over near Père La Chaise there is a street called Rue de la Roquette, it is the Auvergnat Quarter; and as long as Paris stands the Auvergnat will have his cheese. Go over there, but stop your car at the foot of the street; don't go in yourself, let Gabriel do it; and he will find good Crémeries there where Cantal will always be on sale." And so it was as long as we were in Paris.

The Auvergnats are a peculiar people, a race apart as it were, with absolutely fixed ways and habits; and Cantal was one of them. They are mostly *porteurs d'eau* (water carriers), or *marchands de ferrailles* (junk dealers). In the old Quarters of Paris I have often heard them calling, *A l'eau! Oh! Oh! Oh! A l'eau!*; and if you want to read an amusing picture in words of the Auvergnat and his character, get Eugéne Labiche's *Le Misanthrope et l'Auvergnat.* As for his cheese and how it is made, and also his country and its people, read *Un Pâtre du Cantal,* published by the Librarie Delagrave in Paris; it is a gem of a book.

My more intimate relations with Emile Ogier came about through The American Relief Clearing House, which was another child of Mr. Herrick's clear thinking. Speaking at the Sorbonne on November 3, 1916, Monsieur Millérand, at one time President of the French Republic, said, "The group that best synthetises America's charitable work, and constitutes its very nucleus is The American Relief Clearing House." Two facts moved Mr. Herrick to put this organisation in motion. One was that quantities of supplies of all kinds had begun to arrive, much of it addressed to The American Embassy, and the Embassy was in no position, either practically or diplomatically to enter directly into the work of Relief. The other fact was what the *New York Herald* humorously called "too much Committee." Committees of all kinds were being created both in Paris and in America, and as the French Government stood ready to provide transportation and Free Entry of Relief Supplies, it was evident that there must be some centralised responsibility both for rights of transportation and for authority to distribute. So in November, 1914 there was a meeting called at the Embassy, Rue François Premier, and at that meeting Mr. Herrick outlined his proposition. Order must be developed out of the hit-and-miss methods of shipping supplies; all Relief Organisations must have a central Bureau of receipt and issue; public confidence must be protected by assurance that gifts sent were duly received and rightly placed; the French Government must be aided by an American Committee which would control distribution, and must be helped by the stablishing of one centralised authority in Paris which should be the agency for the regularising of free transportation and Free Entry; otherwise chaos would inevitably ensue. The outcome of this meeting was what was called "The Clearing House," which had its offices at the former American Embassy in the Rue François Premier, a building which was generously placed at the disposal of the organisation by its owner, the Comte de Ganay. Mr. Herman Harjes was made President of the Clearing House; and the work which he did was an essential factor in the success of the move. I was made a member of the Board of Directors, as also of the Executive Committee; I was the Chairman of the Relief Committee, afterward called the Distribution Committee; I was a member of the Publicity Committee. And the interests of the Clearing House in all that pertained to the War Orphans Relief was entrusted to Charles Carroll and myself; together we made what the Clearing House records call, "a most comprehensive investigation of welfare work for War Orphans, which resulted in a report which was a monument of conscientious research, and which was of immense value to the Clearing House." In the preparation of this report the aid given us by Premier President Baudouin was invaluable and essential.

At the daily meetings of the Distribution Committee, on whom lay the responsibility for the allotment of monies and of supplies, and at which I presided, there was presented a detailed inventory of supplies and of funds in hand for distribution. Order was then taken for meeting all needs which seemed immediate and that supplies sufficient were on hand; all demands not presenting sufficient data were referred to the Investigating Committee; and needs which presented special problems were brought before the daily meeting of the Board. Co-operating with the Clearing House there was a French Committee with Monsieur Gabriel Hanotaux as

President; a Russian Committee with Monsieur Iswolsky as President, who was represented by Monsieur Sevastopoulo; a Belgian Committee with Monsieur Carton de Wiart as President; an Italian Committee with le Marquis Salvago Raggi as President; and a Roumanian Committee with Monsieur Lahovary as President. The War Relief Clearing House of New York, with Mr. Barton Hepburn as President, functioned as the American Relief Centre, with an Executive Committee composed of Messrs. Andrews, Baylies, Coffin, Greenough, Slade, Taft, Bangs, Preston, Vanderbilt, and others. This Committee centralised all Relief contributions whether in cash or in kind; arranged for warehousing and shipping; and provided the American publicity necessary to the carrying on of so vast a work. When I look at the figures of the completed Report I am simply amazed at what we did, and did without at all realising the enormous enterprise in which we were engaged. It was like all war, you fight in the smoke of the battle, often not seeing either objective or results; and it is only the far-off look which gives any idea of what the reality was. The Final Statement of the work of the Clearing House gives these tremendous figures, showing what our work of voluntary Relief for the Allies meant:

Distributed in Cash	$1,691,247
Valuation of goods in kind distributed ...	8,507,554

or a total of more than Ten Millions of Dollars.

The question of the control of Distribution, to which I have referred as being one of the co-ordinate functions of the Clearing House, was a most important one for reasons which I will now give. It is difficult for an American to realise that relief, gifts, help could not be distributed freely in any country wherever need might be by any generous minded person, as and where he might see fit. It is beyond our point of view that either the United States Government or the State of California should interpose any let or hindrance to any generous minded Frenchman, who might come here in some time of need and start to give away $100,000. to Americans. We would let him do it in his own sweet way, and our only concern would be that we might get our share; but it is not so simple as this in France, and such a procedure in France in time of war is wholly impossible. France is a densely populated country; 40,000,000 people occupying a territory less in area than the State of Texas; you could put Texas down on France and if you were to trim the edges, as the cook used to trim the pie-crust round the dish in which she had made ready an apple pie, you would have enough of Texas left over to make a Holland, a Belgium, and a Denmark. The government of France is a popular government extremely sensitive to the will of the people, and the people are swayed by sympathies and by feelings which are deep and intense. There is no political indifferentism in France; feelings run high, and the Right and the Left, the Catholic and the non-Catholic, the Royalist and the Socialist, the advocates of the Public Schools and their opponents, the party of the Maire and the party of the Curé are always pulling for the advantage. Now take a Commune where the elections are in doubt and let a foreigner come in introduced by some person of prominence in the neighbourhood, so that this person could say, "It was I who got him to give you that Fcs. 40,000," and "pop" would go the ballots in his direction. The situation in the Parlement is so delicately balanced, in view of the fact that it is possible to "interpellate" the Cabinet on any question which may be brought up, and if enough popular feeling can be roused the Government might be defeated on a "Question of Confidence" at any time and this bring about a change of Ministries. It is easy for any one who knows anything of European politics to see, that foreigners, running around the country, giving away goods and money indiscriminately as good natured Americans, knowing nothing of what are the very political necessities of the State and certain to be influenced by social or religious trends, would be simply like small boys playing with fire works on a haystack.

To meet this situation and to exercise this necessary Control of Distribution, the *Comité Central Français des Secours Américains* named a special Commission which was known as the *Sous-Commission de Secours aux Civils,* which met every Thursday morning at the office of the *Directeur du Contrôle du Ministère de l'Intérieur.* This Commission was composed of Monsieur Emile Ogier, the Directeur du Contrôle at the Ministry of the Interior, who was the Chairman of the Commission; Monsieur le Premier Président Baudouin, (Premier Président de la Cour de Cassation means Chief Justice of the Supreme Court, as nearly as the French term can be put into American terminology); Monsieur Roman of the Court of Claims; Monsieur Jaray; Charles Carroll, and myself, (we two to represent specifically American interests). Our first principle of action in directing civilian relief was to help France to be herself. A word is due here as to the personality of Emile Ogier, who was a great Frenchman and a most admirable man. For many years the relief work of the interior government of France had passed under his supervision; later on he became Minister of the Devastated Regions; and when he passed away France lost one of her most devoted public servants. The Distribution of Relief in War time often meant of necessity "passes"; and that meant being accredited to the Ministry of War by some one in position of authority; for passes to go anywhere near the Front were necessarily sternly limited. Here are two examples in point. A Committee doing Relief work for whom the Clearing House had cleared quantities of supplies had received passes for two ladies who were driving a small truck to go near the Front for the purpose of distributing relief to persons in that region; the ladies missed their road and found themselves near a front-line military telephone station; they stopped to make enquiries and to get road directions; were offered hospitality and invited into the hut where telephone messages were constantly passing from one secteur of the Front to another; the officers in question were to blame, without doubt, but the ladies driving the truck were also actually violating Military Regulations in a serious manner; no harm came of it for the lady truck drivers were perfectly loyal; but the fact of their having been in that telephone hut was discovered and was reported to Headquarters, and as their passes came through their being vouched for by the Sous-Commission de Secours aux

Civils, the "chickens came home to roost," and we were "interpellated" on the matter of renewing the passes in question, as being the representatives of American Relief. Another case came up of a lady who was registered as an American and who had asked for passes for distribution of relief; the matter was referred to Mr. Carroll and myself as representing the Clearing House, and neither of us could give any further information than that we had heard her name. The Directeur rang for his *huissier* (ante-room officer, the source of our word "usher") who came in response to the call, dressed as usual in swallowtail coat and with a silver chain of office about his neck; the Directeur sent him for the records of *La Sureté* (Secret Police) covering this person's name: and in a few minutes we had the lady's complete history including the names of the persons present at her last dinner party and also the subjects of conversation at the table, and the names of all her associates in France and elsewhere in Europe.

I learned more of France and of her thinking in those Thursday morning meetings with Monsieur Baudouin and Monsieur Ogier than in all my other days beside. The whole situation of France and of the War was openly discussed; the meaning and the reasons of governmental actions was made clear; nothing was kept in the dark; Mr. Carroll and I might have been Frenchmen and things could not have been more open. In addition to this it was my custom to take Monsieur Baudouin in my car at the conclusion of our meetings at the Ministry of the Interior over to his office in the Palais de Justice, and on the way he would explain to me every thing which I did not at first grasp clearly. Further than that, he gave me lessons in French, in governmental French, in the French of politics which is an *argot* all by itself; so that in time when Frenchmen in the Government Offices talked of government as Frenchmen I came to know clearly what their real meaning was. One of the very interesting jobs which Civilian Relief had to face in War time was the receiving and the caring for and the re-routing of the *répatriés* (the French civilians who were either interned in Germany, or who were in the villages of France to the

North of the battle line). They came down through Switzerland, and the good Swiss fed them; then they were sent to Annemasse, which was the *gare de triage* (sorting station); and from there some were sent home; many of the women who needed medical or surgical treatment were sent to Evian; and many women and children who had need of care for nose, ears, or throat were sent to the Château de la Trombière where a Hospital Service had been arranged. This Hospital was in charge of an American, Doctor Wollison, who had been the leading American Dentist in Petrograd. When the crash in Russia came he made his escape to the Southward, having provided himself with plenty of money for travel, but he was obliged to come away without passport or papers as he had been refused access to the place where he kept them in security. He made his way into France by way of Switzerland; offered his services to the French Government, and was placed at the head of La Trombière as he had studied in France. Often, prior to the débâcle in Russia, I had received remittances from Dr. Wollison to be used for the relief of women and children in France.

One day he was announced at my house in Paris and was shown into my reception room. With him was a wonderfully beautiful girl, an Irish girl with eyes of pansy blue which looked, as the Irish say, as if they had been "rubbed in with a dirty finger": and he told me that this lovely girl was his head nurse at La Trombière, and that they wished to be married and wanted me to officiate. The Director of the Hospital and his wife had been compelled to leave on account of a death in the family and an inheritance which resulted; so that the management of the Hospital in everything would devolve on Dr. Wollison and this lady who was with him. It was essential that they return to the Hospital as soon as possible, and they had come to Paris thinking that the Doctor's civil status might in some way be regularised by the French Government and that he might get some papers to serve in lieu of Passport and Birth Certificate, and that thus a marriage might take place at the American Church, (inasmuch as he was an American citizen) without complying with the French Law which required the filing of papers, and a long wait. I had to explain to him, regretfully, that I was without authority to act in the matter, as in matters of marriage I was under French Law, and I advised him to see the Ministry of the Interior, inasmuch as he was working for them in civilian relief, and to ask them to arrange for him some kind of papers which would cover him legally so far as a marriage ceremony was concerned. I told him that I would go to the Ministry myself later in the morning, and that if he would come back to see me on the following day we would confer further on the subject. When I went to Monsieur Ogier's office at the Ministry of the Interior I found that he was fully *au courant* with the matter, and that he was most sympathetic in his attitude. This was his advice: "We, on the part of the Government, can do nothing at this present in the matter of furnishing the papers which Doctor Wollison needs, but if you will prepare documents and perform a ceremony which will be binding under American Law, you can sign such papers and the necessary Certificate, and declare the couple to be married, and we will see that you are not troubled about the matter." It is a contravention of French Law entailing a heavy penalty to participate in such a ceremony if a *Certificat de Mariage* from the *Maire* has not been duly produced in evidence of regularity. So the next morning when the Doctor and the Nurse returned, I had documents ready for them to sign in which they expressed their purpose to take each other as husband and wife; and declared themselves as bound each to the other; and further declared their intention to have a ceremony of marriage performed in due and legal form as soon as that might be possible. These documents were attested under oath; signed and witnessed in duplicate, and sealed with the seal of the Church. I then gave one to the lady and retained the duplicate in the safe in the sacristy; asked God's Blessing on them, and bid them go on their way rejoicing. I learned that later, when requisite papers had been procured, a ceremony of marriage was performed for them in Switzerland.

One day when Monsieur Ogier told me that he was going

to Annemasse that night to meet an expected *convoi* of 500 *répatriés,* I asked him what would give these poor folk the greatest comfort on arriving in France. He said that the possession of a little bit of French money would be a wonderful gift; so I went to the bank and with some discretionary funds at my disposal I got 500 bright new 50 centime silver pieces (about the size of our silver dime) and asked my friend to give one to each of the *répatriés* in the name of America. The pathos of the stories which he told me from time to time of the arrival in France of these longtime exiles from *La Patrie* was infinitely touching; and none more so than what he told me of the joy which he saw in their faces to hold in their hands a silver coin of France.

One question which demanded solution early in the story of Relief work was the need for artificial limbs, both legs and arms. A meeting was called of a special Committee at the house of Monsieur Gabriel Hanotaux the President of the French Section of the Clearing House at which Charles Carroll and I represented American interests. It was a memorable scene, that committee meeting. The brilliant background was Monsieur Hanotaux's library which was hung with old brocade, and there were books in bindings of blue and scarlet from floor to ceiling here and there. Those present were Monsieur Hanotaux who presided; Monseigneur Odelin *Vicaire Général* in his violet *soutane,* who represented the Cardinal; the Chief Justice of France, Monsieur Baudouin; the great surgeon, Doctor Tuffier; Monsieur Collin, the head of a firm of *bandagistes* (surgical instrument makers), who had occupied the same *locale* and who had handed on the business from father to son for more than six generations; a representative of another firm of surgical instrument makers; and Mr. Carroll and myself. The first question to consider was what was the pressing need and how to meet it. It was estimated that at that time France had need for a least 500 artificial legs a month, and that there was no possibility in sight of meeting the demand. France is a little country in extent of territory—that means few accidents in comparative number; then furthermore crippling accidents are not taken lightly in France; and while it is recognised that accidents are sometimes seemingly unavoidable, yet French opinion considers that usually in an accident some one is responsible, and that some one is held in law. As a consequence machines in factories are carefully safeguarded; and when railway accidents, which are uncommon, do occur, the blame is clearly fixed and the penalty is enforced; hence France had never had in recent times any need for large facilities for the production of artificial limbs. The makers of them who were present estimated that if all possible actual facilities were to be mobilised, the maximum output might be increased to 250 artificial legs a month. It was then asked of Monsieur Collin, "If the Government were to recall all your men from the Front, give you all the floor-space necessary, place at your disposal all material and money that you could use, would you undertake to supply the demand?" His reply was thoroughly characteristic: "I could not do it, for one principal reason; I would not put the name of 'Collin' on a factory product; each article which leaves my door is a piece of specialty work."

Monsieur Collin's reply was so typically French that I want to stress it as exemplifying the principal reason why France is not a commercial nation, and in my opinion, will never be one; and that reason is her fundamental individualism. To take a piece of work and to do it in the rough; then to go back and give it a touch here and a touch there; to adjust and perfect it until the workman is proud of what he is doing so that he feels it to be an expression of his own personality; and all that without counting time or labour or money—that is how the personality of a Frenchman expresses itself. Compare that way of life expression with the mass production process in which each man is but a part of a machine; doing his part but never knowing where what he does goes, and caring less; his chief interest being the least amount of time which he is obliged to give for the greatest amount of money. It is plain that this latter method lends itself to intensive output, and possibly to greater manufacuring profit; but, what does it do to the individual? what is its ultimate vital consequence for the people of whom the workman is a part? Back in the hills beyond Sceaux, on the outskirts of Paris, there was an artist living; he made porcelains and potteries; he lived there and worked there on his little property; he had his workrooms and his kilns there; his name was known to the world of Art, and his mark on a piece of clay or china was admitted evidence of artistic value. One day a visitor found him out in the sunshine beside his kiln; he was breaking to pieces with a hammer a whole benchfull of pieces of his work; most of them were beautiful, but had some slight defect; and when he was asked why he was destroying what he could sell easily at good prices, he replied that he would not let anything bear his name which was not the best that he could do. A representative of one of the great china works at Limoges came to see him one day and offered him a large salary, ten times what he could make financially by himself alone with his little kiln, if he would come to Limoges and take a position with them as chief designer; but he refused. His reply was, "Then Beauty as an essential would have passed beyond my reach."

The Latin's reaching out for Beauty is the keynote to his life; and this is most clearly in evidence amongst the people of France. From childhood the French people have been environed by evidences of beauty in colour and in design to such a degree, that a sense of being destined to be the guardian of Beauty has been ingrained in the national ideal. What the cruel attrition of the War will have done to that beauty concept of life's meaning; what the hard struggle for a place in the sun in an age whose method is that of competition and not of co-operation may ultimately do to French ideals, I do not know; I do not dare to foretell; but if I could be free to do it, and had the strength and the money to do it, I would most of all possible things in life like to make Myron Herrick's wish come true; "I would like to make you Bishop-at-large to preach the Gospel that the reorganised world will need to preserve for mankind that which was so dearly won." I would like to try to make the world see what a real Family of Nations, such as I pleaded for in 1915, would mean to the life of the world; I would like to show to peoples and their leaders that each nation has its own individual contribution to make to the life of the family, and that a garden is not at its best when it is all roses, nor yet when it is all cabbages; that life is a blend and that each separate part is needed to make up a perfect whole. Doubtless I would come to sudden end from heart-break; but it would be worth-while to risk it, if only one could voice life's Beauty story tellingly. Each nation has a character of its own; each nation has that in it which no other nation has; something in each case which the world of human life needs, and which can best be developed in the life of the nation to whom that gift is entrusted. And in the Heart of France there is the feeling that she cannot die, that she must not be crushed, because in her crushed heart there would be wounded to the death that passion for Beauty which she enshrines there, and which no other people senses like the French.

Let us halt our Pegasus now while it is still possible to stop him.

At the meeting to consider the needs of the *amputés,* which took place in Monsieur Hanotaux's library, we had reached an *impasse* when a gentleman arose whom none of us knew. We had all seen him come in ushered in by the maid, and we all supposed that it was some one who had been invited by one of the other principal participants in the gathering. In the best French which he could muster (and its lameness might possibly be reasonably excused in a meeting in the interests of the crippled) he said that he had heard that this meeting was to be called, and that he had thought that possibly he might be of use; he explained that he was from the United States; that he represented a firm in America which manufactured artificial limbs, and that his firm had cornered the available supply of seasoned willow wood; that he was ready to furnish all the apparatus for the amputated soldiers which France might need; that the artificial leg which he proposed was so good that you could do anything with it that you could do with an original member; that you could run, climb a ladder, skate with it. And in order to demonstrate his point, what did our Young America do but there and then in Monsieur Hanotaux's salon dispose of his trousers so that he could display in full the sample leg which he wore (he had been amputated below the knee), and then proceed to hop about the room on one foot so that the gentlemen present could see for themselves just what he was offering. It was amazing, but it was not good business in that assembly.

This matter of the *amputés* brings to mind Dr. Antony Rodiet, who was at the head of the Military Hospital at Dun-sur-Auron (Cher), whom I had come to know through having been in position to supply some of the needs of that Hospital where there were a large number of amputated men. One day at the meeting of the Distribution Committee of the Clearing House, the reading of the list of supplies on hand showed "two cases of single shoes, manufacturer's samples"; and some one said, "That's a lot of junk for the French Government to pay freight on." Our people in America did send over a lot of queer things at times; but this lot was not so bad. I said, "Would you like to turn those shoes over to me; I think that I can use them." The chorus was a unanimous, "Two Cases of unmatched single shoes to Dr. Watson at the Ouvroir Américain." I at once sent word to Dr. Rodiet asking him if he could use the shoes, and the answer was most enthusiastically in the affirmative. It was a great thing for him to have single shoes for his men, instead of having to buy a pair of shoes for a man with but one foot.

As I now look back upon it, my work for the Orphans of the War was the most interesting thing that I had the privilege of sharing. My connection with this work began in this way. I received a note one day from Monsieur Paul Painlevé, who was at the time Minister of Public Instruction, asking me if I could see him in his office on a matter of importance; and the matter of importance was *La Fraternité Franco-Américaine,* or, as it was known on this side, The Fatherless Children of France. The Minister proposed to me that I should become a member of the Executive Committee of *La Fraternité,* and that I should in time be made Vice-President and Chairman of the Executive Board. It was as a result of this conference at the Ministry of Public Instruction that I took up the direction of this big work; and in this matter Charles Carroll was again my colleague. There was always a President of this important distributing Agency of American Relief for the Orphans who was a Frenchman; and at the time that I took on the work the President was Monsieur Louis Liard, Vice-Rector of the Sorbonne, and the practical head of all the work of Education carried on by the French Government: but the presidency was official and involved little in the way of the actual business management of the work. After the death of Monsieur Liard, the next President was Monsieur Lucien Poincaré, a brother of the President of the Republic; and his successor was the Maréchal Joffre. So it came about that in the Orphan Work I served under three famous chiefs.

Louis Liard was a great man; great in his character and ability; and great in what he did for Education in France. To understand at all the inner life of France, social and political, one must reckon with the Law of 1905—the Law of the Separation and its consequences. The Law of 1905 and the putting into effect of its provisions arraigned against the Government of the Republic of that time the sympathies of the larger part of the adherents of the old régime; for it involved not alone the putting of all religious *cultes* (sects) on an equality before the law, but what was more important than that, it made education an affair of the State and took it out of the control of the religious Orders, which had so largely been responsible for it in the past. The Law of 1905 provides that *l'Etat ne reconnait, ne salarie ni ne subventionne aucun culte* (the State neither recognises nor supports financially nor gives grants to any religious sect). It declares that the relations of the State and the Church are from that time on severed, especially in all that concerns the Catholic Establishment; and it abolished the Concordat of 1801-1802, which had been signed between the Emperor Napoleon the First and Pope Pius the Seventh. This abrupt change in the educational life of a people, most of whom were Catholics in sympathy, *croyants* if not always *pratiquants* (the French Catholic who regularly observes his religious "duties" is a *pratiquant;* the others who are in general sympathy with the Church, but whose chief relations with the Church are for baptisms and marriages and burials are *croyants*) called for immediate and effective action on the part of the Government, and especially that branch of the Government called the Ministry of Public Education. It was "up to" the Government to put the Public School System throughout the entire country, not only the universities, the colleges, and the lycées, but the village schools also in condition to furnish a grade of education which should be at least the equal of if not the superior of that which had been furnished to the people by the schools under religious control; and that task had to be accomplished in the face of what was often an unavoidable hostility on the part of many of the people affected by the Law. Changes such as these, involving the abolishing of special privilege, could not but cause resentment against the authority which took away the privilege; and the putting into effect of the new régime meant that the carrying out of the provisions of the Law must be in the hands of men and women, including the teachers themselves, who were willing to take part in this work, and who might therefore be none too gentle or considerate in its execution. In creating France's new system of Public Education, and in providing for the people a scholastic institution, which for thoroughness and for intelligent comprehension of what the education of youth involves compares favourably with any other anywhere, Louis Liard was the effective and efficient motive power. My friend Emile Hovelaque, Inspecteur Général de l'Instruction Publique writes of his great chief: "Better than any other he (Liard) realised the necessity of adapting the old structure to the conditions of modern life; it is impossible to measure the importance of his work; whatever the future may have in store for our universities they will always bear Liard's mark." This sentence expresses most clearly my own recollections of Monsieur Liard. "There was in him at one and the same time the conquering enthusiasms of the old Normans from whom he sprang, and the careful prudence of Norman awareness." In his last hours he was still keen for his work; and a friend who saw him shortly before he passed from earth found him lying on a couch half propped up on his elbow and looking like *un vieux lion couchant* (an old lion recumbent).

In this matter of Education and the Law of 1905 I have touched on another subject which is of deep interest to me, and that is Religion in France. I was obliged to learn and to realise effectively what that word Religion stands for in the life of a people who are intense in all that pertains to the serious side of life. Among my other duties there was that of presiding at certain assemblies at the Sorbonne in the interests of the Orphans of the War; and with the exception of my colleague Charles Carroll, all others but myself were Frenchmen. It was a strange situation for a foreigner to be placed in the position of Presiding Officer in a French Assembly, and to have to say to a great man in France, *"la Parole est à Monsieur Bergson"*—(Mr. Bergson has the floor). My position might have been very difficult but for the considerate courtesy of my French colleagues, and the training in such a duty as that of presiding at a French Assembly which had been given me by my great and good friend le Premier Président Baudouin. It was chiefly his counsel which made the situation intelligible to me. He said to me once:

> "A Frenchman is not only formed by his past: he IS his past: and in weighing what he says and its possible implications one must always take into account his *pré-occupations* (the background of his mentality). This man on the Right is still under the shadow of the Law of Separation; he is a Royalist by tradition; and while he probably never expects to see a King again in France, and possibly in his heart of hearts does not really want one, yet all his thinking is impregnated with that tradition. That man in the Centre cannot help judging men by their possible attitude toward *l'Affaire* (the Dreyfuss Case) and its implications. His next neighbour can never free himself from the historic memories of the Revocation of the Edict of Nantes, and the long struggle which the Protestants made in those days for life itself."

Not that these are living issues to-day, but rather that they are shadows from an unforgotten past in the life of an old man and an intense people who are irrevocably tied to their traditions.

The Confession known as "Catholic" numbers among its adherents the majority of the people of France, not so much because of the idea involved in the word "catholic" as because of old association in a time when Catholic and Christian meant much the same thing in France; and also because the outward form of the Latin rite is sympathetic to the native instincts of the French people, who are artistic by temperament, monarchical through long habituation; who love beauty and splendour and ceremony. And in all this the Catholic Church satisfies them. In actual fact the word "catholic" in France is an exclusive rather than an inclusive term; it stands for a *method* of faith rather than for an absolute content of the Faith. The word is commonly used by the people to mean what is regular, and what is as it should be. My chauffeur Gabriel would sometimes stop the car, get down and listen to the motor. I would say, "What is it, Gabriel?"; and his reply would be, *"Eh, bien, Monsieur, il y a quelque chose ici qui n'est pas tout à fait catholique"*; (Well, Monsieur, there is something here which is not quite catholic).

Like all else in Gaul, the Catholic Party in France is divided into three parts: there is the Right, which is ultramontane in sympathy and royalist in feeling; there is the Centre which is the conservative element; and there is the Left, which is not Left by choice but by necessity, having been forced into this position by the opposition of the Right. Of this Left Wing *le Sillon* was one of the expressions: a movement unlike the destructive Modernism of the Continent, but rather a movement of deep spiritual import, an effort of spiritual interpretation, a trying to explain the Catholic mind to the Catholic heart.

Then there is the Protestant element in France: a strong, cohesive body of people, with an influence all out of proportion to its numbers. (It must be borne in mind that in France there are no "57 Varieties," as there are in America.) Protestantism includes *l'Eglise Reformée de France,* the

French Reformed Church, with its Calvinist wing, its moderate centre, and its Left wing which approaches more nearly the Unitarian point of view. Moreover, it is interesting to note that Protestanism in France is largely a matter of geographical distribution; there are Departments where there are scarcely any Protestants; and there are Departments where the Protestants far outnumber the Catholics; and so deep does French sentiment go that sect influence makes itself felt in little details of life. Monsieur Henri Boland writes of being in one of the towns of the Department of the Tarn-et-Garonne, and one evening while he was looking in a shop window a passer-by said to him, "Are you a Protestant, Monsieur? for if you are I can direct you to a shoemaker of your Faith." "I am one of those," writes Monsieur Boland, "who find that the quality of his natal soil explains in some measure the man. There is a correlation between the people and that on which they tread and from which they gain their sustenance; there is an upward mounting of a sap from out the land apparently so movementless (yet which is in reality alive with movement), a sap which saturates the very being of those who are rooted in that land, who came from its dust; who must go back to it again." The story of Protestantism in France is written in those words. The Protestants, like Israel of old, are hill-people; they were driven from the populous and rich centres of the seaboard, from the cities which were Royalist in sympathy, by the persecutions of the Religious Wars; they took refuge in the rocky valleys of the Centre, and they found cover in the purple shadows of the hills and vales; they forced an inhospitable soil to yield them unwilling sustenance; "the iron entered their souls"; there was nothing in their contact with Nature to soften the stern character so created, nothing in the shadows of the hills to brighten the austerity of their Credo. Yet time, the great healer, has done much for them. Great changes have come to the spirit of the Protestant Body in France; and among them there are some of the noblest of the sons and daughters to whom France has given birth.

And again, to understand the background of French life,

the Jews of France must be taken into the reckoning; and it is in France, I think, that the Jew is at his best. I have often said to them that they are the better Frenchmen for being Jews, and the better Jews for being Frenchmen. There is a similarity of experience in the life struggles of Jew and Frenchman, as they have battled for centuries for the right to be themselves; and because intellectual achievement has been one of the doors open to him that he may live a life of proved worth to the community the Jew in France has become a factor to be reckoned with in the realm of thought and letters. One has only to cast a passing glance at the list of the intellectuals of France to recognise how many of them are of Jewish origin.

The picture is not complete without taking into the reckoning the *Libre-Penseur:* not that I would class the *Libre-Penseur* as being definitely a religious element in the life of France; yet his relations to France's religious life are very definite; for he is *Libre-Penseur* because of what the others are. The term *Libre-Penseur* can no way be rendered by the English term Freethinker, for the Freethinker of England and the *Libre-Penseur* of France are wholly unlike in origin and in meaning. There are *Libre-Penseurs* without doubt who are openly iconoclastic; yet the most of them are simply *religious orphans.* Jews they cannot be, for that is a matter of race and blood; Protestants they cannot be for the theology of French Protestantism is an intellectual impossibility for them; and as for being Catholics, the Catholic régime means to them Control from Without; and to them and to their forebears Ultramontanism and all that it stands for is a bitter memory. Hostile to religion they certainly are not; but they are unyielding opponents of any system which means the abnegation of any single portion of their intellectual or political heritage in *La Patrie.* One of them who was one of France's most devoted public servants once wrote me: "I believe with you that France is fundamentally religious at heart; but the 'merchants in the Temple' have tried to make of religion an instrument of Party gain; and it is against them and not against religion that France has rebelled."

When we remember that education in France, of necessity, on account of France's history and especially on account of the Law of 1905, involved the question of religion; that the education of the Orphans of the War was necessarily committed by the State to the Ministry of Public Instruction; that the Ministry of Public Instruction was of necessity, at the time when the Law of 1905 went into effect, largely manned and directed by *Libre-Penseurs;* that the whole question of the Public School system involved deep feelings and prejudices on the part of the traditional supporters of the monarchical idea, the idea of class and of a hereditary *noblesse,* on the one hand, and on the part of the opponents of this idea on the other hand; that France is a country where feelings run high, and that you cannot touch a public issue without needing to be on your guard against being used by conflicting elements in the life of this eager people: it is easy to see how in the conditions thus set forth all the elements are provided for a drama which might have in it some bitter scenes; and how necessary it was that a foreigner entering into this work of the education and care of the Orphans of the War should make use of both knowledge and caution. I had to know the elements of the popular life which entered into play in the educational question; and above all I had to know whom to trust. I was Vice-President of the *Fraternité Franco-Américaine* (Fatherless Children of France), and Chairman of its Executive Committee which arranged the distribution of the monies which came from America for the Orphans. I was a member of the Committee of the *Secours National* (National Relief) which distributed France's voluntary gifts for Orphan Relief. I was elected a member of the French Governmental Commission for the Distribution of the money voted by the Parlement from the National Treasury for the care of the Orphans of the War, as the result of a ministerial decree conforming to a parliamentary ruling of date of March 31, 1917. The question at once suggests itself, How did a foreigner, and especially one occupying my official position in Paris, come to be mixed up with so many seemingly governmental affairs? The prime reason was this; I was the only

American there in an official position in 1914 (and the Rectorship of the Church in Paris was then a very *official* position), who was not obliged by the necessity of his post to be a neutral. Embassy, Consulate, whatever their personal feelings, had to observe the semblance of neutrality. I was free from any obligation of that kind, free to follow the dictates of my feelings and my judgment; my feelings were motivated by an attachment to France which was in part a matter of heredity; and my judgment was that Right lay on the side of a nation which had been attacked from without. At the outset of the struggle France wanted American sympathy far more than she wanted American aid; she wanted an American advocate before the bar of American public opinion; she wanted to put that advocate in position to know what France was doing and what France was suffering. My voice had been openly raised in France's behalf both there and in the American press; and James Gordon Bennett had given instructions that his New York News Service should reprint all that appeared over my name in American papers, or all that concerned my part in Relief Work in France. As a consequence it was but natural that I should have been drafted by the French Government into such positions as would render my advocacy the more effective; in fact, so much importance did the Government attach to that advocacy on my part that when I was promoted Chevalier of the Legion of Honour, the Decree reads: "Who has given himself with utmost devotion to the work of the defence of France and her Allies." And the Minister of Foreign Affairs, Monsieur Pichon, wrote me later: "You have been amongst the foremost in taking up actively in the United States the defence of Right and of Liberty; and your influence in the intellectual circles of your country has been of strong effect in enlightening your compatriots." Furthermore, it was well known that I had always preserved an attitude of strict impartiality in all that pertained to France's internal affairs. (Mr. Herrick said to me, "For you as for me, the existing Government, whatever it may be, *is* France.") I had made it clear that in the administration of whatever Relief came under my own personal control—

and it was large—no question of religion or of politics had ever been allowed to influence a decision. At 23 Avenue de l'Alma we ministered to Catholic, Protestant, Jew and Libre-Penseur; to those of all creeds and to those of none; all that was asked was assurance of the existence of actual need; and never did any worthy cause present itself there without getting help of some kind. This certainty that I was alien to all of France's internal differences made me the better witness as to the impartiality of France's official Relief for her own, and was a chief reason why I was appointed to membership in Commissions which were wholly French.

No one who has not lived through a war at close quarters can realise what utter absence of perspective comes down on one like a cloud; how feelings normally intense blaze at such a time into unreasoning expression; how easy it was for Right or for Left to think that "their widows were being neglected in the daily ministration," or that Relief was being used as a leverage to deflect the Party loyalties of widows, or that education was being made a means of detaching the children from ancient alliances. Hence my presence as an active, voting and responsible member of these governmental agencies was, as it were, a hostage given by the Government to the people as an assurance that a just impartiality should prevail. Furthermore, my being chosen to preside at sessions of Orphan Relief Boards at the Sorbonne and at the Ministry of Public Instruction was an easy solution of the ever present Party question—the choosing of a foreigner as Presiding Officer, one who had no local or sectional allegiances, avoided the necessity of giving the preference to any one of the differing elements in French politics.

It was my constant practice to refer to Monsieur Baudouin the Chief Justice; and to Monsieur Ogier the Director of Contrôle at the Ministry of the Interior, all cases where I needed counsel or advice; and I never made any public utterance or put my name to any printed statement which involved France or French issues, without having it edited by the Chief Justice first. Monsieur Baudouin, in reply to my request for his advice whether I should accept a certain position which I had been urged to take, said, "We, (meaning the Government) are asking of you a great service in this matter; you can do nothing more helpful for France than to accept the post; it is a position of responsibility, and at times your decisions, given as they will be in line with your frank American habit of speaking and acting, may entail unpleasant opposition, and even hostility; but I will see that your position is sustained; and you may feel free to come to me at any hour with any problem which you find difficult." Without the constant counsel of the Chief Justice I could not have carried on; and when he passed away it left me with a feeling that my work for France was bereft of what was an essential element for its continuance; and that conviction was with me till the day that I resigned my post. He lived in an old building where once lived the Comte d'Artois; and I well remember the many times that I went there to see him, always to find a ready welcome; sometimes to find him annotating a score of orchestral music, or busy compiling the statistics pertaining to the hundred or more of the volunteer Orphan Relief Committees which shared in the Government's aid; and always I would go away with my troubles lifted because of having been shared with one, whose shoulders were already bending beneath the weight of years and the sorrows of the War and the heavy responsibilities of a position unique in France. To me Manuel Baudouin was a prince amongst men.

My colleagues on the Fatherless Children of France Committee were all of them men of interesting personality. The Treasurer was an oil refiner and financier, Emile Deutsch de la Meurthe, one of the finest Jews whom I have ever known; and I knew him intimately. His personal generosities were known to few, but the Fatherless Children work could not have succeeded as it did but for him. One day we went to his Château des Boulains to take déjeuner. There were sixteen of his family present, children and grandchildren, and all of them spoke English with the exception of Monsieur Emile, as he was affectionately called by his associates, among whom he graciously permitted me to class myself. One day when I was going to a meeting of a Committee of Orphan Relief, I put in my pocket some cheques which had come in the morning mail and which I had endorsed to Monsieur Emile Deutsch as Treasurer. When I came in to the room, the Treasurer was telling those present of the serious shortage in funds with which he was faced at the moment. I drew out from my pocket one cheque and then another and handed them to him; he looked at them and then at me, and then he came behind me and put his arms about my shoulders affectionately and put his fingers in another pocket and took out another cheque and held it up to the view of our colleagues and said, *"Il est tout cousu d'or, ce bonhomme."* (He has his pockets full of money; this fine man.) Monsieur Emile telephoned me one day asking me if I would be good enough, if it were possible, to stop at his office when I came into the City. It was at a time when we had been trying to arrange for interested personal surveillance of the home care given the children whom we were helping; and to that end we had organised a Central Committee of French women, to be known as *le Commité de Dames* who would have correspondents in all the towns and villages and who would help us in maintaining the little homes of France. For our first object in Orphan Relief was to keep the child with its mother, and to that end to "keep the home fires burning"; and our little fifteen francs a month for each child did just that; it kept up the morale of the mothers by reminding them that they were not forgotten. And in order that it might be France which brought that monthly gift we sent it always in the form of a *Mandat de Poste* (Post Office Money Order, paid at the house by the Postman) so that the mother might see that it was France herself in the person of the carrier who brought the help. For this *Comité de Dames* we had need of an effective *Madame la Présidente.* Some of them wanted *la Comtesse* ———, who represented the *noblesse* and the Right; others wanted *Madame* ——— who was the wife of one of the *Députés* of the Extreme Left; both of them were fine women, but too partisan in their interests to be generally acceptable. Our choice finally fell on a lady whom I had known in other Relief work, and who was representative enough to be acceptable to all. Monsieur Emile had not been present at the meeting when this choice was made; and when I greeted him at his office his first question was, "Monsieur le Président, who is this lady whom you have put in as *Présidente du Comité de Dames?"* I told him her name, and the names of some of her associates in other Relief; but that was not enough; he wanted to know just who she was in French life; and I told him that I could not answer that question. "Well," he said, "I can easily tell you"; and he pushed a button on his desk and a keen looking little gentleman came in who was introduced to me by Monsieur Emile as *"mon Je-Sais-Tout,"*—(I know everything). He told *Monsieur Je-Sais-Tout* the story, and then he said, "Now, who is she?" His aide turned to me and said, "Where does she live, Monsieur?" I told him the street and number. "Ah," he said, "now I can tell you what you wish to know, Monsieur Emile. Madame ——— is the widow of a former President of the Conseil d'Etat"; then turning to me, "You do not know, Monsieur, I suppose, just what the Conseil d'Etat is?" "Yes," I replied, "I have even been present at a session of the Conseil d'Etat." "But you have not had any business to be judged by the Conseil d'Etat, I hope, Monsieur"—(The Conseil d'Etat has as one of its functions the adjudication of certain cases in Equity). "No," was my reply. *"Alors,"* he said. *"Je vous en félicite: car on dit qu'en France la Justice est boiteuse: mais je peux vous dire que le Conseil d'Etat n'a pas même de jambes."* The bon mot is so perfect and the wit so keen that it must be set down here just as it was spoken; and the English of it is this: "Then I congratulate you; for they say that in France Justice is lame; but permit me to say that the Conseil d'Etat has not even any legs."

One evening shortly before I left France I was taking Monsieur Emile with me in my car after a meeting of the Fatherless Children Committee in order to leave him at his house which was near where I lived, and he was telling me something of the Jew in France, and in answering him I said a few words in Hebrew. With a voice broken with emotion he said, "And you know that too!" Then he said quickly, "Will you do our people a great honour? there will be a solemn ceremony to-morrow, the eve of the Sabbath, at our Synagogue in the Rue de la Victoire, when our people will be praying for the young men dead in battle. Will you come with me to that service and sit with me in the seats of the Elders of the Congregation?" I went; and the scene is still vivid in my memory: the great Synagogue with its thousands of worshippers; the wonderful chanting of the Canticles in Hebrew; the eloquence of the Grand Rabbin, who was an Alsatian, as shown in his accent (many of the Jewish people in France are Alsatians who left Alsace after the War of 1870); the women by themselves on one side, and the men on the other, all the women in black. And although by race I was a stranger I felt a wonderful nearness to those people there. There is an intense sense of the reality of the Divine in the Hebrew Faith and Ritual, which you go far to find elsewhere; and the deep emotion of that hour overwhelmed me; and I am grateful to Emile Deutsch de la Meurthe for the privilege which he shared with me a Gentile.

On the evening before I left Paris he came to my house; greeted me French fashion; and said, "I am so happy that these books came from the bindery in time, for I want you to carry them to America with you; they are a message to your heart from the heart of Israel in France." And he handed me a package which he had brought. The books are before me as I write, and on the title-page I read:

LA BIBLE
traduite du texte original
PAR LES MEMBRES DU RABBINAT FRANCAIS
SOUS LA DIRECTION

de M. Zadoc Kahn
Grand Rabbin

This is the most perfect translation of the Hebrew Scriptures ever made into any language; it was made by men to whom the Hebrew was as the breath of their life; it is a translation voiced in that most perfect of literary expressions, which is French at its best; it is the union of two loves, that French Hebrew Bible—the Jew's love of his racial meaning, and the Frenchman's love of Beauty. I must quote from it here; and whether the reader knows French or not, he will respond to the melodic rhythm of the words, and will feel how the beauty of expression transcends that of any other version:

PSAUME XXIII

L'Eternel est mon berger, je ne manquerai de rien.

Dans de vertes prairies il me fait camper, il me conduit au bord d'eaux paisibles.

Il restaure mon âme, me dirige dans les sentiers de la justice, en faveur de son nom.

Dussé-je suivre la sombre vallée de la mort, je ne craindrais aucun mal, car tu serais avec moi; ton soutien et ton appui seraient ma consolation.

Tu dresses la table devant moi, à la face de mes ennemis; tu parfumes d'huile ma tête, ma coupe est pleine à déborder.

Oui, le bonheur et la grâce m'accompagneront ma vie durant, et j'habiterai de longs jours dans la maison du Seigneur.

And it is with those words which he loved that I say *Au revoir, mon ami!* to Monsieur Emile Deutsch.

I have three other books on my shelves which bring back French memories of especial interest; three little volumes in red binding, *Contes de la Gascogne,*—Tales from the Midi. And this is how I came to find these rare treasures. A Gascon friend of mine was at dinner with us one evening; the candles on the table were our only light, for we were rationed in electricity. Over cigarettes and coffee he began telling stories heard in his boyhood, stories which his *nourrice* had told him, fascinating stories of days when that mystic side of life which now we only half sense at times was vivid; and I asked him if those stories had ever been put in print. He said that he had often thought that he would write them out for he knew that they ought not to be lost; but that his life was more than busy. I asked him if there was a book in print which contained similar tales; and he told me that years before a publisher in Paris had brought out a small edition of a book entitled *Contes Populaires de la Gascogne,* but that he did not think that the book could be had any longer;

however he would give me the name of the publisher. At my first free moment I hunted up the *Libraire* whose name he had given me, only to find that the business had gone into other hands; but that information gave me another address to which I went, to find there that the owner was an old gentleman who lived in a little town where Jeanne d'Arc stopped on her way to Orleans; that his two sons were at the Front; and that all the books of his stock had been taken to his house in Paris. So there I went next to find the *concièrge* (perhaps I should say *concièrgine*) in charge; a fine looking handsome woman of the Midi with flashing black eyes; I talked with her but with small results; however I left a message for the *patron* and asked her to deliver it to him when next he came to town. Ten days later I went back to the house and she told me that the *patron* had been in Paris, that she had told him of my visit, but that he had left no word for me. Then some *compliments* passed, "from me to her," and she asked me to sit down in the *loge* and have a demitasse of coffee; and under that benign influence she asked me, "Just what is it all about, Monsieur, this matter of yours with the *patron?*" I told her who I was; where I lived in Paris; why I was interested in the folklore of the Midi; and that I would gladly buy the books for which I was looking, if her master would let me have them; and I told her the name of the books. And before I went on my mournful way there passed—not "over the tea-cups" but under a coffee-cup—a five franc note with the plea that she would bring my affair to the *patron's* favourable attention. A few days afterward when I came home one evening, I was met at the door by Louise (the *bonne*), and I could see that she was visibly disturbed. She had a package in her hand done up in new paper wrappings, and she said, "Monsieur, there was a woman here just now, and she left this, and she said it was for you, and she wanted fifteen francs for it, and I did not want to give her the money, for Monsieur had not told me that any package was coming; and she said, 'You'd better take this and give me the money, or if you don't when your master comes home he will beat you': and she talked so fierce, Monsieur, that I was afraid, so I gave her the money;

but if it is not all right with Monsieur, I will pay it myself, for it was my fault." In the package were three little books, the books for which I had been hunting; and the woman who brought them was evidently the *concièrge* of the house in the *Quartier Latin.*

Those books! they are a treasure of ancient story. In them I found "Puss in Boots," "The House that Jack Built," "The Sleeping Beauty," "Cinderella," "Blue Beard," and many other tales "dear to my childhood"; but told in the original, told as the "folk" told them, not laced and furbelowed, but with all the crudities and Rabelaisian adornments of the simplest of times, and all in peasant talk. In this form they were the source of *Grimm's Fairy Tales,* and of Perrault's *Contes de Fées;* and the charm of them lies in the simple wit, the naïveté which is often half lost in the adornments and the *brodéries* with which more artificial compilers have "dolled up" the plain speech of the peasant and the children's nurse of the Southern hills. One evening when Paul Painlevé was sitting in our salon after dinner with a little pot of black coffee by his side which Louise would fill whenever necessary, and smoking his cigarettes, I brought out my treasure-trove and showed them to the Minister. With his love of old France and his keen literary sense he was delighted to see my three little red books, and he asked me if it were possible to try and get a set of them for him. Some days later I went back to the House in the Latin Quarter; but whether it was that there was another concièrge, I cannot tell; suffice it to say that the one who met me did not know me, and she knew nothing about books —"Monsieur must surely be mistaken in the house."

XIII

PRESIDENTS, PRIME MINISTERS, AND OTHERS

AMONG my close relations with men in public life in France none are of happier memory than the hours which I spent with Paul Painlevé. More than once when he was giving a dinner at the Ministry of War when he had among his guests some of the editors of the *Revues,* he asked me to be of the company. And at the table he placed me beside him and would tell me what the other guests individually represented in French opinion; then there would be brought out incidentally, as it were, some policy which the Government contemplated putting into effect; for the *Revue* has a much more potent influence on public opinion than do American newspapers or the French dailies. Monsieur Painlevé was Minister of Public Instruction when I first came to know him; later he was Minister of War, and also Prime Minister; and when his Government fell I sent him a great sheaf of red roses; it was my tribute to the fine qualities of the man—a Prime Minister to whom the "Roses of Picardie" would bring the message of my feeling for him when he bowed to defeat in the Chamber in the vicissitudes of political strife.

I was associated with Monsieur Painlevé on two of the greatest days of my public service. One of them was Christmas Eve of 1917. The Government had arranged a great ceremony at the Sorbonne, as a tribute of recognition of the help which had been sent for the Orphans of the War; and *La Fraternité Franco-Américaine* had the place of honour. The great auditorium of the Sorbonne was packed with the people of Paris. The Presiding Officer was the Maréchal Joffre; and the official speakers were Paul Painlevé, Louis Barthou, Eugene Brieux, Misses Schofield and Fell, and myself. The President of the Republic was detained by duty, but was represented by Madame Poincaré and by his Official Military Aide; the Musique of the Garde Républicaine played; and the Boys of the Choir of Holy Trinity sang with wonderful effect Victor Hugo's touching hymn:

"Ceux qui pieusement sont morts pour la Patrie
Ont droit qu'à leur cercueil la foule vienne et prie.
Entre les beaux noms leur nom est le plus beau:
Toute gloire près d'eux passe et tombe éphémère,
Et comme ferait une mère,
*La voix d'un peuple entier les berce en leur tombeau."**

I made an address which was afterward printed in full in *La Revue Hebdomadaire* entitled *"L'Amérique Amie des Enfants de France"* (America the Friend of the Children of France). Before beginning my more formal speech, I turned to Maréchal Joffre and offered him America's tribute to his great services in the War, and I assured him of what it meant to the children that he was part of this day's meaning in personal presence as well as in heart and sympathy. For minutes the hall rang with applause for the white haired Chief as well as in appreciation of my words. The Maréchal had risen when I addressed him; he was deeply affected, and he stood with hands stretched out to the people until silence fell and he could master his emotion sufficiently to reply in a few affectionate words. It was a wonderful ovation that France's "Great Old Man" received that day; and the memory of my part in it makes me very grateful. At the conclusion of my address I paid a tribute to Myron Herrick. I told the crowd of his love for children, and of the cruel blow it was to him when his little grandson, Myron Herrick, II had been suddenly killed; and then I told them that the boy had taken back to America with him a little French flag which he kept hanging over his bed entwined with the American Colours; and that each night he used to

* Those who have given their lives for la Patrie
Receive but their due when at their tombs we kneel and pray.
Their names stand chief amongst all glorious names:
Beside their fame all glory is a passing dream:
And as would a mother, so
The nation's voice would chant their cradle song.

say a prayer which he had learned in France from his French nurse:

> *"Protégez-moi, mon ange gardien,*
> *Puisque Dieu le dit."*

For, when he spoke to people in general, he spoke in English, but when he spoke to God it was in French that he spoke; and that story touched the crowd to the depths of their hearts.

Among the many words of appreciation which came to me after that speech the most telling of them all, to me, was the tribute paid me by Louis Barthou, then Minister of Justice. He took my address as the theme for his own, and turning to me he said: "Monsieur Watson, you have spoken of France as a son loves to hear some one speak of his mother. She is so dear to your heart that your very words are fragrant with the perfumes of all the flowers of France." And the naïve compliment which Gabriel paid me was: "To think that when *le patron* first came to France I was his interpreter; and here to-day he speaks in the Sorbonne itself to thousands of French people who listen eagerly to his words!"

Another great day when I spoke for France was the Fourth of July, 1917; it was the day when American troops appeared for the first time in the streets of Paris.

When the War broke on France there were a number of young Americans in Paris who were eager to enlist in her service, students and others who had been beneficiaries of that culture which France offered so willingly to all who sought it; but, being citizens of a nation which was at that time "neutral" in the conflict, they could not be received into the Regular Army; as a consequence they took service in the Foreign Legion. General Gouraud said of these men: "A distinction should be made between duty and heroism. We Frenchmen who fought in the War were performing a duty required of us by our country; but when men who have no obligation to fight risk their lives in defence of a cause because they hold it dear, those men are showing real heroism." A group of these young men went to see the Ambassador to ask him what they should do in this matter of enlisting in the defence of France and of Freedom. Mr. Herrick first freed his conscience by getting out the Code and reading them the Law on the duty of "Neutrals"; then he freed his heart by saying: "That is the Law, Boys; but if I was young, and were in your shoes, by God, I know mighty well what I would do." Then to the Rue de Grenelle came the "Boys"; and they were our first American Volunteers. On the 12th of May, 1917, I wrote to Monsieur Painlevé:

"Monsieur le Ministre,

"For the love of France and of Liberty a little group of Americans enlisted in the Second Regiment of the Foreign Legion at the commencement of the War; and for the three years of 1914, 1915, and 1916 they fought beside their French comrades. Always they carried with them the Stars and Stripes which they floated above their dugouts during their hours of rest, and when they went 'over the top' they carried the flag with them.

"This flag was worn as a girdle about his body by René Phélizot of the Second Regiment, Sixth Battalion, when he was killed. Two other men of the same Company, of whom one was killed and the other was seriously wounded, wore it in the same manner.

"Their flag has been entrusted to me by the representatives of these fellow citizens of mine, with the request that I present it to their beloved France in the hope that it may be placed in the *Musée des Invalides,* should that be possible.

"The flag is accompanied by a plaque in bronze which bears the following inscription:

DRAPEAU
porté par les
Volontaires Américains
du 2ème Regiment de la Légion Etrangére

* * * * *

C. R. Phélizot	F. Capdeville
Edward Morlae	Dr. Van Vorst
Edgar Bouligny	P. A. Rockwell
J. W. Ganson	K. Y. Rockwell
D. W. King	Charles Sweeny
J. J. Casy	F. W. Zinn
F. Wilson	Prof. Olinger
G. Casmèze	R. Soubiron

Bill Thaw	W. B. Hall
H. Chatcoff	J. J. Bach
Charles Trinkard	Dennis Dowd
Bob Scanlon	George Delpeuch

F. Landreaux

* * * * *

"I deeply appreciate the honour of being the representative of my compatriots in begging you to accept this flag in the name of those Americans who gave their all to save France.

"I beg you, Monsieur le Ministre to accept the assurance of my warmest regard,

"S. N. Watson."

I knew well enough what the Minister of War would like to do, but—Could he do it? that was the question. America had just come to take her place with the Allies. It was a very tense moment. To exalt the flag and the deeds of those Volunteers of 1914; to glorify those Americans who through those three terribly long years helped to hold open the door until America could gather her force and her *élan;* men who, in the words of Myron Herrick, "to many of us seemed the saviours of our National Honour"; men who were offering themselves for a cause in which the heart of their country was already enlisted—Could France say that, in the face of the arriving American troops? True or not—Could it be said? I did not know. Therefore, in order to avoid any needless embarrassment to my friends in the War Office, I sought an intermediary. I went to see my good and great friend General De Lacroix, and I laid the whole proposition before him, and asked his opinion. Could this flag be accepted by France now? Should I make the offer? General De Lacroix was heartily in favour of my proposal, and urged me to proceed with it. "Then, *Mon Général,*" I said; "when you go to the Council of War this morning, will you take with you my letter to the Minister of War; will you tell him privately what it all means; will you ask him if he wishes to formally receive the letter? If he thinks that it is unwise or lacking in tact to take up this matter at this present moment, just put the letter back in your pocket, and forget it; but, on the other hand, if Monsieur Painlevé approves of it, will you then present the letter in due form to the Minister of War in my behalf?"

The following documents tell the rest of this part of the story:

"Paris, the 16th June, 1917

"Monsieur le Recteur,

"I am happy to transmit to you the enclosed card which I have just received from the Chef de Cabinet of the Minister of War.

"Please accept, Monsieur le Recteur, the assurance of my high regard and my sincere devotion.

"H. De Lacroix."

"14/6/'17

"MINISTÈRE DE LA GUERRE
Cabinet du Ministre

"Mon Général:—

"The proposition of *Monsieur le Recteur Watson* is accepted.

"The emblem of the American Legionnaires will have its place in the Salle d'Honneur of the Musée.

"Be pleased to accept, *mon Général,* the assurance of my deep respect and my personal regard;

"signed by the Chef de Cabinet"

"REPUBLIQUE FRANCAISE
Ministère de la Guerre
Cabinet du Ministre

"Paris, the 14th June, 1917

"Monsieur le Recteur;

"In the name of your compatriots enlisted as Volunteers in the *2ème Etranger,* you have graciously offered me the Star Spangled Banner which was their guide in battle for almost three years, in order that it may be deposited, together with a commemorative plaque in the Musée des Invalides.

"I accept with deep appreciation in the name of the French Army this glorious emblem, for which General Niox the Governor of the Invalides has ready a worthy place in the Salle d'Honneur of the Musée de l'Armée.

"This flag will thus stand forever as a striking testimony to the devotion shown to France by those American Volunteers who at the very outset of hostilities came to fight in our ranks for Right and for Civilisation.

"I am entrusting to the Military Governor of Paris the duty of arranging with you and with General Niox the ceremonial which will be used for the turning over of this American flag to the custody of the Invalides.

"Be pleased to accept, *Monsieur le Recteur,* the assurance of my personal regard:

"Paul Painlevé."

It was a wonderful sight: the background the Court of Honour of the Invalides; the galleries all filled and more than twenty thousand persons assembled; in the immediate foreground (I have the official photograph before me as I write) Monsieur Painlevé Minister of War, Monsieur Poincaré President of the Republic, the American Ambassador Mr. Sharp, the Maire of Puy in the Lafayette country, Monsieur Deschanel President of the Chamber of Deputies, Monsieur Ribot Minister of Foreign Affairs, General Pershing, Admiral Lacaze, General Dubail, General Pétain, General Foch, Maréchal Joffre, General Niox; the President of the Senate and the Diplomatic representatives were seated on a raised platform; and in the front and centre were Charles Carroll carrying the flag, and I who was to offer it to France. It was a little flag, a very cheap piece of bunting in itself; but it carried all the honour of a great nation in its brilliant folds. Some one had given it to the Volunteers when they first enlisted; I saw them crossing the Place de la Concorde with it; it went with them to Rouen where they first made camp, then when Rouen was threatened their Regiment was sent to Toulouse; and from there the flag went with them to the Front. I had had a rich rosewood staff and ropes of heavy silken cord made for it. The Ceremonies began with the entrance of the troops: first the *bleu-horizon* of the French, then the khaki of the Americans; an American Band played the *"Marseillaise,"* and a French Band played "The Star Spangled Banner." Then there was presented to General Pershing a general's *guidon* as a gift from the descendants of soldiers who had fought beside Washington and Lafayette, and another similar flag from Le Puy which was the *chef-lieu* of Lafayette's home country. After which I addressed General Pershing:

"It is my privilege, General, as representing our American Legionnaires, those Americans who for the love of France and of

Liberty entered the French Army in 1914, to present to France this flag, their flag and our flag. They were the pioneers of that great American Army which is coming following your lead as their General. And now they, the Advance Guard, are leaving to you and to your troops the task which they began so bravely; now your new Standard will replace their bullet-pierced flag; whilst theirs is confided to France whom they loved with deathless eagerness, and it will be guarded forever in that Shrine of the Nation, the *Musée des Invalides*."

Then to General Niox, the Governor of the Invalides, I addressed these words:

"*Mon Général,* it is my duty as well as an honour which I appreciate most deeply to bring you to-day, on behalf of a little group of my countrymen, this flag which they loved. They wrote their names on its bars of white, and they signed it with their blood. It was not their privilege to carry it with them as a battle flag when they went 'over the top,' but at such a time one of them wore it, as a *ceinture de sauvetage:* and more than one of them was wounded, more than one of them was killed with this flag wrapped about his body. It was thus that our Stars and Stripes received their Baptism of Blood in this struggle for Right against Might. I beg that you will accept it in the name of France, and I ask that it may be placed where it will be a perpetual inspiration to those who follow on to be worthy of those who have gone before them to pay the eternal price of the Liberty of Nations."

Then Charles Carroll handed the flag to General Niox, and the Ceremony was ended.

I felt deeply my responsibility in being, in a sense, spokesman for both America as well as for France at such a critical moment, when ill-advised words might have stirred up reactions because of feelings already sensitive. And I was immensely relieved when I found that the French Government gave unquestioned approval to what I had said. Monsieur Painlevé, Minister of War, was one of the first to come forward and to take both my hands in his and to express his great satisfaction. Then came the Directeur of the Protocol, the arbiter of diplomatic etiquette, who said to me in a voice broken by emotion, "*Monsieur le Recteur,* I trembled for you and for France when you began to speak for I knew well the difficulties of your task. Your words were in perfect taste and in glorious moderation. From the depth of my heart as a Frenchman I thank you. It was splendid; it was splendid." And so drew to a close one of the great days of my life.

I want to note here my cordial relations with Monsieur Raymond Poincaré, who was the President of the French Republique during my days in France. When I crossed to France in 1912 I was talking one day to Myron Herrick of the probabilities of the coming Presidential Election in France. And Mr. Herrick said, "The choice will probably fall on Raymond Poincaré; and no man in France is better qualified to serve the Republic in a difficult hour than he." It was an unconscious prediction, the significance of which we then little understood; but it was a judgment which was amply justified by Monsieur Poincaré's leadership in time of France's great struggle for her life, as also by his masterly effort to rehabilitate France's financial position. And again I would note what was one of the finest of Mr. Herrick's gifts, his power of weighing the worth of men. It takes this long back-look to give one a clear picture of what Monsieur Poincaré's task was, and of how finely he accomplished it; and further one needs a clear understanding of what the office of a President of France really is, and how limited in actual authority, are his powers. Think of him as a Frenchman devoted to his country's welfare, with high ideals of his nation's destiny; and, during a period such as that of the great War, seeing his country in a position where she sometimes dared not speak or assert her rightful claims, tied as she was for weal or woe to the political and military policies of other nations, and that, regardless of her own convictions as to their practical wisdom; himself shorn of any large power of individual initiative by a system of government which makes the Executive responsible for the vagaries of the Parlement, but with small control over parliamentary action; sure to be blamed for the faults of others, and equally sure often of missing the credit due to the accomplishments of his own statesmanship—such was Monsieur

Poincaré's position as President. And, as one who was an eyewitness at close range of his political sagacity, his personal modesty, his brave and lofty patriotism, I can echo with fullest assent what Madame Poincaré said to me one day in the garden of the Elysée: "Ah! Monsieur, if the President only had the power which his wisdom and his worth deserve, what wonderful things he could accomplish for France!"

Among the literary treasures which I value most highly is a gift which came to me at Bordeaux bearing the seal of the Elysée, while I was waiting there on my return to America in 1918. It is a little fascicule which contains, each one under a separate cover and each one signed, "R. Poincaré," a number of brochures, the War time speeches of the President of France. Better than the pen of any biographer or the pencil of any artist could these speeches delineate the man, his character, and his vision. I have re-read them with a renewed admiration for the scholarship and the literary ability which they exhibit. One of them brings clearly to my memory a brilliant scene: it is the speech which Monsieur Poincaré made "A La Gloire de Rouget de l'Isle"; Rouget de l'Isle who wrote the "*Marseillaise,*" France's "Battle Hymn of the Republic." He died in 1836, and his body was then laid to rest at Choisy-le-Roi; but the Government decided to make a picturesque spectacle of War time by bringing his body to *Les Invalides.* It was the *Quatorze juillet* of 1915; and what a summer that was in Paris! In my *Quartier* nearly every one was gone; my house was one of a scant dozen on the whole of the Avenue de l'Alma which remained open; the *étrangers* were all gone; scarcely a taxi was to be seen in ten minutes on the Avenue des Champs Elysées; and those of us who had been in Paris so long used to say, "What a pleasure to have this quiet Paris all to ourselves!" The Front was quiet too; the opposing Armies facing one another in their trenches, simply waiting. The atmosphere of the City had taken on a tone of semi-translucence; and I remember well standing one day on the Island of Refuge in the middle of the Place d'Iéna, looking up the Cours la Reine at the Sacre Coeur and seeing it as an opalescent vision, a temple in the sky such as Bernard of Cluny sang of. It was on a day like that, the sky lightly overcast, and the beautiful city clothed in the loveliest of opal tints that down the Champs Elysées the cortège passed; a squadron of officers of Cavalry; the 23rd Colonials next; then a gun-carriage with the body of Rouget de l'Isle; then the members of the Government; the President of the Republic, the Prime Minister, the Ambassadors and the Diplomatic Corps. At the Arc de Triomphe superb voices began the "*Marseillaise,*" accompanied by the Musique of the 30th Territorials; down the length of the Avenue the crowd took up the strain, and at the Pont Alexandre the boatmen on the Seine joined the chorus. All day long the casket rested at the entrance to the Saint Louis Chapel of *Les Invalides;* and at five o'clock silence fell on the City as the poet's ashes were placed in the crypt of the Chapel. And all this to do honour to a man who had done what? who had written a song. But that is France. And of the song itself Monsieur Poincaré said:

> "Wherever its strains are heard there rises in men's hearts the image of a people master of itself; whose passion for independence is such that any and all of its sons would make deliberate choice of death rather than servitude. And not only for us, the people of France, does the '*Marseillaise*' have this glorious meaning; its Liberty cry is the cry of mankind, and its wondrous poetry voices the heart-notes of the world."

On the Fourteenth of July, 1916, a year after the moving demonstration which I have just described, the Government of France ordered that a solemn ceremony be held at the Grand Palais at which Diplomas of Honour should be presented to the families of the Nation's dead on the Field of Honour.

That year of 1916 was one of the turning points in the struggle for Freedom; and the question was being asked, Would France hold out? The answer came from the battle front. Through the streets of the capital, before the eyes of the people came the fighting men of all the Allies. And what a sight it was! On the Esplanade the troops were reviewed by General Dubail, General Cousin, and General

Galopin, who were the escort of the President of the Republic, the Minister of War, and the Diplomatic Corps. Later in the morning came the procession through the City: British troops singing "Tipperary," Anzacs, Scotch with their kilts; then the Hindus with beautiful horses and shining lances; then the Belgians, and the crowd grew still in reverence; then came a roar of sound, and the Russians surged along singing a full-throated hymn; then the great host of the Army of France; little Annamites and Tonkinois, Algerians, Moroccans, Senegalis, Territorials, Cuirassiers, Chasseurs-a-pied, Frenchmen all of them, keeping fête in Paris until the sun was set, then back to the trenches to keep tryst with France again—perhaps to keep tryst with death. It was of them that Monsieur Poincaré said that day in his address to the people:

> "As one man they rose to the cry of their Country endangered; they rushed To Arms; they hurried to the frontiers, young men and old; the boys with their fathers; from the fields and the factories they came, labourers and professional men together; priests, and those who never prayed but in secret; children of the Midi, and sons of the Western Ocean: one and all they are worthy of the endless gratitude of the race."

It was in the month of October of 1916 that France again kept solemn watch with her dead. The Bar of Paris had arranged that three religious ceremonies should be held in memory of the members of the Bar who had fallen at the Front. There was to be one at the great Synagogue of the Rue de la Victoire; one in the Protestant Temple of the Rue de l'Oratoire; and still another, of deep historic significance in La Sainte Chapelle at which the Cardinal Archbishop officiated. (Some one said,—That provides for the Jews, and the Protestants, and the Catholics; but how about the Libre-Penseurs? Where will their commemoration take place? And a wag replied, "In the Chamber of Deputes, without doubt.") It was at this Ceremony for the Bar that Monsieur Poincaré said:

> "What a throng of intimate associations with the past the sight of this place brings before us! Within as without the

Palais de Justice you are in constant touch with the very elements of our story as a people. Just beside us here, at the western point of the old City, on the ruins of a Roman fortress, are the walls of the first palace of the Capet princes: here, under the same roof lived for long years Justice and Royalty; but a few steps from where we are now, under the double ogival vaulting of the Great Hall of other days, before the famous marble table, there took place the solemn reception of foreign ambassadors, and the publication of the Treaties of Peace, after wars; it was in the Place Dauphine that the Revolution received such throngs of volunteers offering themselves to fight against the hostile coalition of Europe; and the sombre scenery of the Conciérgerie was the background of the stage on which the Terror mounted so many fearful dramas. If there are anywhere those who can have doubts as to what France is, I would counsel them to come to this spot to learn here her lessons of fidelity, of constancy, and of energy."

I wish that I might have the privilege of translating into English, and of publishing in one volume, all of the War time Speeches of Monsieur Poincaré. It would be a very real contribution to the world's best literature; and it would also be a tribute on my part to the touching courtesies which were shown me by both Raymond and Henriette Poincaré, for both of whom I have feelings of deepest admiration and gratitude. Their last gifts to me were their signed portraits; portraits of a man of intellect, of power, and of courage; and of a woman of grace, of beauty, and of charm.

In his *Memoirs,* Mr. Herrick speaks of the American news-writers who were in Paris in the early days of the War, and of their difficulties, being sent over to France to get news, and no accurate touch possible, while home offices were clamouring for reports. Sometimes these gentlemen came to me for points of view or asking my aid in establishing contacts. There was first of all Victor Murdock, the nationally known Kansas journalist. He said that he wanted to learn firsthand something of the effect which the War was having on the spiritual and religious life of the French people; that he had been to the great churches of Paris, but that he could gain no accurate impressions from what he saw there; and he had been told that I could help him out. That

I was of real assistance to him became evident; for depending on his own spiritual intuition and the experiences which he quickly learned to interpret aright, he wrote an article in the very beginning of the War, setting out what France meant as a spiritual power in terms of marvellous clearness and accuracy.

The next to come was Will Irwin. He told me that he simply must make contacts with the Minister of War, and with Monsieur Joseph Reinach the noted War Critic of *The Figaro;* and could I help him to gain these interviews. No one could have made such a request of me with greater surety in advance that I would do all in my power for him; so one morning Will Irwin and I went to the house of Monsieur Millerand. I had met the Minister of War casually at large official dinners, but this was the first opportunity which I had of a personal talk with the man who was then at the head of the War Department, and who was after to be President of the French Republic. His powerful, intellectual looking head; his earnest look; his readiness to respond to my questions made an impression on me which I have never forgotten. And among other grateful memories which I have of Will Irwin is this, that he made the opportunity for me to know better the man who, when asked by General Gallieni the Military Governor of Paris, how far resistance to a possible enemy attack on the City was to be carried, answered, "You will defend Paris to the last ditch."

Then we went to see Monsieur Reinach. We found him in the library at his house looking out over the lovely Monceaux Quarter. The library of a French man of letters always woke my admiration. There is a certain sense of dignity, an appreciation of values on the appearance of books which are bound for a purpose; books so bound that you know that the owner thinks them worth the keeping. The French custom of issuing books in paper covers, even very valuable books, crown octavos and quartos printed on fine paper, and then leaving it to you to say whether they are worth the binding and the keeping is a custom which we might well copy. Where is the sense in paying for the binding of a book which you never intend to keep and which is but the pastime of an otherwise weary hour, when paper covers would serve equally as well. I have some beautiful books which were given to me unbound. I am thinking especially of the *Life of Pasteur* and, the *Life of Madame Pasteur,* both of them given to me by the author, Monsieur Vallery-Radot who was the devoted son-in-law of Pasteur, and each of them signed with a dedication from the author. Further, the appearance of a room filled with books, often as in the library of Monsieur Reinach, reaching from low armoires to the heighth of the ceiling, befits the tastes of a book lover. Monsieur Reinach was a student of politics in all its phases; and in Europe that means War in its origins and its consequences; and during the Great War, his articles in *The Figaro* were the clearest commentaries which we, in Paris, could find. My visit to him with Will Irwin that day, listening to his clear cut visions of the situation, past, actual, and to come, stands out in my memory as a uniquely privileged moment.

Among my treasured souvenirs of valued acquaintances and War-made friendships are some of Will Irwin's books which he gave me. In one of them he has written this dedication:

"Dr. Samuel Watson,
mainly responsible for Chapter I,
from his accomplice
Will Irwin."

"May 1917."

My daily papers came to me from a little woman who kept a kiosk on the corner of the Avenue de l'Alma just above my house. My morning diet was *The Figaro,* the *Echo de Paris, Le Matin,* and *L'oeuvre.* Whenever I wanted to get the latest and most accurate news from the Front I got *Le Journal de Geneve* (that Swiss daily gave us lots of news of the conflict which never appeared in the Paris papers). My evening pabulum was *Le Temps, L'intransigeant,* and *La Liberte;* and for a lesson in the pronunciation of French just listen to the newsboy on the street calling "*La Lee-bear-tay.*" My little newsvender at the kiosk at the corner used to do a particularly graceful thing. When she brought my morning papers to the house, *L'oeuvre* was always carefully wrapped up inside *Le Figaro;* she knew well that *le Patron* could well read anything that he cared to read, but it was not for the *personnel* of the house to see such dangerous literature as *L'oeuvre;* or, for that matter, even to know that *le maitre* was reading it—he might lose caste. In all matters of opinion I got more satisfaction from *L'intransigeant* than from any of the other of my papers; and the reason for that was to be found in the clear and independent thinking of its editor, Monsieur Léon Bailby.

One name suggests another, and one story leads to another. I came to know Monsieur Bailby first through *Les Petits Lits Blancs* (the Little White Beds), which was a very beautiful Charity in which he was deeply interested, and of whose Committee I became a member; the name means little white beds for children with bone-tuberculosis; for as the War dragged on its weary length, and more and more milk and eggs and warm clothing and heat for the houses were lacking bone-tuberculosis in children climbed in maiming percentage—from 27% to 68% in the poorer *quartiers.* Along the streets of the cities and along the country roads one may see them limping, dragging their shortened limbs, *clopin-clopant,* and these were all once children with bone tuberculosis; and to try to save France from the dread increase of this trouble, and to try to give the Country sound bodies of men and women instead of cripples, *Les Petits Lits Blancs* was founded. The Little White Beds were first in the wards of L'Hôpital Saint Louis; and Dr. Pinard with his aides and some of the Committee would go through the wards where were lying the children suffering from this malady, and he would say, "This one can go"; "That one cannot." But why this discrimination? Simply because we could not care for them all, and so only the curable ones could be taken. They have beautiful dark eyes, most of the French children of the *quartiers;* and there was an especially pathetic loveliness in the eyes of these little sufferers. They knew what that ward visit of the Doctor meant, and their eyes would follow him as he went from bed to bed with a silent pleading which was heart-rending; you so wanted to take them all and comfort them with fresh hope. For it was to Roscoff in Finistère that they were taken, where the climate is so mild that lemons will grow there. There there were more little white beds for the night times; and in the day times the children were taken to the beach and placed in open barracks with full eastern and southern exposure where the air coming off the rocks covered with algae was saturated with chlorine and bromide and iodine. The record of cures made by *Les Petits Lits Blancs* is a joyous thing to read. The first group of children sent to Roscoff had warm dressing gowns which were made in our *Ouvroir* in the Avenue de l'Alma; some one had sent us fifty yards of beautiful scarlet cloth, and Jeannette had it made up into wrappers for these children. Madame Henri Lavedan was Présidente of *Les Petits Lits Blancs,* and Léon Bailby was its Vice-President; and on the Committee there were also René Vallery-Radot who was Pasteur's son-in-law; and also Edmond Rostand. Monsieur Rostand wrote some lovely lines called *"Complainte pour L'Oeuvre Des Petits Lits Blancs":*

"L'homme du Front n'est bien vainqueur
Que grâce à vous, femmes du coeur!

A quoi bon sauver le terrain
Si l'on ne sauve pas le grain?

Nous sentons que derrière nous
*L'Avenir est sur vos genoux."**

How rich we felt as Committee of *Les Petits Lits Blancs,* when at the close of the first year's work we found that nearly a hundred thousand francs had come in for the crippled children; and since that day two millions of francs were the result of just one Christmas Fête at the Opera in just one evening. And all of this lovely Charity is due primarily to

* " The man at the Front can win the victory only by your gracious help, Women with hearts full of love.

Why try to save the fields, if one save not the seed with which to plant them?

And we, we feel that the future is safe for you, hold it on your knees."

the initiative of Madame Henri Lavedan. Monsieur Lavedan was one of the Forty Immortals, a member of the Académie Française, one of the editors of *L'Illustration*, and a writer of note. In one of his books, *La Famille Française*, he wrote on the fly-leaf:

> "*à Monsieur le Docteur Watson, avec l'admirative et reconnaissante expression de mes sentiments tout dévoués.*
>
> "Henri Lavedan."

"Juin 1917."

My further acquaintance with Léon Bailby came next through a dinner to which we were asked by Rachel Boyer. Rachel Boyer was a *doyenne* of the Comédie Française; she was *Présidente-Fondatrice of L'Union des Arts* as also of *L'Orphélinat des Arts;* her house on the Boulevard Inkermann was just across from the Lycée Pasteur in which was housed our American Ambulance Hospital. I came to know her first by being in a position to find some valued help for these fine Charities in which she was so deeply interested; and we went more than once to her house to dine. At one of these dinners there was an especially distinguished company, (at her house one always met people who were out of the ordinary). There was the Military Governor of Paris; there was Léon Bailby of *L'Intransigeant;* there was a Judge of the *Cours des Comptes;* there was Albert Flament of *L'Illustration;* there was Lucy Arbell of the Opera; there was Lise Berty, and others whose names all spoke for the brilliancy of the company. And that we might show our appreciation of it on our part we asked them all to dine at Avenue de l'Alma that day week; and they all came.

Then later we had an invitation to a dinner at the house of Monsieur Bailby on the Boulevard Saint Germain; and there again we met an interesting group in French life; Monsieur and Madame Lavedan again, and Monsieur Albert Flament. My dinner companion was the Princess Murat who was the daughter of the Duchesse de Rohan; she had just come back from Russia where she had been, in order to find out what was the true state of affairs in Russia;

she gave a thrilling account of her visit, and told of what she had learned about the monk Rasputin who played such a sorry part in Russian Court life.

Rachel Boyer was a woman of large heart and wide influence; and her influence gives one an idea of the hold which all which belongs to *Les Arts* has on the French people. There was to be a reception at *L'Orphélinat des Arts* for its friends. The children cared for there were the orphans of artists who had been killed at the Front; and "artist" means musician, or painter, or sculptor, or singer, or dancer, or actor; and for an object lesson in heredity those children were wonderful. The art instinct, for it is that, an instinct, is inbred in these *artistes* of France; they are born to it, they live and breathe it, they sense it and see its output. Even now the *artistes* are a class apart in French society; and they are as tenacious of their position and their privilege as are the *noblesse* or the *bourgeoisie.* And at *L'Orphélinat des Arts* all this was taken into account; the children were being educated and trained along the lines of that especial type of art appreciation which they showed as their heritage; a more graceful and beautiful group of children than the orphans whom Rachel Boyer gathered there that day could not be found. When she asked me to come to this reception I replied that I would gladly come, but that I did not believe that I could go so far, (it was outside the City). "But, you have a Military Pass, have you not?" she said. "Yes," I replied, "I have a Pass, but I am very short of *pétrol* (gasoline). I have been to the Bureau at the War Office several times to have my *bon de Pétrol* (Gasoline Permit) renewed; but there is some delay about it." "You will have your *bon de Pétrol* before noon to-morrow, I will assure you of that," she said, "and then you will come to my reception, *n'est-ce-pas?"* I answered most gladly in the affirmative; and about eleven o'clock on the following morning came an orderly in uniform to my house, bringing me the bon de Pétrol which was so essential in my work. Once again the influence of the Theatre on the Public Authority showed itself most interestingly; and that was in the matter of the Hospital for Convalescent soldiers at Tessé-la-Madeleine. Madame Brolemann, a good friend of ours and the wife of the *Maire* of Neuilly-le-Vendin, was deeply interested in this hospital; she and her daughters worked there constantly and had done much to make the hospital a success. Another interested worker in that hospital was the Marquis de Frotté a distant kinsman of mine, whose home was the old Château de Couterne close by, a fine old building built in the 16th Century by the poet Jean de Frotté a chevalier of Marguerite de Navarre. And word had come that the Hospital at Tessé-la-Madeleine must be closed. Pursuing a necessary policy of concentration in order to cut down expense, the *Service de Santé* (the Surgeon-General's Department) was closing many of the smaller hospitals which the generosity of the people had organised earlier in the War. Tessé-la-Madeleine was one of these; and the Brolemanns were disconsolate and told me their sorrow over it when we visited them at their Château de Vaugeois. One day when I was at dinner at the Boulevard Inkermann, I told Rachel Boyer about it, and asked her if there was anything which could be done about it. Her reply was that she was going the next day to Bagnoles-de-l'Orne with her mother who went there to take the waters, and that if I would give her a card to the Brolemanns she would go and see the hospital for herself. A few days later I had word from her saying that the matter had been arranged, and that if I would go and see the Chef of the Service de Santé, the necessary papers for keeping the hospital would be issued. It is a great thing for a nation to have as part of its government a Ministry of Fine Arts; and in my opinion the Ministry of the Beaux Arts is as important an element in the educational life of France as is the governmental function which concerns itself with what might be considered as specifically scholastic attainment.

One of the men in the public eye in France whom I have occasion to remember appreciatively is Edouard Herriot, Senator of the Rhone, Maire of Lyons; a one time Prime Minister. I received a card from him one day asking me if I would come to see him at the Senate. I went with great readiness; it was my first opportunity of seeing the Senate in session. Monsieur Herriot wanted all sorts of firsthand information about American Relief; what the American Relief Clearing House was doing; what I was doing for Relief from the American Church and from the Ouvroir which we maintained. In a book of his, *Agir,* there is a chapter entitled *"L'Amitie Americaine"* in which he says:

> *"un homme admirable, le Reverend Watson, pasteur de l'Eglise Américaine, avenue de l'Alma, installe un ouvroir qui a envoyé depuis le debut de la Guerre plus de cinq cent mille articles aux oeuvres de secours et aux soldats. . . . Il me cite un chèque de 5 dollars adressé pour les blessés français par un petit groupe de négresses du Liberia. Une autre offrande provient d'une quête faite dans une école de dimanche en Chine; elle est expediée par de petits garçons chinois pour les petits orphelins français."*

All this I told Monsieur Herriot in the midst of a running fire of questions on his part and of answers on mine; and I knew then how my questioner could be Senator of the Rhone and *Maire* of Lyons at the same time, and still have the needs of all his little people in his heart all the time. Then next Monsieur Herriot tells the story which I told him about Abbé Hutin. This good priest was a real father to his people; he had charge of two little villages which were tucked away in the valleys of Les Eparges; the people were a mixed population in origin, many of them being descendants of a wave of refugees who fled the hill countries after the Revocation of the Edict of Nantes; and the rest of them were mostly Catholics. The Abbé told me: "I minister to them all; for I am the only *pasteur* they can have; I baptise them, I marry them, I bury them; when a couple are married who come of Protestant stock I always give them a Bible in French; when a child of one of these families makes his first Communion I give a New Testament in French. I want them to feel that I am really a shepherd to the flock." Shortly before Christmas of 1915 it was that Abbé Hutin first came to see me. He had been commended to me by my good friend Jean Linzéler who, when stationed in that region of the Front had stayed at Abbé Hutin's *presbytère* for a night or two; and he told me of the needs of the people, and how the enemy had over-run the villages and had carried away nearly everything. I sent him cases of clothing, some blankets and some bed linen, and I gave him some money. Shortly after Christmas he wrote me:

"Monsieur le Recteur; you kindly permitted me to buy some things for my Church out of that money which you gave me: well, among other things I bought a fair-linen cloth for the Altar; I used it for the first time at the Midnight Xmas Mass; and I thought sadly that our Saviour was better sheltered that night so long ago in the stable of Bethlehem than in our poor church *toute endeuillée* (there is no English to translate the delicate meaning of the French words, "all in mourning" would be best) from the War and its consequences, with its windows shattered by the obus, and its roof in holes from the shells."

Then, after this pathetic note, so quickly does the French mood change from the sublime to the laughable, he continued:

"Last night there was a council of the women of the village; they came to ask me to write you so that you might, if possible, send us one rooster and three hens of American stock (for they have great confidence in the American spirit). And I myself believe that with six hens and two roosters we could succeed in re-populating the deserted chicken coops."

In response I sent him a dozen English Orpingtons, telling him that it was a long fly for American birds across the water, but that I hoped that their English cousins would do their duty by France.

Now that I have mentioned Jean Linzéler I want to pay a tribute to *la famille Linzéler*. They were our first French friends, and gave us our first welcome inside the closed-in garden of the *haute bourgeoisie* family. Our first dinner at the house of Madame Frédéric Linzéler in the Rue d'Astorg was noteworthy; she was the grandmother, the *bonne-maman* as they say endearingly in France; and the life of the family centred about her. There were a dozen or more of the family at the table, and at the beginning of the meal our hostess said that she wanted her children to share her pleasure in having for the first time *des étrangers* at her table.

Etranger in France means any one who is not French; and the English derivative of the word carries with it something of the idea, "strangers"; strangers to the old traditions of a French household; and it meant a great deal when Madame Linzéler welcomed us, *des étrangers* to her *foyer* and to her table. More than once I was asked by Americans in France to arrange for them that they might have the entrée to a French family circle of the old stock; and I would have to explain that it was much easier to have an invitation to a "five-o'clock" at the house of Madame la Comtesse or Madame la Marquise than to be received in one of the homes of the *haute bourgeoisie* of France. While in a certain sense I regretted this attitude, and while I have a certain sympathy with the move toward a larger *Fraternité,* I am still inclined to the opinion that the old ways are better for France, although I am certain that French traditions of family life are so firmly ingrafted on the hearts and minds of the people, that there is little danger of alien habits and alien manners creeping in and changing that personal reserve which is so necessary for the preservation of French character. We in America can have little idea of what all this means; our life is such a wholly different one; we are such a composite people, whilst France is a people of one blood, of one racial tradition. France exists and endures because of that tradition of a racial ideal, a racial meaning; her habits of reserve are a needed barrier against the deterioration of that ideal; and the casual introduction of foreigners into that *foyer* which is more a Frenchman's castle than an Englishman's HOME is such to him entails dangers which the *haute bourgeoisie* of France were ever on their guard against. We visited Madame Linzéler at the Château de la Voisine; and again we were guests at the Château de Carsix which was Robert Linzéler's place in Normandy; and at both places I took photographs of the girls of the family; one of a lovely young girl who was Simone coming in from the garden with her basket full of flowers and fruit for the noonday déjeuner; and others of Jacqueline and of Marie Thérèse, and of their cousin Alice. The pictures of Jacqueline and of Marie Thérèse I sent to Robert their father, who was at the Front. In a volume of poems which he wrote and which was entitled *"En Lorraine,—1914-1916,"* a copy of which he sent me with this note: *"en hommage respectueux et reconnaissant, Robert Linzéler"* there is a poem, *"A Ma Fille Jacqueline pour ses seize ans pendant la Guerre"*; and another, *"Sur un portrait de ma fille Marie Thérèse."* Jacqueline's begins:

"Je reverrai l'éclat soudain de tes grands yeux,
Ton calme et lumineux sourire" *

And of a photograph showing the three girls gathering roses from an overhanging vine he wrote this of Marie Thérèse:

"Sous l'épais cordon
Des légères roses
J'aime cette pose d'indécision
. . . . .
Mais reprends ton rire
Libre et sans remords:
Que les vieux soupire!" †

And here is to me one of the wonders of the French character. Here is an active business man in time of peace, an officer on the Lorraine Front in time of war, and from out the muck of the trenches he writes most charming verse. *La chère Bonne-maman* (which is familiar French for grandmother, and prettier too) was the guiding spirit of the household always; she was *petite*, refined, elegant, cultivated, and just like the ladies of her generation in my own family; and the evening gatherings in the salon at Carsix where each one worked or played games was the dear old life of the families of the 1800's. That salon was panelled with carved woodwork, each panel showing the strong relief of a Grinling Gibbons; the corridors in the Château were of stone as were

* "I shall see again the quick flash of your great eyes, Your calm and luminous smile."

† "Beneath that heavy wreath of light roses
I love your pose of indecision:

But smile again, freely without regret;
Let us older folk do the sighing!"

the stairs, the centres of whose treads were so deeply worn in the centres by generations of feet that you had to "mind your step"; in our bedroom the walls were of panels of chestnut each one carved with a different motif; and the great bed, too heavy to be moved, was in an *alcove* so deep that we wondered how the maid could ever make it up, until she showed us a little sliding door in the partition which formed the *alcove* which could be pushed aside.

That visit to Carsix has left lovely memories. Robert and Jean were at the Front; and when we left it was a real parting to say *au revoir* to Madame Linzéler and Madeleine Jean and Madeleine Robert and Jacqueline and Simone and Marie Thérèse and Alice and *l'oncle* George and his family; but we were on our way to Lower Brittany and our leave was short. We went by way of Séez, and I took a photograph of its splendid Cathedral front, as I was standing on the marble counter of a *charcuterie* (by the graciously accorded permission of the proprietor). From Séez we went by way of Tours and Angers to our intended destination which was Pornic. We were going to Pornic because Browning wrote "*Fifine*" there; but Fifine had gone before we arrived; and the hotel had the sad odour of an old fashioned Monday washday; so the morning after our arrival I compromised with the landlady and we started on our way again. "Where are we going, Monsieur?" said Gabriel. "To La Baule, by way of Nantes," was my reply. "But that is in the War Zone, Monsieur." When we came to the bridge across the Loire, Gabriel said, "But, Monsieur, we are sure to be arrested at the bridge." "Good," was my reply, "that will get us where we want to go." But the unexpected happened; we were not arrested; we were not even asked for our "papers"; so we drove to the Préfecture. I always carried with me a card which had been given me by Monsieur Ogier at the Ministry of the Interior and which was addressed simply to Monsieur le Préfet, without specifying any Préfet in particular, and commending me to that potent official's good graces. In this case I found that Monsieur le Préfet was in Paris; but his Chef de Cabinet was most courteous.

I told him that I had come to ask the Préfet to get me a military pass so that I might go on to La Baule for my ten days holiday. The Chef de Cabinet said that he could not do anything personally about it; that the pass would have to come from the Commandant de la Place; so I asked him if he would kindly telephone the Commandant and ask him to let me have the pass. And I heard the conversation which ensued: "But, Monsieur, it is for an American gentleman who is well known and who gives all his time to Relief Work; he is a Chevalier of the Légion of Honour; we ought to arrange it for him." With the final result that he hung up the phone and said to me: "You have heard, Monsieur; the thing is impossible; he says that it cannot be done without sending your papers to Paris." I thanked the courteous Chef de Cabinet and asked him to give me a card to the Commandant, and to send his *huissier* with me in the car to see that I got in to see the officer in authority at the place. All this was done with the same result; my papers must go to Paris. After thanking this officer for his courteous reception of me, I asked him his name, which he told me; and I then said, "Are you by any chance a relative of Monsieur ——— of the Ministry of War?" He was;—and did I know him? I replied that we had dined together at the Ministry but a few evenings before. After a few more minutes of pleasant conversation I had my Laissez-Passer; a big blue sheet with red lines crossing it diagonally, and duly embellished with three photographs; and without further delay we were on our way to déjeuner at the Restaurant Prévost in the Place Graslin, where we were much comforted for the morning's fatigue. Then in the afternoon we were off for La Baule; and in all the trip, to La Baule and back again, through Lower Brittany, and across the Loire, and through the Vendée and the Deux Sèvres those military papers never came out of their *serviette;* they were never even asked for.

My friend the landlord of the hotel where I used to stay, —and in those days La Baule was a simple little Brittany *plage* and there was but one hostelry *de premier ordre*— told me when I saw him in the evening that there was an American ship on the rocks between Pouliguen and Le

Croisic; that it had been torpedoed by an enemy submarine a few days before, and that the crew had taken to the boats and were all saved. The next morning I went down to see the ship. It was a five-master, a wooden schooner; and I took some photographs of her with her five masts sticking up above the water: but as it was then high tide I could not get close enough to her to make out her name. Now a five-masted schooner was sufficiently rare, so that my memory recalled having seen a five-master launched. It was in the summer of 1906, the year when I was sailing the *Lula-Marion,* a 42-foot sloop, on Penobscot Bay, and in that year she won me a fine cup, the first prize in the "Fisherman's Class" in the season's races of the Bucks Harbor Yacht Club. We had been up at Castine for luncheon, and as we came back we saw a five-master on the ways at the edge of the water, so we sailed over close enough to see her make her graceful slide, and we could read her name which was *Dirigo,* the motto of the State of Maine; and also to see her figure-head. In 1907 I was sailing the *Lula-Marion* down Eggemoggin Reach, and just off Pumpkin Island Light I passed the *Dirigo;* she was loaded with ice and on her way from Sargentville for New York; and she was a beautiful sight with all sails set. When I could finally reach the American ship on the rocks I went down at low tide to the coast below Pouliguen and I climbed out on the rocks quite close to her. She was the same *Dirigo* that I had seen launched in Penobscot Bay eleven years before: she had been loaded with cotton in bales, and with pig iron; the sea water had swelled the cotton which had burst the hatches, and the shore all the way to the Bourg de Batz was decorated with bales of American cotton which had been washed ashore.

I could write pages on that old town of Batz, known as Le Bourg de Batz, and locally pronounced "Bah." There is a Musée there which contains interesting examples of ancient Breton furniture; it has a unique collection of the costumes of the *paludiers,* as the workers in the neighbouring salt-marshes are called. I have a set of beautiful water colour sketches of these costumes which were painted for us by

Yvonne Duguereau; by the costume of a *paludier* and by the hats or the coiffes one may tell whether the wearer is bachelor or maid, widow or widower, and what is the social station of each. The rights to the harvesting of the salt in the *marais salants* (salt-marshes) was once a royal prerogative; and these rights have been farmed out to descendants of the same families for hundreds of years; and all salt so collected pays a tax to the State. Saillé, the oldest village of the *paludiers* is completely surrounded by salt traps. This village is known in history because here was celebrated the marriage of Jeanne de Navarre to Jean IV. In ancient times the principal town of the region was Guérande: its Church of St. Aubin was founded in 852; and before its high altar in 1365 there was signed the peace between Charles V of France and Jean de Monfort. Guérande is one of the best types of the old fortified cities of the Middle Ages; its walls with their ten towers intact and their four gates piercing the walls date back to 1413. Around the walls there is what was once the deep trench of the ancient moat; and on the farther edge of the moat there is a fine promenade beautifully shaded with trees; and on that promenade I have seen more than 2000 of the citizens of Guérande marching in solemn procession on La Fête Dieu, wearing the costumes of the olden days; and there were at least five little infant Saint Johns in the procession, and each one with his own little woolly lamb.

Guérande is on the way of a pilgrimage which we used to make from La Baule to the *Calvaire de Pont-Château.* This Calvary was built by the inspiration of *le bienheureux Grignon de Montfort* in 1709; it was destroyed by order of Louis XIV; and it was then rebuilt in 1821. It is a complete presentation of the life of the Christ from the Annunciation to His Ascension, and it takes more than an hour to visit all of the Stations. The Calvary itself is a hill in the midst of a plain, and this hill is made of great rocks which were dragged there by the peasants until an elevation of at least 200 feet or more had been constructed. On the summit of this hill there are three crosses which stand out against the horizon; and in the side of the hill there is the Tomb in the

Garden, and the figures of the Resurrection group; then some hundred yards further on is a figured representation of the Ascension; seen from some distance the figure of the Christ seems to be literally floating off in the air; and in the group of the bystanders there is a figure of the Blessed Virgin with the most exquisite face that one could imagine. The beginning of the Way of the Cross comes just after passing the Judgment Seat of Pilate. This last is a sculptured group at an elevation of about fifty feet from the plain, and Pilate on his throne stands out against a bas-relief of sculptured figures which is very impressive. There are three stairways that lead to the platform on which Pilate is seated; and the centre one of these stairways is a *Scala Sancta*.

The first time that we went to La Baule I asked mine host of the Inn where the Calvary was and also some information about it. There were two little girls in the doorway of the hotel at the moment, and the landlord said, "These little children know the Calvary well, and they will be glad to show you where it is": so Didi and Janine were our guides that day. "Didi" was short for Marguerite; she was the little daughter of Doctor Millet who had given up his private practice at Vincennes in order to be free to give his services to the Hospital which had been established in the Casino on the beach at La Baule; and Janine, who was Jeanne in full letters, was Didi's little girl friend. Didi was *brune* and *svelte* and *spirituelle;* and Janine was round and rosy and *pratique*. When we came to the front of the terrace below the Judgment of Pilate, Janine started to walk up the middle stair (the *Scala Sancta*); but Didi pulled her back saying, "Janine! you must not do that!" "Why not?" said Janine. "Because you must go up there on your knees; every step of the Holy Way which you go up on your knees will be worth to you a week of Purgatory." Janine remained a moment in thoughtful hesitation; then she dropped her little pink, plump knees on the cold, wet, mossy steps, and began the slow and disagreeable climb; it had been drizzling a cold drizzle, and the stone steps were very wet and very cold. After a discouraging climb of four steps Janine, *pratique*, little blonde Janine gave it up; and turning to her friend she said, "Didi, it isn't worth it."

On coming in to the Hotel at La Baule one day after having been to look after the needs of the Hospital in the Casino I sat down on one of the chairs on the terrace before the door, and there I was soon joined by a man wearing the uniform of the A.E.F. We got into conversation and he asked me if I liked the hotel; if they took good care of me and if they had given me good rooms. Then after seeming to consider my replies, he said, "You are an American, and I am an American; may I ask you some plain questions?" The prelude did not seem to me to augur well for the music which was to follow. I had found some of my compatriots quite dissatisfied with their reception in France; they thought that they were giving France a great deal, and that apparently the fact was not being recognised as they thought it should be. However, I told him that I would be glad to give him any information that he considered would be of use to him, and I asked him what it was that he wanted to know. "It is this," he said. "I am an American officer, and you are an American; you are not French though you speak French; now I would like to know why I am treated so differently from the way in which they treat you around here. I was at the Restaurant Prévost in Nantes yesterday when you came in; every table inside was marked RESERVED; but you went in, were given a good table, and I had to sit outside with the chauffeurs. May I ask if you had reserved a table?" My reply was that I had not. "Well, that's one thing," he said. "Then here at this hotel; I came here before you did. You tell me that you have a good apartment, with a bath; I could not get one. You have one of the best seats in the dining room looking out across the garden to the Ocean; and I have a table from which I have an excellent view of the kitchen. Will you tell me what it all means?" I deliberated a moment as to what to say. Experience had taught me that it is a fool's job to attempt to un-prejudice a homesick and biased mind; you simply do not get anywhere. Kipling's "Never the East and West shall meet" is just as true of some types of *English-speaking* minds, (and that is not a slip of the machine; it is just as I mean it). English-speaking minds and the mind of the man of France do not understand alike, and never can they. But, there was one thing which I had noticed, which made me think that possibly my American officer had a knowing heart, despite his biased mind. I had noticed him making friends with a little French boy and girl outside the Hotel; and I decided that if he could make a little child his friend, his heart might redeem his mind. So I decided on the instant to make the venture; and this is what I told him: " 'What it all means' "—to quote your question—"is this. You are a gentleman at heart, and yet you have in the background of your thinking the feeling that your money counts. 'I am paying for it' is the common expression heard so often on the lips of our countrymen; while the truth is that nothing that is real or worth while in life *can* be paid for." We heard so much of that point of view with regard to food in France during the War. When I reminded American soldiers that they were fed by France which did not have food enough for herself, I have often been told, "But, we paid for it." But really it was not money, not anybody's money that paid for that food; it was life, the life of French families, the life of French children. There was not enough, and prices kept on going higher, and the little families of the land could not buy the food at those prices, and so child life was crippled and sacrificed, as all who were in that horrible affair were sacrificed. Money paid for food in those days, when milk and eggs went up 10%, 30%, 50%; that was not all the price. There was that which money could not buy: a whole generation of French children were paid as part of the price of that food. So I told my A.E.F. friend: "Your trouble is that you have an instinctive idea that you can buy what you want in the way of hospitality; while the French Inn-keeper's mental background is that you are his guest and that he is your host, rather than that you are a customer and he a dealer."

It is an interesting fact that in French the word *hôte* means both guest and host; and that the word *hôtel* in

France used to mean simply a large house; and a large house is called to-day *un hôtel particulier,* a private hotel. Hence in olden times strangers were entertained in the large house of the village, for there were no hotels in the modern sense; the traveller was received as a guest (we have the relic of the same tradition in the habit of speaking of persons who are staying at a hotel as being "guests"). And when the traveller went to his room he found on the bedside table a plate on which was money, small pieces and large; if he had plenty he was expected to leave on the plate when he left the house some gift, an *honorarium,* to help some other traveller more needy than himself; and if he was in need he was welcome to take from the plate enough to supply his wants for the next day's journey. That same tradition of life sharing was the glory of the learned professions in older days; and it was even continued by some professional men in my days in Paris. I had occasion once to consult a skilled oculist about my eyes; he wrote pages in his record after examining my eyes. On leaving the salon where I had been received when I came, I found a maid by the door, and beside her on a pedestal there was a plate, and on the plate there were gold pieces and bank notes; and I left an honorarium comporting with my financial status. I had been told in advance by the general practitioner who had referred me to the oculist just what to expect; that this brilliant professional man refused to keep any financial accounts with his patients; that under no circumstances would he ever send a bill; his services were not something which could be paid for, and money could not buy them; what he received was what your sense of honour suggested to you as fitting, it was an *honorarium.* Each patient was expected to leave on the plate a twenty franc gold piece at least; and on the occasions of my visit to him I saw there many gold pieces, some 50 franc and some 100 franc notes, and occasionally a 500 franc note.

And there were Counsellors at Law in France in my day there, who had the same high sense of the meaning of their professional relations. I did not explain all this to my American Officer friend, but I did try to show him that point of view when I said to him: "In a French hotel of the olden type you, as a visitor, are not buying anything; you are a guest; and you simply did not know that. I can only imagine what happened at the Restaurant Prévost from what I noticed this morning. You went into Madame's private Bureau with your hat on and smoking a cigar, and you acted as if you had a right there, as if your money warranted your assuming trade relations; so I can well see why you have not gotten the room you wanted nor a seat in the dining room which is to your liking. I will risk being thought officious by telling you the difference in my own case, for that is the only way I know of explaining it to you. When I came to the Restaurant Prévost I took off my hat and went in and asked if Monsieur Prévost could see me; he was busy at the time in the kitchen preparing some delicious *entremet* or other, and it was a minute or two before I could see him. When he came I told him of how much I had enjoyed my déjeuner in his cool dining room on the occasion of my last visit to Nantes, and that I remembered the *sole frite,* and the omelette, and the cool pitcher of *petit vin rose* which he had brought me from the cellar; and I expressed my disappointment at not having the pleasure of eating with him at this time. 'But, why not, Monsieur?' was his reply. 'Because I see that I am too late, and that all the tables inside here are marked *réservée.'* Instantly he drew out a chair from a table near a window and taking up one of the *réservée* cards, he said, 'But, yes, Monsieur, this one is reserved for you.' And when I came to this hotel I asked the concièrge to see if Madame could receive me, and when I had been ushered into her little Bureau and she had greeted me cordially, I said that I hoped the hotel was not so full but that I could have a room with a bath, such an apartment as I had so much enjoyed on the occasion of my last visit. 'Monsieur shall have the very same one,' was Madame's reply. 'And for a table in the *salle à manger,* would there possibly be one free on the ocean side and near a window?' 'If there is not one free then an extra table shall be put in for Monsieur,' said the Hostess." I had the pleasure afterward of receiving the hearty thanks of my American friend;

and I felt that he had really become my friend; for he told me that it was all a wholly new point of view for him; and that it would make his work in France much easier for him thereafter. Never in my years of association with the French people did I find the time when courtesy did not bring a courteous response. Often, it is true, the courteous response would be the prelude to something like what is told of the man in the parable who said, "I go, Sir; and went not"; but, I like it better that way. One of our old *serviteurs* at the Church would always say, *Soyez-tranquille, Monsieur,* to my sometimes repeated requests to have some thing attended to then and there. I never could be wholly sure that the thing was done after all; but I liked the *Soyez-tranquille,* just the same.

Monsieur Chevillot of the Hôtel de la Poste at Beaune in the Côte d'Or country is another one of the *bons hôteliers français,* who is associated in my mind with interesting and fragrant memories. I arrived once at his hospitable door at about six o'clock in the evening, and he came out to meet me as soon as he heard the motor snorting up; and his first words after greeting me were, *"Je n'ai pas oublié le brochet, Monsieur."* The last time that I had been there I had complimented him on a fish which he had served for dinner; so when he received my telegram announcing my impending arrival, he hurried off to have another one like it for me. It was just another instance of that cordial relationship between host and guest which is so very attractive; really, you are not just host and guest; you are friends meeting after an interval of absence. On that hot summer evening our dinner was served in Monsieur Chevillot's private sitting room; and between courses he would come in himself to see that we were being well cared for. After dinner he brought us a *liqueur* which he himself had made from his own *eau-de-vie,* the product of his own grapes, with the aromatic herbs which the old women of the village gathered for him on the hillsides; and as we inhaled its fragrance he told us that it was called *Fleurs-de-Rosée.* He then asked us if we would not stay over the following day and see the *vendange,* the gathering of the grapes; that he would begin cutting them in another large vineyard in the morning. I thanked him for his invitation but told him that we were on our way to Peyrieu where we were expected; and further that we had just been visiting at the Château de Joncy in the Saône et Loire, where I had helped at the *vendange*. It was a most interesting vision of old patriarchal French life in all its simplicity, that grape gathering at Joncy. I went out with the young Vicomte in the morning as he went through the vineyards to see that each one of the workers was cared for; with his own hands he would tip the scales so that old Madeleine might get a little more pay; and when Jeanne, whose husband had been killed at the Front, came a little late, he saw that she had a place to pick where the grapes were thickest. It was the Parable of the Labourers in the Vineyard over again; the Master saw that each one got the penny that he needed.

Then Monsieur Chevillot thought of something else that might interest us. "Had we ever seen the wine in making?" "Would Monsieur and Madame like to come with him now and see how the wine is growing in the vats, full of the produce of the last vineyard whose grapes he had gathered?" Monsieur and Madame would,—and did. Without headgear of any kind we walked out into the little Place in front of the Hôtel, thinking that we had but a few steps to go; instead, we went down a side street for two squares, then under a great stone archway; then across a courtyard into another inner court in the far side of which there was a heavy door which our host opened, and in an instant the air was full of the perfume of the fermenting grapes. There were vats nine feet high; you could hear the gentle bubbling of the fermentation, and as we went in we felt a curious warmth. At Monsieur Chevillot's suggestion I mounted a ladder which he held against the side of one of the vats and looked down into it, and the gas which flowed was so strong that it blew the flame of a candle which I held in my hand, and the liquid in the vats was warm with the heat of the fermentation. On coming out from the vatting rooms, Monsieur Chevillot said, "And now you must come with me and see where my fruit of the grape is being aged after its first fermentation is over"; and again another hatless voyage of exploration through the silent streets of the old town in the warm August moonlight. And as we crossed the place again, the procession was augmented by two additions, a lame man and his fox-terrier; the lame man was a personage, none other than the Maire-Adjoint, the Maire himself was off at the War, and Monsieur l'Adjoint being lame could not go. We were charmed by his cultivated manner and by his erudition, for, after due presentations to officialdom in which I was qualified by all the titles which Gabriel furnished for me (and my titles never lost any glory in Gabriel's rendering of them), the Maire-Adjoint accompanied us. There was a golden harvest-moon that night, which gave the old Cathedral a most unreal look as we made our way up the winding street behind it to where were the ruins of the old Monastery. There we turned down steep stone steps which led to the Monastery cellars where the monks had used to keep their wines; which cellars had been leased by our friend Chevillot for the aging and the storing of his wines. First a great steel door was unlocked and we were given candles fitted into old iron sconces; then an iron grille was freed from its padlock and we went down more steps into the cellar itself. On the sides, under the stone arches, and as far as the eye could see there were rows and rows of casks; and in the centre between the casks were thousands and thousands of bottles lying on their sides and piled in the form of pyramids like cannon balls; and the date of each vintage was marked in whitewash on the butts of the piles of bottles.

On the way back to the Hôtel and in his little salon after we got back, Monsieur Chevillot told us the Romance of the Wines; how a wine is a living thing, having its infancy, its youth, its maturity, its old age; it even has its diseases, and sometimes we can cure them. You can kill the living wine with alcohol if you will, so he told us. "Americans," he said, "often want wines which are simply pickled in alcohol like pathological specimens; and so they are disqualified wholly from appreciating the deliciousness of our living wines, many of which are of so sensitive and delicate a life that they cannot be shipped even from one part of France to another for they have so little alcoholic content." It was like listening to a fascinating story of a life which we had never known before.

At one time our best of friends, Mr. Edward Tuck, sent us part of a purchase which he had made of a *petit vin français,* Mont-Louis, a Mont-Louis of 1911, the hot summer when the harvest was small but the grapes of superb quality. This *petit vin,* just lightly sparkling, was so delicate that it could not bear transport from the Touraine to the Côte d'Azur. When I came away from France I gave away all the fruits of the vine which various good friends had given me; and I sent for Mr. Tuck's butler and asked him to take back the Mont-Louis which I had left to the kindly giver who was then at his place in Monte Carlo. One day after Mr. Tuck's return to Paris the butler at luncheon offered him wine saying *"Mont-Louis, Monsieur, 1911."* Mr. Tuck said, "But there is no more of it." The wise butler persisted *"Mont-Louis, Monsieur, 1911"* only to get the same reply, "But I tell you there is no more of it left"; and again came back the butler with *"Mont-Louis, Monsieur, 1911."* And this time he was successful; he filled the glass of *le patron,* who after tasting it, said, "Why, it is; where did you get it?"; and then Mr. Tuck learned that it was some of his original gift to me which had come home again. And he wrote me, "I've often heard of bread cast upon the waters coming back; but this is the first time I ever knew it to happen with wine."

We were on our way to Monte Carlo for our winter vacation from work which we usually spent with Mr. and Mrs. Tuck: it was the winter of 1917, and a very cold winter for France. We drove to Fontainebleau for the night in order to make an early start in the morning, intending to reach Beaune for the second night; and at Fontainebleau we stayed at the Hôtel de France et d'Angleterre with that charming hostess Madame Dumaine, whose collection of prints and engravings is famous. It was Christmas night, and before we went to our rooms Madame Dumaine took down from the wall an old etching of a Bishop of Durham made by Josiah Wedgewood which was one of her treasures, and she gave it to us for a Christmas present, knowing our British ancestry. This etching I have given to my dear friends Doctor and Mrs. Richard Evans. Doctor Evans has been my devoted medical adviser; both he and Betty have exquisite taste; so that Madame Dumaine's etching has found another appreciative owner. The next morning the sky was overcast, and when we reached Auxerre there was a feeling of snow in the air, and by the time that we came to Avallon the road was white in places with patches of snow. When we came to Saulieu where we planned to take our déjeuner there was a foot of loose snow on the road, a strong wind was blowing, and it was quite a pull for the car to climb the hill. While we were at déjeuner the *patronne* telephoned for me to Monsieur Chevillot at Beaune, to know how the roads were between Saulieu and Beaune and to ask whether we would better stay where we were instead of trying to make Beaune for the night. The reply was that there had been several army camions through and that the road should be passable; so after déjeuner we started on.

We had intended to take a branch road a few kilomètres out of Beaune in order to go by way of Pouilly, and so avoid the rough country of the Morvan by taking the military road from Dijon down; but in the snow we missed the turn and the next thing we knew we were in Arnay-le-Duc with nothing to do but to go on by way of Bligny-sur-Ouche. At Bligny the climb began, and we made that well enough, coming out on a plateau of the Morvan which is all desert *landes*, with no fences or anything else to mark the road except the tracks of the vehicles and they were by that time almost obliterated by the drifting snow. After a time—it was about five o'clock in the afternoon—there was a skidding of the wheels and we were off the road and head-on in a drift. For three quarters of an hour we tried to dig the wheels out so as to get purchase enough to back the car, but that well-known dismal whirr of spinning wheels was the sole result. So I said to Gabriel, "There's nothing to do but to see if we can get some horses at Lusigny (a little village a few kilomètres on) to pull us out of this. Do you think that you can make it?" Certainly he could; so our good Gabriel started off on foot feeling the hard surface of the road beneath the snow as his guide; and we shut ourselves up in the car, with nothing at all to eat and nothing to drink but Listerine. The snow had stopped drifting, but the wind was blowing, and it was so cold that the windows of the car were covered with frost a half-inch in thickness; and we sat there and shivered, listening to the concert of the wolves howling in the woods beyond us. It was two hours later that we heard shouts, and looking out I saw Gabriel coming; and this was his story: "I found a little *épicerie* in the village and I made arrangements there for the horses, and while the boy went to get them I telephoned to Monsieur Chevillot, telling him where we were and asking him to keep dinner for us as we would be late in getting into Beaune. His answer was that he had feared we might be in trouble as the snow had begun again since he had telephoned to Saulieu at noon; that we would have no need of horses as he had his car at the door with ropes all ready and that he and his chauffeur would come up and pull us out. So," said Gabriel, "I sat down by the stove with some bread and cheese and a little *pichet d'ordinaire* and waited until Monsieur Chevillot came along to bring me back here." "But, where is he?" I said. "If Monsieur will look down this way about 200 metres, the lights of Monsieur Chevillot's car may be seen; he is head-on in the other end of this same drift which caught us; and he has sent his chauffeur back to the village to get some men and shovels to dig us out." Soon came along Monsieur Chevillot in person, and after greeting us he produced a "little brown jug," the same sort of a jug as the ones which John Gilpin carried on either side of him as he rode, with their ears held by his belt-strap; and in that jug which Monsieur Chevillot brought there was rum punch, once on a time hot, but which had even then, two miles from home on that cold night, wonderful capacity for warming; and under our feet he put a big pewter container full of hot water; and so the near-tragic part of this tale draws to its close. At

11:15 we were in the courtyard of the Hôtel de la Poste at Beaune; and in their warm little salon was a table all spread for us, and Madame Chevillot and her daughter ready to see that we were well served. Monsieur Chevillot had disappeared, but soon he came hurrying back with the "first-aid" which he poured into goblets, one for each of us. "This," he said, "is the blood of the grape; drink it all, the whole glass full as you sit by the fire, and by the time that we have dinner on the table it will have quickened the blood for you, and it may save you from a serious illness." And who were we to dispute the prescription of so wise a counsellor? The dinner was delightful, as good as the Burgundy which preceded it; and by 1:00 a.m. we were tubbed and in bed with a comforting *édredon* over each of us. The next morning we rose late after *petit-déjeuner* in bed; and then came our *déjeuner-à-la-fourchette* served in the petit salon again. "Monsieur Chevillot," I said, "will you tell me what is this cold meat which we have been eating?" "That," he replied, "is roast *marcassin* (young wild-boar); I shot one a week ago just a hundred yards from where you were caught in the snow last night."

The reports were that the roads were still too heavy with snow for us to keep on our southward way by Bourg-en-Bresse, as we had intended, so we decided to go by way of Lyon and the Valley of the Rhone. Before retiring for the night I asked Monsieur Chevillot if he would kindly let me pay my reckoning that night, as we wanted to make an early start in the morning; so he brought me a memorandum of it. "But," I said after looking it over, "there is nothing down in this statement for the Burgundy which you brought us when we arrived; nothing for your coming to get us in the night and the snow; nothing for your chauffeur's services, and nothing for the *pétrol* which you must have used." His reply was characteristic; "Will Monsieur please not mention those things; he and Madame are our guests; Monsieur may pay the reckoning for the rooms and for the meals, and, if he wishes, he may pay for the men who came with shovels from the village to dig us out; but I would count it a favour if Monsieur would not mention the rest; it is our privilege to do this for Monsieur." "But, Monsieur Chevillot," I said, "you came out late at night to save our lives, and you did just that, and at some personal risk to yourself; and I do not feel right to let that go without recognition of some sort; is there not something which I can do to show my appreciation?" After a moment's hesitation he said, "Yes, there is something which is very dear to my heart. There is a Hospital for wounded soldiers here at Beaune, and during the week, as Monsieur knows, my *estaminet* (bar-room) is closed; but on Sundays I open it and have it warm, and I send and get twenty of those poor chaps and bring them down here, and they have good food and their wine and their cigarettes: but the War is long; I have small custom at the Hotel, and I do not know how much longer I can keep on doing for the soldiers. If Monsieur felt like doing something for them for a Sunday or two, he would be doing it for me." In these words I have given you a picture of *un bon hôtelier français;* he was my *host,* and I was a *guest.* The following morning on our way to Macon where we were to get our *déjeuner* at the Hôtel de l'Europe et d'Angleterre I said to Gabriel, "Tell me, what is the name of the *patron* at Macon? I know him for I have been here before, and I want to greet him personally when we arrive as it makes such a lot of difference." Gabriel pondered awhile, then said, "I cannot remember it, Monsieur; perhaps I will later." Then a half-hour afterward he said, *je l'ai, Monsieur—le nom du patron; c'est celui qui écrivit le Catéchisme; Monsieur le connait sans doute";* (I have it, Monsieur—the name of the hotel man; it's he who wrote the Catechism; Monsieur certainly knows). And then it came to me, Dupanloup. There was a well known bishop, a Monseigneur Dupanloup, Bishop of Orleans, member of the French Academy; after 1870 he was a *Député;* then in 1876 he became *Sénateur inamovible* (senator in permanence), and it was he who was the author of instructions required to be learned by the children of the Church. So I won a ready welcome when I greeted Monsieur Dupanloup by his Episcopal name when we reached his Hotel in Macon; though I did not tell him that "it was he who wrote the Catechism." From Macon we went to Lyon;

and learning that the roads were blocked at Vienne and at Montélimar (the home of Nougat), and that Valence had had no milk for two days, we decided on the train, and went first to Cannes where Madame Brett took good care of us; —care which I was much in need of, for I had acquired a serious bronchitis from the exposure of that night in the snow.

XIV

RECOGNITIONS AND REMEMBRANCES

AT CANNES I received a telegram which had been forwarded to me from Monte Carlo, and with it came another telegram which was a message of congratulation from Mr. and Mrs. Tuck, the Monte Carlo Telegraph Office having communicated to them the purport of the first telegram knowing that they were close friends of mine. That first telegram was an announcement of the fact that The President of the Republic had awarded me the Cross of a Chevalier of the Legion of honor; it asked me to be in Paris on the 23rd of January when *"Ministre Justice vous fera Chevalier Honneur"* (Minister of Justice will make you Chevalier). The Minister of Justice at that time was the brilliant orator Monsieur Viviani. I felt compelled regretfully to reply that I could not return to Paris for the 23rd, as some days of rest were obligatory if I were to avoid a serious illness. I lay the break in my health which eventually compelled my leaving France in 1918 to the exposure and fatigue of that night in the snow in January 1917, for I never fully regained my strength after that. It was at Nice when returning from that visit to Monte Carlo that I heard the news of the break in diplomatic relations between the United States and Germany; and it was at Cannes that I received my first decoration. Madame Brett came to the train to see us as we passed through, and brought me a little bow of red ribbon. The formal ceremony of Decoration took place at the American Relief Clearing House on the 8th of February, 1917. It was Monsieur Gabriel Hanotaux, one time Minister of Foreign Affairs, who gave me the *accolade.* In transmitting to me the Cross of the Legion on behalf of the Government, he "gratefully acknowledged the exceptional services which Dr. Watson had rendered to the French nation by his generous activity, tireless labour, conscientiousness and tact"; and, continued Monsieur Hanotaux, "every time we have had a delicate mission to carry out we have always turned to you to act as our ambassador; and your perspicacity and the confidence your personality and your sacred office inspired have invariably crowned your efforts with success." Monsieur Hanotaux is a member of the French Academy, the President of France-Amérique, and he was *Président du Comité Central Français des Secours Américains.* A man of charming personality, a brilliant writer and historian, his *History of Cardinal Richelieu* is considered generally to be his outstanding literary work; but, for me, it is his *Life of Jeanne d'Arc* which best reveals the man, and shows the sensitiveness of his spiritual nature as well as the charm of his literary style. I have a letter addressed to *Monsieur Hanotaux, Membre de l'Académie Française,* which is signed "BRIAND," and which reads:

> "You have kindly recommended to me for the Cross of Chevalier of the Legion of Honor Monsieur le Docteur Watson, *recteur de l'église américaine de Paris.* I take great pleasure in informing you that the President of the Republic has just conferred on him this distinction. I have been most happy to second the interest which you have taken in Monsieur le Docteur Watson, and I will be grateful to you if you will transmit to him the emblems of our Nation's Order which accompany this letter, as well as the Official Notification enclosed."

This Notification was in the form of a letter addressed to me and signed "Briand Prime Minister and Minister of Foreign Affairs," and conveyed to me Monsieur Briand's official and personal congratulations. As statesman, orator, political leader, France has had few sons who were Monsieur Briand's equal. As member of several Ministries, as Minister of Foreign Affairs, as Prime Minister, then as representing France at Geneva, and crystallising by authoritative declarations the peace-loving instincts which are deep in the heart of France, he made himself a place and an enduring place in French history and in world history; and I am grateful to have his name among the many who sent me their tributes of regard when France awarded me the distinction which a Frenchman values above all others. From every side, from every rank and station in life, from priest and pastor, from noble and peasant, from the Army and from the Bourgeosie, from educators and writers and from artists congratulations came.

I have a book beautifully bound in Neapolitan leather entitled *Livre D'or de la Legion D'honneur* which holds them, and as I run through its pages I am moved deeply as I find this evidence which tells me the pleasure of my friends, in that France had enrolled me as one of her sons by adoption, as I am in fact by far-off lineage. The first letter in this book, after that of the Prime Minister, is one from Madame Baudouin written shortly after the death of her husband who was *Premier Président de la Cour de Cassation* (Chief Justice of the Supreme Court), which says: "How my dearly loved husband would have been happy! He was awaiting with impatience the realisation of his desire, to see you receive this distinction so merited." There is a letter from the son of this family, himself *Président du Tribunal de la Seine;* and again another from a daughter of the family which says: "This decree realises his dearest desire. How happy he would have been to have given you the *accolade!*"

Among the many names there recorded are Henriette Duchesse de Vendôme, Princesse de Belgique; the Princesse Geneviève d'Orleans; the Marquise de Mun; the Marquise de Talleyrand; the Marquise de Scribot de Bons; the Comtesse de Cossé-Brissac; the Comtesse de St. Gilles de Raymond; the Comte du Pavillon; the Baron and the Baronne de Beyens; the Baronne d'Hangouwart; the Comtesse de Reinach; General de Lacroix; General Dubail Military, Governor of Paris; the Colonel and Madame Philippe Bunau-Varilla; the General Major Frans, of the Belgian Army; Monsieur Laurent, Préfet de Police de Paris; Alfred Dumaine, Ambassadeur de France; Emile Ogier, Directeur du Contrôle, Ministère de l'Interieur; Jean Branet, Directeur Général de Douanes; Monsieur Ternaux-Compans, Président des Medailles Militaires; Hugues Leroux, Sénateur de France, and Madame Leroux; Fernand Bordas, Directeur Ministère Travaux Publics; Alphonse Deville, Ancien Président Conseil Municipal; André Payer, Conseiller

Municipal; Alfred Roll, Président Association Nationale des Beaux Arts; Louis Liard, Vice-Recteur de l'Université de Paris; Louis Mill, of *le Temps;* Fernand Laudet, Directeur de *la Revue Hebdomadaire;* Xavier Léon, Directeur de *la Revue de Metaphysique et de Morale;* André Weiss, Professeur à la Faculte de Droit; Edouard Champion, Editeur; Maurice Roman, Conseiller à la Cour des Comptes; Etienne Grosclaude, of *le Figaro,* and, *l'Illustration;* E. Lavignon, Président, Oeuvre des Orphelins, Ville de Paris; Charles Voigt, Agent General des Eglises Reformées; les Docteurs Collin; le Docteur René Gaultier; le Docteur Antony Rodiet; Rachel Boyer, Présidente l'Union des Arts; Emile Deutsch de la Meurthe, Trésorier Fraternite Franco-Americaine; Pasteur Charles Wagner. And to complete the list would take pages more just for the French names.

To these should be added, as a further part of this record, the names of some of the many Americans who sent me their appreciative remembrances at this time: Madame Waddington; Mrs. John Mackay; Mr. and Mrs. Robert Woods Bliss; Percy Peixotto; Bertram Winthrop; James H. Hyde; Wm. S. Dalliba; J. Leroy White; Maj. F. A. Mahan; Jas. H. Perkins; Ridgway Knight; Arthur Hugh Frazier; Bishop Brent; Bishop Tuttle; Bishop Gailor; Bishop C. D. Williams; Mr. and Mrs. J. J. Hoff; Mr. and Mrs. Labouchère; Mr. and Mrs. Walter Gay; George Munroe; Cleveland Coxe; James Mark Baldwin; Charles and Susanne Carroll; Helen Baird; Florence Matthews; Alice Hubbard; Julia Depew; Mr. and Mrs. Whitney Warren; Mr. and Mrs. Edward Tuck; Geraldine Millet; Stuart Knott; Endicott Peabody; Mrs. D. Cameron. In addition to these names and many others who sent written messages, there were numbers of friends who came to bring their greetings in person.

And last but not least I want to record the tributes of our *personnel* at the *Presbytère.* Gabriel wrote with characteristic humour: "I have learned of your nomination to the Legion of Honour. But who in the world worded the citation? It is as cold as this winter weather is; it talks of honouring the President of this and of that, whereas it is the man that you are which has won the honour. Happily, all those who know you will interpret it aright." Alexis wrote from the Front: "I am both proud and happy to congratulate you. I have shared the good news with my comrades in the trenches, who are glad with me that France takes to her heart one who has devoted himself to us since the beginning of the War." And his wife Louise, our housemaid wrote to me at Cannes: "Since Sunday the mail has been voluminous; and there has been a constant stream of visitors coming to congratulate Monsieur on his Decoration."

My promotion to the grade of Officer of the Legion of Honour was by a Decree dated the 19th of November, 1926. This gift from France, coming to me as it did some years after my return to America, was peculiarly gratifying as being an eloquent witness that the memory of my work for France during the War lasts on in the hearts of the men of the Government with whom I worked and served. It is as if France had said, *Nous autres français, nous n'oublions pas* (We French folk, we do not forget). I have a letter addressed by the Minister of Foreign Affairs to Monsieur le Sénateur Brangier of Les Deux Sevres saying: "I have the honour of advising you that the President of the Republic has conferred, on my proposition, the Cross of Officer of our National Order on Monsieur le Révérend Watson whom you were good enough to recommend for this distinction. And I am sending you herewith the Brevet of this rank which I will ask you to forward to him." The letter bears this endorsement, *"Merry Christmas et meilleurs souvenirs, P. A. Brangier."* I owe much to Senator Brangier for his initiative in this matter; and I also have reason in this connection to remember Messrs. Poincaré, Painlevé, Barthou, and Herriot, who were members of the Council of Ministers when this action was taken.

I have a letter from the Minister of Foreign Affairs of Belgium saying: "Monsieur le Docteur, it has pleased the King, my august Sovereign, on the proposition of the Minister of the Interior and of mine, to confer on you the Cross of Chevalier of the Order of Leopold. I have the honour to send you herewith the emblems of this Order as also the Royal Decree of date of the 20th of May, 1918. This Decree is signed, *"Donné en Notre Quartier Général le 20 mai, 1918,—ALBERT."*

It was the Comtesse de Reinach who sent me word from Salonica that the King of Serbia had conferred on me the Decoration of Chevalier of the Order of Saint Sava. Later, in 1918, I received an Official Brevet from Serbia to the effect that I had been promoted to the rank of Commander of this Order. I had met the King at the Serbian Legation in Paris while he was Crown Prince; and I had been able to be of service to *la Mission de Co-ordination de Secours aux Armées d'Orient,* and also to the Relief of the Serbian Orphans. When in Paris in 1918, I went to the Serbian Legation again to greet our devoted friend Milenko Vesnitch, Serbian Minister to France, and I gave him a communication which I had received, to the effect that the emblems of the recent promotion had been sent me. Monsieur Vesnitch opened the safe in his office and took out the Collar and Cross of a Commander of Saint Sava, and said, "I have them here, and I am most happy to confer them on you, assuring you of Serbia's gratitude." Shortly before a visit which Monsieur Vesnitch was to make to America in the interest of Serbia's cause, he asked me if I would do him a favour, viz:, to translate from the Serbian into liturgical English the National Prayer of the Serbian people. He wished to make use of it when speaking in America, and while his conversational English was sufficiently exact for ordinary conversation, he hesitated somewhat as to the wording of such a liturgical form as the Prayer. I at once expressed to him my readiness to comply with his request, but said that my only difficulty would be that I knew no Serbian. "I will translate it for you from Serbian into French," he said, "and you can then make the translation from French into English." All of which came duly to pass. On crossing to America one of my companions at the Captain's table was Mrs. George Blumenthal; and one day at luncheon she passed a piece of paper across the table to me saying, "I would like you to read that, Doctor." I read it, and smiled my reply. "But why are you laughing," she said; "that is one of the most beautiful things which I ever read." "I am smiling because I wrote it," was my reply. "But," she said, "it was given to me by Monsieur Vesnitch the Serbian Minister; it is the National Prayer of Serbia." Then I told her of how it came about that I had furnished the wording for it.

The nations of the Allies paid their own tribute to the work which Jeannette had done in the War. She received the *Médaille de la Reconnaissance Française* from France; *la Médaille de la Reine Elizabeth* from Belgium; and *la Médaille de la Pitié* from Serbia. My own work was most largely official and in connection with governmental agencies of Relief; while the personal and direct ministrations to the suffering, the needy and the helpless which centred at the Avenue de l'Alma were all under Jeannette's direction. She also was primarily responsible for the creation of *l'Oeuvre du Soldat Belge* and its co-ordinated branch *l'Oeuvre des Orphelins Belges de la Guerre.* I was one of the Vice-Presidents of *l'Oeuvre du Soldat Belge,* but in all that great work of Relief for Belgium, which meant principally relief for Belgian refugees, and which was administered by that little group, headed by King Albert's sister the Princesse Henriette Duchesse de Vendôme, and which met weekly in the Sacristy of Holy Trinity my work was chiefly that of financier and counsellor at large. The actual administration of the countless largesses of Relief came chiefly from an *ouvroir* which Jeannette organized in the first month of the War, and of which she was the efficient manager. The first weeks of the War saw the dress-making shops of the Rue de la Paix closing their doors, and their little *midinettes* were obliged to seek work, which meant bread, elsewhere. We took in fifty of them; borrowed sewing machines; and put them to work in the big upstairs hall of the Parish House. At first we gave them a fixed wage in cash with a *supplément* for their *déjeuner;* but we soon found that they would often eat nothing or next to nothing at noon in order to save the money. So I arranged with a little restaurant in the neighbourhood that I was to have the restaurant and its entire service for half an hour each day from 11:30 on, and we sent our *Mimi Pinsons* over there, and I paid for the luncheons in one sum for the group. As they would file out on to the Avenue de l'Alma at the noon-hour, accompanied by their *directrice* and their *première,* the neighbours would smile and say *Voilà le couvent de Madame Watson!* (there go the girls from Madame Watson's Convent).

One great service which that *couvent* rendered is something which I look back to with deep feeling, which was this, the making of shrouds for our soldier dead at the American Ambulance Hospital. The decent disposal of the dead was a problem which confronted us soon after the first wounded men came in; first some arrangement of the bodies so that they were presentable when their relatives came for one last look; and later, for their interment. Coffins were too costly, even if they could have been gotten, which they could not; and at first we were obliged to use sheets; then later at the Ouvroir there was designed a beautiful shroud in the form of the robe and hood worn by the Prophet Hosea in Sargent's mural in the Boston Public Library, and thereafter every one of the brave fellows who left his body in our Ambulance Hospital was given for it a decent robe of fair cloth with a great cross in violet on the front of it. That especial work Jeannette took charge of personally; and in addition she saw to the preparation of the layettes which went out day by day and every day; with her own hands she arranged more than 2500 of them. This was a difficult task at one time, this making of layettes, for finding the material for them in Wartime Paris was not easy. But one day a glorious gift came; Mrs. Levi P. Morton asked what we needed most, and in response to our reply, she sent us beautiful white flannel to the value of $1,000; and another $1,000 worth of dried milk; soft white flannel for baby clothes, and milk to feed the babies with—that was a princely gift.

And one day a Princess came when the flannel was being unpacked, saw it and felt its fine texture, then said, "You know, we cannot get soft white flannel any longer in France; these children of the poor will be more softly clothed than will be the little grandchild whom I am expecting soon to come to my daughter, the Princess"; the answer to that was that Jeannette made up the layette for the little princeling. Here is another touching story about a layette from the *ouvroir*. The son of the Marquise de Scribot de Bons came in one day, to ask if one of his men in the trenches could have an *imperméable* (rain coat); and when that was readily offered he asked if he could have one thing more, a layette for the same soldier's wife, who was expecting a little one very soon; they were people who had once been well off, but the War had taken all they had. So a beautiful layette was packed and made ready to send, and in another package by its side in the shipping room was the rain coat, but by some jest of fortune the packer mixed the addresses: the expectant mother received the rain coat, and the soldier in the trenches got the layette. A week or so later the officer came in to tell us what had happened, and instead of regretting the mistake he was overjoyed at it. "It was a jest of the Good God," he said; "my men were weary, they were homesick, long hours in the mud and the cold had almost crushed their courage, and by nightfall they were hopeless; then in the morning comes the sergeant bringing the mail; he calls the name of the man to whom you sent the package: the poor fellow was not listening for he was not expecting anything; his comrades called him,—'A package for you!', and he came up wearily to get it; he unwrapped it, the tarred paper first, then the heavy wrapping paper, then the tissue paper, and he stood amazed as the comrades crowded around him saying, 'What is it? What is it? Put it up there!', and they point to the shelf of clay dug into the side of their *cagibi* (refuge); and there it was put, the soldier's package; and the grimy men looked and saw little baby clothes, and little knitted baby-socks, and a little blue blanket with little white rabbits scampering over it; and they fell on their knees as before an altar shrine, and they kissed the little things tenderly; and with shining eyes which spoke as eloquently for their feelings as any words could they said, 'That is what we are fighting for; for the little ones who come after us; for the France of to-morrow.' "

Magali Besnard heard the story in the *ouvroir* and wrote some lovely lines which begin:

"Deux chaussons de bébé, si légers, si laineux,
Faits de neige attiédie ou de toisons celestes,
Mettant leur chaleur blanche entre ses doigts calleux
Qui pour les effleurer, trouvent de nouveaux gestes.
Et l'homme, ce soldat, demain sera Vainqueur
Puisqu'il ne se bat pas rien que pour des paroles.

Mais pour les petits pieds portant chaussons, sabots,
Pour tous les petits pieds d'enfants de la Patrie
Dont il est le gardien: . . . et des ineffables mots
Aux lèvres du soldat montent, dans la féerie" *

Of Jeannette's Decorations there is a worth-while story to tell. We were in New York in the autumn of 1918 after several months of resting and speaking, and we were awaiting notification from the authorities of the ship by which we were to return to Europe, whether to France direct or to France by way of England we did not know. You went to a hotel, then left your address at the shipping office and were told "you will go on No. 25," or some other number which meant nothing to you as to what the boat was or where it was going; and you were told, "We will telephone you where to find the ship; keep within reach of the tele-

* "Two baby-socks, so light, so soft,
Woven of snowy wool or fleecy clouds;
To feel their downy warmth numbed fingers
Find life coming back to them again:

And the soldier of tomorrow dares to hope to win
Since he is fighting for something more than words:

It is for the little feet in sabots or in socks,
For all the little feet of France he fights:
He is their guardian; . . . and to his lips there come
Voiceless words, as if t'were there a fairy land."

phone, for the hour of embarking will not be made known long in advance";—no information as to ship or sailing being given out on account of submarine dangers. Our passports were ready; at the French Control my Legion of Honor got me a quick visa; but at the British Control Office it was another story. There we waited a long time before we were admitted to the august presence of the potentate who controlled our destinies and destination. He was a grim old seadog of a Vice-Admiral, and after questions at length which he put to me, he said: "I will endorse your papers, Sir; but Madame cannot go." Whereat I demurred, and I argued, only to be met with a still more positive refusal to endorse the papers for Jeannette. About this chilly time in our interview a valet came in and addressing the officer, said, "Tea, Sir?"; and he said, "You'll have tea, of course." With tea the atmosphere grew less chilly, and Jeannette loosened her heavy coat and threw it back, thus exposing the ribbons of France, of Belgium, and of Servia which she wore on her dress. The Admiral looked at them in surprise and said, "What are those ribbons which you are wearing, Madame? Decorations which you received in France? Why the devil didn't you say so before, Madame? Of course, you can go. I didn't know that you were a War-worker; I thought that you were a lady." And the papers were signed without more ado.

Jeannette's own story, *Our Sentry Go,* which was published in 1924, tells more than I can possibly tell her of what her work was; she was the personal side of the work, which supplemented with life and heart my tasks which were so largely official.

At Easter time of 1918 I was completely exhausted, after nearly four years of incessant strain and responsibility. The Church had an increasing duty to the Americans who were arriving in numbers, a duty which I knew that I was unable to cope with in my state of worn heart and nerves. Furthermore, I could not abandon the French and Belgian responsibilities which had accumulated on my hands during the years before the Americans arrived. As a consequence I made a quick decision to return to America. The following document is self-explanatory:

"Paris, March 20th, 1918

"To the Reverend S. N. Watson, D. D.,

"Reverend and dear Sir;

"Your unalterable decision to sever your connection with the Church of the Holy Trinity has left the Vestry no alternative.

"We can only express to you once more our deep regret, and endeavour to put into words our high appreciation of the invaluable services which you have rendered to the Church during the past six years.

"At the beginning of your Ministration you were confronted with serious problems. For these, your wide experience and efficient administration were assuring us of an early and successful solution.

"War came; and with it a wholly new and disturbing situation, which threatened to greatly imperil the activities and usefulness of the Church.

"Looking back, it is even now more than difficult to see how such a result could have been avoided but for your presence which may legitimately and reverently be described as Providential.

"Not only has the work suffered no break, in spite of financial and other impediments, but its scope has been greatly extended without regard to the heavy additional burden.

"The Church has become widely known by your initiative, and the active and far-reaching work for relief and usefulness in various directions, especially from your devoted and efficient service, side by side with the French Authorities, in connection with the Relief Work both French and Belgian necessitated by the War, and for which both you and the Church have received such distinguished recognition.

"We are glad that our happy associations are not to be entirely severed, and that you have accepted the honorable position of Rector Emeritus.

"You will understand our wish to add our further tribute of respect and gratitude for the untiring devotion with which Mrs. Watson has supported and facilitated the execution of your plans.

"We hope that you may soon find needful rest and fresh energy for the work which you may next undertake; and we beg to offer to Mrs. Watson and to yourself our very sincere wishes for your welfare and happiness.

(signed)

"J. LeRoy White, *Sr. Warden*
G. Munroe, *Jr. Warden*

John Ridgely Carter — Robert Turner
Chas. H. Whiting — Andrew D. Lillie
G. Schlatter — F. G. Fenton"

In 1919 I received the following letter:

"HOUSE OF BISHOPS

"October 25, 1919

"My dear Dr. Watson:

"It is my pleasant duty to inform you that the following Resolution, offered by the Bishop of Erie, was adopted by the House of Bishops in Session on October 21st, by a unanimous vote:

" 'Whereas, the Reverend Samuel N. Watson, D.D., former Rector, and now Rector Emeritus, of the American Church of the Holy Trinity, Paris, France, by his self-sacrificing and arduous labors during the late War presented to Europe the all-embracing compassion of this Church: Be it resolved, that this House desires to place on record its appreciation of the work of the Reverend Dr. Watson.'

"May I avail myself of this opportunity to express to you my hearty congratulations on the noble record which you have made in Paris.

"With best wishes, faithfully yours,

Geo. F. Nelson,
Secretary."

The Bishop of Erie was Bishop in Charge of the European Churches during the later period of my work in France, and was my intimate friend and adviser; and it was with his consent and collaboration that I made arrangements for the transfer of the work of the Church in Paris to my successor.

It had been my great privilege to have with me as a colleague at the Church the Rev. Dr. F. W. Beekman, who had come over to France to take the direction of the American Soldiers and Sailors Club, a foundation of Mr. Rodman Wanamaker; and in that work both Dr. and Mrs. Beekman had done valued service. At my request the Vestry asked

Dr. Beekman to take a position on the staff of Holy Trinity; and when I found it necessary to transfer the responsibility of the ministrations at the Church to other hands it was a most opportune aid to have with me at the time one already familiar with the work and who was already attached to the Parish. With the approval of the Bishop of Erie, this transfer was made; and so, with no break in administration, Dr. Beekman took up the Church's service in Paris where I relinquished it.

I knew many fine, brave, devoted men who came to France to work during the War, and my heart holds them all in gratitude; but of them all I cherish most the memory of Rogers Israel, Bishop of Erie. His wisdom, his deep spirituality, his recklessness of all save God and His Service (he would walk out on the street from my house on an evening when the sirens were howling their warning and the bombs beginning to fall and he would laugh at our urgent pleas that he stay with us and not return to his hotel that night); and but for him and his understanding faith and his constant devotion I do not see that I could have carried on. The tribute which I know that he likes best that I should pay him here can best be rendered in the words of a wounded soldier in a hospital where Bishop Israel gave his last service in France: "Oh! Bishop, I know I could not keep on living without you here, and I sure could not die without you."

Bishop Israel had a keen sense of humour, and he so valued the power of the French to mix, almost in a breath, the sublime and the amusing, that I must tell a story of him as it was told to me. He was at the Front; he went there whenever he could get there, sometimes with "passes," and sometimes with his uniform as a Red Cross Chaplain as his only voucher—(he was waiting for his Hospital Unit to come across from Pennsylvania). At Headquarters it had been arranged that he should be convoyed back to Paris for supplies which he needed by a staff car which was to meet him at a small village near-by; but the Staff Car missed connections, so the Bishop went to an *auberge* (French Inn) in the village to find food and shelter. It was the hour of the evening meal when he came in to the common living room, which served as dining room as well; and at one end of the room was the *fourneau-de-cuisine* (cooking-stove), and at the other end there was a sink where a boy and a cat were washing and licking up the dishes as fast as they were being used. The Bishop was in interesting company; there were several young French officers; several *commis-voyageurs* (what we would call "drummers," travelling salesmen); and also some members of a Variety troup who had come out from the City to entertain the soldiers when they should be off duty; and the Bishop's neighbour at the left when they sat down at table was a jolly girl *(jolie* quite likely), a little *soubrette* from the theatre. When the *café* was served it was put on the table in bowls before each guest, and the sugar was passed down the table from one to another. When the sugar came to the little lady who was the Bishop's neighbour, she passed it first to the American officer (the Bishop), with the intention of showing courtesy to a foreigner; and the Bishop declined it, saying, *"Merci, pas sucre,"* in a French which he said afterward was none too good either as French or as pronounciation. The little lady insisted, thinking that he did not know that it was sugar meant for the coffee, and she took a spoonful and tried to put it in his cup; but the Bishop pushed her hand back gently saying, *"Ã la guerre"*; it was a common expression, *"à la guerre, comme à la guerre,"* to indicate "the necessity of war"; and what the Bishop meant was that he was not taking sugar on account of the War; but his pronounciation of *à la guerre* must have sounded like *à la Gare* (which in Americanese might be rendered, "Beat it, You baggage!"). The little actress showed quick signs of being both hurt and offended; but one of the French officers across the table from them, who had been watching this by-play with amusement, explained to her that the American officer had not said what she thought, but that he was such a friend of theirs that he would not eat sugar which might be needed for the men who were fighting. Whereon she put her arm about the Bishop and patted his cheek and told him that he was *un brave garçon* (a fine fellow).

What the dying soldier said to Bishop Israel in the hospital brings me a realisation to-day, at this long distance from the scene, of something which I often thought of while the War was going on; viz: the fineness of character which the War brought out into the open where, otherwise, it would have been little likely that it might ever have been known that the men possessed it. And I realise again that there is nothing on this earth which is wholly good or wholly bad; nothing wholly bad, not even war. I am thinking of the sublime songs which came from human hearts out of the dismal depths of conflict; of the superb faith and aspirations which men showed, and which that breaking of old inhibitions (which was war) called into utterance, with the result that all human life thereafter is immeasurably richer. I am thinking of Alan Seeger, of Charles Peguy, and of a host of others who dreamed such lovely dreams of life when they were down there *dans la boue* (in the mud); and my meaning is well illustrated by some words of a letter written by one who came of a fine race and of a fine family. And as I record them here I pay a tribute of gratitude on my own part to his father and mother also, to whom I am indebted for many kindnesses. In October 1918 Lieut. Kenneth Mac Leish, U.S.N.R.F.C., was brought down above Schoore, in Belgium; he was one of the "flying-men" who dared all and who gave all; and in March 1918 he wrote:

> "If I find it necessary to make the supreme sacrifice, always remember this: I am so firmly convinced that the ideals which I am going to fight for are right and splendid ideals that I am happy to be able to give so much for them. . . . So you see I have no fears, I have no regrets; . . . I have only to thank God for such a wonderful opportunity to serve Him and the world. The life which I lay down will be my preparation for the grander, finer life that I shall take up. I shall *live*."

Peace has its triumphs, its moments of splendour, when the spirit out-leaps the placid stream as the trout leaps up into the sunshine; but there are soul-revealing moments in war which let the God who is in man come forth, and we see and know that there is no more two, God and Man, but just ONE, God, and man in God.

"Car la mort n'est rien dans la somme des choses,
Et la vie n'est rien dans la somme des choses,
Et la chair n'est rien dans la somme des choses,
Mais l'homme en Dieu est tout, et Dieu dans l'homme." *

We sailed from France shortly after Easter of 1918, and on landing in New York went directly to White Sulphur Springs for medical care and for rest. While there we had the pleasure of visiting with Myron Herrick and Mrs. Herrick; and later in the year we were their guests in Cleveland. Invitations to speak came in great numbers, but with the sole exception of making the Memorial Address at the Commemorative Service for James Gordon Bennett which was held in Grace Church, New York, I was unable to accept any of them. After some weeks of care at White Sulphur I was able to move on, and we settled in Glencoe (Chicago), Illinois, for the summer. During that time I spoke at the City Club in Milwaukee, where I was a guest together with an old friend, Edward S. Van Zile and his wife who was May Bulkeley of Hartford and whose charming hospitality at the family home on Washington Street "under the Elms" I remember so well. It was Ed Van Zile who wrote those thrilling lines, "The Battle Hymn of Democracy":

"What hear we in the world today?
A paean wild and sweet,
The peoples' song of Victory:
And where the nations meet
Not King shall call to brother-King,
But race shall call to race,
And man no longer slave to man
Can look God in the face.

" 'T is a Marseillaise so wonderful
The world is singing now,
As the peoples find their power and fulfil a sacred vow,

* "For death is nothing in the sum of things,
And life is nothing in the sum of things,
And flesh is nothing in the sum of things,
But man in God is all, and God in man."

That the stars that dance along the sky
Its rhythm seem to feel,
And the universe is throbbing with
A glad triumphant peal."

My touch with the Church in Paris was kept up by letters from John Ridgely Carter who was one of the Vestrymen and a member of the Finance Committee, and who had been a close friend of mine in College days. He wrote me in June of the financial needs of the Church and "to express the hope that we can still rely on you, as Rector Emeritus, not only to continue to help us with your appeal for the Church, but also with your advice." As I regained my strength I spoke in many places for the Church and its work in Paris, and also for the Relief Work which we had carried on in France and in Belgium and in Serbia. I also published statements of what work had been done and what its needs continued to be, and the response to these statements was immediate and most generous. Then in October I was able to send Mr. Carter checks for $7,050; in acknowledging which he wrote me, "Your work in America for the Church has been quite extraordinary; the Vestry should be deeply grateful for your brilliant achievement; which I am sure they are." In addition to gifts made specifically for the Church in Paris, generous contributions came in for Relief of American Soldiers in France; Relief of American Civilians in France; The *Pauvres Honteux* ("ashamed to beg"); French Children; French Orphans; The Poor Gentle-folk of Belgium; Belgian Orphans; Serbian Orphans.

It amazed me to find the widespread interests of which we were made trustees by friends in America. These gifts were so large and many of them so personal in their character and requiring such personal administration, if we were to discharge our responsibility both to the donors and the beneficiaries. There were gifts such as Frs. 35,842. for the *Pauvres Honteux* in France; Frs. 14,295. for the *Pauvres Honteux* of Belgium; Frs. 14,845. for French Children; and Frs. 35,310 for Belgian Orphans, that we felt that our responsibility as trustees was imperatively engaged, and that we must go to see personally to the distribution of these gifts, although that meant an added strain for which we were not physically ready. We sailed for France then in the autumn, going by way of England; and we went up to London in a railway carriage whose windows were largely missing as they had been recently shattered by an air bombardment. In Liverpool we had great difficulty in finding a hotel which would house us as the city was very crowded; but finally, in company with a Quaker friend and his wife who were on their way to work in the Belgian trenches, we found rooms in a dingy kind of a doggery, a sort of 2nd class "Pub." When we went to the station to register the baggage in order to make an early start in the morning, the old porter said, "And did ye find a room for the night?" I told him where we had put up, and noticing a quizzical look in his eye, I said, "It's an all right enough kind of place, isn't it?" To which the old boy replied humourously, "Oh, h'anny port in a storm, Sir!" Liverpool was dreary, as always; and Liverpool was cold and hungry, and London was both; and as, for so short a stay as we hoped to make, it hardly seemed worth-while to go to the Police and register for Food Tickets. We followed an ancient example:

"Methuselah ate
What was put on his plate;
He ate it because it was 'chow' ":

The provender as provided "by the Laws of this Realm" was meagre indeed.

The only possible crossing for civilians at the time was by way of Southampton and Havre, and one boat each night was the extent of the service. So I spent much time going back and forth, to and from booking-offices, to see if anything had been given up in the way of reservations. On my last visit to Cook's a gentleman who just preceded me at the counter laid down two tickets for the Southampton-Havre crossing and asked to have them redeemed; and as he looked good-natured I covered the tickets with my hand and said, "These are for me, are they not, Sir?" "They certainly are, if you want them," said he. So that was settled. It was then eleven o'clock of a Saturday morning, and I had to get visas from both French and American officialdom, and the offices closed at noon on a Saturday. At the American office my way was made smooth by a good-natured coloured porter who got me an immediate hearing. I then rushed off to the French Control, reaching there at a quarter to twelve, only to be told by a *sous officier* who was acting as Cerberus that *Monsieur le Commandant* was just leaving, and that the office was closed for the day. I saw my last chance to use those coveted passage tickets going glimmering, unless I could in some way "rush the gate"; so I uttered such an emphatic protest that *Monsieur le Commandant* himself came to the fore. When he saw the red of my Legion of Honour he was most courteous; but so far as the visa was concerned he was adamant; my papers must go to Paris. I finally got myself invited into his private office and got him to look over the papers in my brief case, but the result was nil; even a letter which I had from the Archbishop of Canterbury drew only a respectful but interested comment. However, in an inner pocket of that brief case I found a letter which won me the day; and again I have to thank the gracious writer of that letter for another courtesy. It was the letter which Madame Poincaré had written while we were in Bordeaux last, sending us as *cadeaux d'adieu* signed photographs of herself and of President Poincaré, together with personal messages. That letter was enough; I got the visa; and that same evening we went to Southampton, got supper aboard the boat—everything which we had wanted in London and could not get, good bread and butter, fine cold roast beef, cheese and jam and clotted cream, and then with some "central heating" in the way of tea ("central heating" in London had been *vox, et praeterea nihil,* which is defined in the dictionary as "sound without sense"), we were warm for the first time since setting foot on my ancestral soil of Britain. I was just tucking in under the blankets when there was a tap at the door, and to my "Come in!" there appeared the duckiest kind of a little Welsh maid in cap and apron, who said, "What time shall I bring your tea in the morning, Sir?" And to my query of, "What time do we dock at Le Havre?," she said, "Well, Sir, if we get across, we should be in by seven." "Then I'll have some tea at six, please":—"Thank you, Sir," said she; and how I relished that British politeness! In due time the boat got away, and for an hour and then another hour, she twisted and turned and backed and crawled around the mines, and when she reached the open water we were off with such a burst of speed as I had never felt—the boat fairly leapt in the water; and, we went duly to sleep, and reached Le Havre as we expected; and in due time we arrived in Paris again.

My first errand was to the Ministry of the Interior to ask my friend Monsieur Ogier, *le Directeur du Contrôle, to* arrange for our *permit de séjour,* which he readily agreed to do. Two days later, not having heard from these most necessary documents I went again to the Ministry to receive from Monsieur Ogier a most welcome piece of news, viz: that he had taken up the matter with the *Sureté* (Secret Police); that both the *Sureté* and the *Préfecture* had been advised, that we could go and come as we pleased in France. It was like feeling ourselves a sort of Diplomatic guests of the country. In due course, all matters of Relief Distribution were arranged; the Armistice had come and gone: President Wilson had established himself in Paris; and the new regime had begun.

It was a regime which was strange to us, and I was glad that we could be free to leave it all and to return to America; to leave that sad series of tragedies; the tumultuous rejoicings, then the changing attitude of the people; the heroic struggle of the American Idealist, a struggle which began in a sublime belief that HE could bring Peace to the world, and which ended in the slow realisation that he and they "over there" did not see "eye to eye" and never could, did not speak the same language, and never would; that they were not seeking the same ends, he and they; then the sadly slow acceptance of the dreary compromise which was the prelude of his return to America, to disillusionment, and to heart break. It had all been foretold to me by French statesmen long before, just what would happen and how. They were world students, those men, not men of one land or one language; they knew that no man, however sublime his courage or however divinely true his visions of Humanity's Utopia, could bring a world peace then; and more than that they knew Europe; they knew the background of its peoples; they were skilled in the methods of the Chanceries; they knew that it would be long, very long before peoples, who were still mentally compelled by the thought methods of the monarchical regimes from which they had but partially emerged, would welcome a Peace of Democracy, such as that of which Ed Van Zile had sung. And it was with the sad knowledge which was born of bitter experience that they realised beforehand that in the end they, the idealists of France, and that greater idealist from the New World would find the only possible outcome of Councils and Conferences to be, not a Treaty which should establish a lasting Peace, but instead of that only another "Scrap of Paper," which could not long stand unviolated because between the lines of its crafty verbiage there could be read the motif of it all, which was not an intent toward peace, but rather that old maxim of material prudence: "Let him take who may, and let him keep who can."

Our second home-coming after the War was not with the "Au Revoir, but not Good-bye," which was James Gordon Bennett's farewell to us. This time we knew that we were leaving friends whom we would probably not see again, such friends as one makes rarely in a lifetime. And friends have always meant more to me than places; it is the friends who have hallowed and endeared the places whose memories I cherish. Chiefest among those friends in France, among our own compatriots were the Tucks, the Hoffs, and the Carters. John Ridgely Carter was the friend of my boyhood; and that friendship renewed in manhood and in times of stress and strain took on a deeper meaning than a boyhood friendship could ever have. The charm of our walks together on the Avenue du Bois after working hours were over lingers with me yet; and his wise counsel and his courteous understanding in difficult moments were an invaluable help to me. To have a friend in difficult hours who always takes you for granted, who asks for no explanations, whose world experience has schooled him in restraint of expression—that meant more to me than I can set down in words; and all of that John Carter was. When policies clashed and other men were impatient he was the one who always kept his equilibrium. At the Clearing House and in the councils at the Church my interests were his; and one cannot ask more of a friendship than that.

Our visits to Mr. and Mrs. Tuck in summer at the Château de Vermont, and at Christmas time at Monte Carlo are delightful memories. These interludes of rest and refreshment made the load of the work lighter always; and we could not have done what we did in France but for the ever generous sharing of it with us by Mr. and Mrs. Tuck. I have known many men of large wealth in my long lifetime, but I have never known one to whom possession meant less, in and of itself, and to whom money meant more simply just that finer spiritual something into which wealth of things may be transmuted.

Among those Americans who have given France full reason to appreciate their country's meaning and worth John J. Hoff and Grace Whitney Hoff hold high place. They are so lovable in themselves, and they radiate a soul quality which makes their friendship precious to those who are honoured by it, and we were of those elect ones. I always think of them at Bréau, or at Peyrieu, where we were so often their guests. Le Château de Bréau sans Nappe, to write it at full length, and so to distinguish it from the other Bréaux, was a former hunting lodge of Henry IV; it is a foursquare ivy-grown manoir with *tourelles* on its four corners pierced by *meurtrières* which overlook the moat; and there is a fine old *pigeonnier* in the park. Under the feudal regime in France the right to construct and maintain *pigeonniers* was reserved to the nobles; and the *pigeonniers* of that period were usually built in the form of cyclindrical towers which covered with a conical roof; and such is the form of the *pigeonnier* Le Bréau; more than once I have been shown with pride by the *châtelain* of an old place his ancient *pigeonnier*. Of Le Bréau sans Nappe it is told that the

King on coming in one day from hunting and passing on the way an old stone table which still stands in the centre of a *carrefour* (cross-roads) in the forest, told his lackeys to throw the game down around this old table, saying *nous déjeunerons ici sans nappe* (we will lunch here without a tablecloth, without ceremony), hence the name of the property. I have one brilliant memory of Le Bréau which outshines the others; it is of a day when we went out there to bring in some of the fruits and vegetables which were at our disposal for the relief of our Paris poor and which the old caretaker, Monsieur Thouzé, had gathered for us. In the garden there were some trees of *mirabelles* (unfortunately we here in America do not know, apparently, what *mirabelles* are; they are a cherry-plum, and they merit their name of "wonderfully beautiful"); and under the trees the ground was thick-covered with the lovely pink and golden fruit, and the bees and the wasps were drinking their fill of the honeyed sweetness of the juice which oozed from the fruit cracked by the sun and by their fall from the tree.

Le Château de Peyrieu has also its fair memories. In going there we often went by way of Bourg-en-Bresse and Monsieur Rebière's hospitable Hôtel de l'Europe; and that meant also a visit to one of the loveliest architectural treasures of France, the Church of Brou which was begun in 1506, but which was completed in its present form by Marguerite of Austria who was the daughter of the Emperor Maximilien the First. Marguerite was one of the *Grandes Dames* who brought about what was known as *La Paix des Dames* or the Treaty of Cambrai in 1529, when Queens brought about a Peace which Kings and Councils could not arrive at. As a child, Marguerite was a pawn in the game of statecraft. She was first betrothed to a king's son in France and sent to Paris to be educated in Court ways; and from that peril she escaped by the death of the old king. Then she was sent to Spain to be betrothed to the Infante; and he died; and so she escaped that. At last she made a love match of her own with Philibert le Beau, the Duke of Savoy; and he was killed by a fall from his horse while hunting. It was while on her voyage to Spain and when the ship which was carrying her thither came nearly being crushed on the rocks of the French Coast, that Marguerite wrote an epitaph to be used for her resting place in case of need, humorously worded in order to amuse her terrified companions; and these were the lines:

"Ci-git Margot, la gentille demoiselle;
Qui eut trois maris, mais mourut pucelle" *

When Philibert was killed Marguerite built herself a little house and oratory at Brou, and gave up her life to building its exquisite Church, the rood-screen of which is like a piece of lace in stone. I persuaded the *gardien* that I was *persona grata* to the Ministry of Beaux Arts and so I succeeded in getting some remarkable photographs, inaccessible to the ordinary public. A world at strife would not let Marguerite rest in peace; it insisted that she should come back to the North and rule her principality of Flanders; and when she died there her gentlemen-in-waiting carried her body on their shoulders all the way in the snow to Brou (as Queen Eleanor's body was carried; and where it rested in the City there King Edward built a Cross, *La croix de la Chère Reine,* Chère Reine Cross,—Charing Cross). And in the Church of Brou Marguerite has a lovely tomb just where she can look across and see the tomb of Philibert, the most beautiful of all the tombs there in the centre of the Choir.

From Bourg and Brou we would come by an easy drive to the country of the Bugeyand, all its little towns which end in *"ieu";* Belley is its *chef-lieu d'arrondissement* (county-town). And it was at the railway station at Belley that the Hoffs had their Christmas tree set up, for the soldiers who passed through Belley on the trains on their way to or from the Front, so that every soldier who came that way might have his bit of Christmas cheer. Then on a little way from Belley we came to Peyrieu and its Château perched up on the hilltop overlooking the Valley of the Rhone; this is the home of the Hoffs in the Department of the Ain; and in all the countryside about the *chatelains de*

* Here lies Margot, the dear girl
Who had three husbands, yet died a maid.

Peyrieu are loved and honoured. The poor and the sick are their special charges; and the picture is clear in my memory of Mrs. Hoff starting out in the morning with her dog and her stick, ('Mulus stayed at home to look after me) on her way to the nearby villages where she was a special Providence. Among Mrs. Hoff's treasures there is a great roll of cyclamen coloured silk, woven for her specially by the people of the silk mill in the village; and on each metre of the silk her name is woven in the selvedge. It was always hard to leave Peyrieu and its atmosphere of rest and charm; something of the spiritual vision of the *châtelaine* seemed to pervade the atmosphere of the place. * * * It was hard to leave France. * * *

It is hard now to stop this Memory wandering when there is so much more that I could tell, and which I would like to tell. But I have told enough to give a vision of La France Vièrge, La France Guerrière; still the vision seer like Jeanne d'Arc amongst the apple trees of Domremy; and like *la Pucelle* still often misunderstood.

I have not written this story with any set purpose; I have let it tell itself. I have let the dream unroll itself from my Memory book, just as the pictures came to my mind day after day, like England's poet who "lisped in numbers, for the numbers came." But as I re-read its pages I sense a conviction that I have all unconsciously repaid in some slight measure all that France gave to me by painting a picture in words of what it means in a nation's life to have a clear consciousness of its meaning in history.

So now, To Bordeaux and the Boat!

AVE! VALE!

FRANCE BIENAIMEE!

XV

HOME AGAIN

IT WAS in January 1919 that we came to America again, and after landing in New York we came straight out to sunny California, and again we were too worn to do anything but sit in the sun. We took a little house in Montecito Park and there we stayed for four months; and then we started Eastward. After another summer spent in Glencoe (Chicago), I accepted the offer of the Vestry there and became the Minister of the Congregation, but with no idea of remaining there longer than a year, and with a tenure of office which was limited at my request to a service of month by month. It was five years before we moved again. In Glencoe, as elsewhere the place meant the friends we made; and the people there were very good to us.

First of all there were the Brighams: no clan of old Europe had a stronger sense of belongingness than that family had: you felt it; you admired it when you were privileged to be a guest," when good men get together," at one of those re-unions of the blood which Henry so loved to call around him; and for all the fact that you could not help realising that you were not a Brigham but only a grafted-in twig on the tip end of a Brigham limb, that feeling really meant, as you saw them all together and knew what they meant to each other and to life, that you could not help honouring their pride of family, simply because its outward fruitage was a compelling sense of *noblesse obilge.* Fine men all, the men of that family; Douglas with his capacity for effective administration; George with his wide sympathies, his unreckoning generosities, his "unco" rigid respectable prejudices, and his dry wit and sense of humour; and Henry, the acting head of the Clan, a doer of great things and a dreamer of great dreams, with the sweep of an oldtime patriarch in his feeling of responsibility for the wellbeing of the youngsters of his generation; a man whom one would have liked to see dowered with years on years to enable him to carry into effect "a good time to be had by all." I am grateful for what they all gave me of welcome and of affection; and for George I have a deep feeling of kinship because of 'Rilla who shared her life with ours from her early childhood. She came to Glencoe one summer's day to ask that words of blessing might be said on her life, and on another life to be joined to hers. Jeanne, then a little girl, was to be the bride's attendant; she had carefully practiced her "step" to the rhythm of "Dum,—DUM—de Dum" before she left Saint Louis; but 'Rilla had refused to come in as a "Dum, DUM—de—Dum," and had chosen a real wedding-y kind of a thing. As George said in a tone of annoyance which faintly veiled his paternal pride, "Wouldn't you know that she would do something like that!" And when someone asked, "But, Jeanne's step? she's practiced it for that old march!" "Let her alone," said George, "Jeanne will invent one of her own"; and Jeanne did just that. "Trust it to Jeanne," as Jim would say.

The Cassels and the Sutherlands come together in my Glencoe memories; there was something in our comradeship which found its source in far-off Scotland. Mr. Sutherland was first degree Scotch; Mr. Cassels was one degree farther removed; Jeannette's Grants, and MacLeans came next; and my Montgomerys trailed respectably after; but inasmuch as "Bobbie Burns" received us as "belonging" when we went to see the Sutherlands, our standing with the clans was unquestionable. When we came to leave Glencoe it was the leaving these dear comrades, grown-ups and children, which made the parting real. For after my one proposed year in Glencoe had lengthened into five, my good medical adviser Doctor Wiley said: "These weeks in bed have helped, but your heart is still weak; my advice to you is to stop work and to go and live in California." And seeing a bit of gloom on my countenance, he added, "It's not such a bad prescription to take; I'd take it myself if I could."

So we started again on our wanderings and reached Santa Barbara again on the second day of August, 1924. We went to the Arlington Hotel where we found a welcome waiting from a friend of mine of the long ago, Mrs. C. E. Perkins whom I always remember as part of my boyhood associations in Burlington, Iowa. When we were in Montecito in the winter of 1919, just after coming from France, the telephone in our little house in Montecito Park rang one day, and a voice asked, "Is this Doctor Watson?", and to my affirmative reply said, "Is this the Reverend Doctor Watson?", and again I said, Yes. Still another question, "Is this the Sam Watson whom I used to know as a little boy in Burlington?"; and then after I had joyfully confirmed my identity, came the next message, "I am Mrs. Perkins: Will you come and lunch with me on Saturday at Sandyland?" In the beautiful edition of her mother's *Letters and Journal,* which Mrs. Cunningham gave me, Mrs. Perkins wrote:

> "Sam Watson, whom I had not seen for thirty-nine years, and whom I last saw at one of our Xmas-trees in Burlington. . . . He and his wife have just come from Paris where they have been doing War work. They are here for a rest, for they nearly killed themselves. I saw a notice of their arrival in the paper, and I thought I would take a chance; so I asked him, and said, if he was the Sam Watson I used to know, perhaps he would come and see me on my sand-dune; . . . if he wasn't, I begged his pardon, and hoped he would get the rest he came for. . . . He almost got here before I did."

As I re-read Mrs. Perkins *Letters and Journal,* living documents which the loving care of a daughter has opened to those who loved her mother, I am lost in admiration of the spiritual insight, the literary taste, the breadth and depth of reading and thinking of which they give evidence. And with that admiration there comes a regret which I have felt before with regard to other choice natures, regret that time and years did not give me the chance to know her more intimately and more constantly. We miss so much, we others, when we make but casual contacts with souls who have such hidden treasures of heart and mind to share; and when, through press of things, or in hesitation lest we be importunate, we pass them in the all too short days almost like "ships that pass in the night"; only to realise later, perhaps, a loss which cannot be repaired in this Here and Now. The gift which Mrs. Cunningham made me of these books was but another token of her generous courtesy to both Jeannette and me. And I will never cease to remember gratefully her kindnesses to us both when the hour of the parting of life's ways came.

Soon after our arrival in Santa Barbara came a telegram from Akron, from Charlie and Mary Raymond, asking us to go to their house on Channel Drive and to make it our home until we found a place in which to live. After a few weeks of rest there, we went to "Siamasia," a cottage hotel in Montecito, and there we had plans prepared for a home for ourselves. It was really Jeannette's home, as she supervised all the building of it as I was not able to do more than make the necessary business arrangements; the house was built on ground which was the gift of Mary Raymond. The house was all ready for our occupancy with the exception of the interior decorating when the Great Earthquake of 1925 occurred; but the house was so well built that it stood the shock without any damage. That earthquake came early in the morning. I was in my little bed, and there I stayed, for after all the experiences of the preceding years, earthquakes were "no treat to me." Some one asked me afterward if it was not a terrifying time; and my reply was that in a few years space I had lived in a city which was constantly being bombed from the air (for what military purpose I cannot discover); I had crossed the ocean in a leaking ship, and with submarines appearing now and then; I had missed a cyclone so closely that the road ahead of our car was strewn with broken trees and timbers from unroofed houses; I had been in a train wreck when the dining-car in which we were sitting was de-railed and its front end telescoped; and now this earthquake. None of them were experiences which one would want to repeat; but of them all the earthquake was the least demoralising.

We established ourselves in our house on Hill Road in August of 1925; and there followed then some years of real living in a house which Jeannette used to describe as

"A house full of books,
A garden of flowers,
And the sight and the sound of the sea."

We were so near the ocean that we were, as one of my French friends puts it, *"Bercés des chansons des vagues,"* (Sung to sleep by the songs of the waves).

Santa Barbara meant more new friends, and better still it meant renewing old friendships in closer intimacy.

We had known Edward Alling Oviatt and Zelle in our Akron days; then it was an acquaintance; here in California the acquaintance flowered in an association of close friendship, so that in the days when I needed friends, most what I needed was done by them before my wearied heart could ask it; and time has brought no change to their devotion. A permanent record should be made of what Alling Oviatt has given to this community in farsighted and constructive service: the Montecito Public School, its fine earthquake-proof building, and its ample children's playground are a witness to his care for the living; and the Chapel in the cemetery and the added beauty of its surroundings are his tribute to the love which cannot forget its dead. (We call them *dead,* though they are far more living than we are).

Here I want to pay tribute to my friends so generously devoted, my doctor friends in Santa Barbara. It is a great privilege to live in a community which has drawn to itself men who stand so high in sympathetic knowledge of the "ills that flesh is heir to," as do the men of the Medical Faculty here; and also to have access to a hospital which is so perfectly managed and directed as is Cottage Hospital. When I last found myself in the East and realised that the disabilities incident to seventy-one years of age, plus four years of War, were demanding most imperatively that I admit them to reckoning, I said to myself, "Back to Santa Barbara! In a hospital where I was not known I would be but a number, and to the doctor here I would be a case; while in Santa Barbara your doctor is your friend, and days in a hospital come as near to being home-like as devoted personal attention can make institutional life." My doctor friends here have made me feel the depth of the fraternal feeling which ideally underlies the calling of "the Good Physician," and my personal contact with many of them, and chief of all with Doctors Evans, Nuzum, Robinson, Ullmann, Geyman, Mellinger, Brush, Lewis, Stone, McGovney, Franklin, and Johnston has quickened my admiration for a calling which has something of the Divine in it.

November 25, 1928, was Jeannette's birthday. On November 22nd we went to The Strollers Club in the evening. On the morning of the 25th she was so far from well that I sent for her brother and her sister. On the 3rd of January 1929, just as the morning was beginning, Light broke for her on the Larger Day. Her last tribute to earth was made when we laid away a casket in Santa Barbara Cemetery in a lovely spot, where the Southward look is toward the infinitely living Sea, and its Northward vision is toward the comfortingly eternal mountains; and that memory place is marked by lines which she had written in her Prayer Book:

"THERE'S SUNSHINE ON THE HILLS OF GOD."

There has been placed in the Hoover War Library at Stanford University a unique collection of papers and other memorabilia which I brought back from France, through the courtesy of the Directeur Général Des Douanes, Monsieur Jean Branet. This Collection includes bound files of the Paris edition of the *New York Herald;* of *L'Illustration;* and also twelve folio volumes of documents and correspondence which were part of my office records in Paris. It is to be known as

"The Samuel N. Watson
Jeannette G. Watson
Collection."

Printed in the United States of America